Textures of Renaissa

MANCHESTER
UNIVERSITY PRESS

Textures of

Renaissance Knowledge

EDITED BY PHILIPPA BERRY

& MARGARET TUDEAU-CLAYTON

Manchester University Press

Manchester and New York

distributed exclusively in the USA by Palgrave

Published by Manchester University Press
Oxford Road, Manchester M13 9NR, UK
and Room 400, 175 Fifth Avenue, New York, NY 10010, USA
www.manchesteruniversitypress.co.uk

Distributed exclusively in the USA by
Palgrave, 175 Fifth Avenue, New York, NY 10010, USA

Distributed exclusively in Canada by
UBC Press, University of British Columbia, 2029 West Mall, Vancouver, BC, Canada V6T 1Z2

British Library Cataloguing-in-Publication Data
A catalogue record for this book is available from the British Library

Library of Congress Cataloging-in-Publication Data applied for

ISBN 0 7190 6464 3   *hardback*
     0 7190 6465 1   *paperback*

First published 2003

11 10 09 08 07 06 05 04 03   10 9 8 7 6 5 4 3 2 1

Typeset in Minion with Tagliente display
by Graphicraft Limited, Hong Kong
Printed in Great Britain
by Bell & Bain Ltd, Glasgow

—contents—

List of illustrations—*page* vii
Notes on contributors—ix

Introduction   PHILIPPA BERRY
& MARGARET TUDEAU-CLAYTON—1

v

CONTENTS

—illustrations—

—contributors—

PHILIPPA BERRY is Fellow and Director of Studies in English at King's College, Cambridge. She is author of *Of Chastity and Power: Elizabethan Literature and the Unmarried Queen* (1989) and *Shakespeare's Feminine Endings: Disfiguring Death in the Tragedies* (1999), and co-editor of *Shadow of Spirit: Postmodernism and Religion* (1992).

DYMPNA CALLAGHAN is Dean's Professor in the Humanities at Syracuse University. She is author of *Woman and Gender in Renaissance Tragedy* (1989) and, most recently, *Shakespeare without Women* (2000). She is editor of *The Feminist Companion to Shakespeare* (2000) and a casebook on *The Duchess of Malfi* (2001).

STEPHEN CLUCAS is Senior Lecturer in English and Humanities at Birkbeck College, University of London. His recent publications include a translation of Paolo Rossi's *Clavis Universalis, Logic and The Art of Memory: The Quest for a Universal Language* (2000), and *The Wizard Earl's Advices to his Son*, co-edited with Gordon R. Batho (2002).

DAVID COLCLOUGH is Lecturer in English at Queen Mary, University of London. He has edited a collection of essays on *John Donne's Professional Lives* (2003), and is completing a book on freedom of speech in early Stuart England. He is editing *New Atlantis* for the Oxford Francis Bacon.

MARIE GARNIER-GIAMARCHI is Professor of English Literature at the University of Paris VIII, where she lectures on seventeenth-century poetry and drama, and modernism. She has published a number of articles and book chapters, mostly on Shakespeare, Traherne, Milton and Joyce. She is author of *George Herbert: The Temple* (1997) and *Jardins d'Hiver* (1997), a book on literature and photography.

LIZ GUILD is College Lecturer in French at the University of Cambridge. She has published widely in French Renaissance and seventeenth-century studies, in journals such as the *Romanic Review* and most recently *The Cambridge History of Literary Criticism* volume III. She is currently working on sacrifice and the extreme act in early modern France.

ANN LECERCLE is Professor of English Literature at the University of Nanterre. She also teaches seminars on Shakespeare and Renaissance studies at the Ecole Normale Supérieure, Paris. She has published, mostly in French, on theatre, critical theory and the Renaissance.

WILLY MALEY is Professor of English Literature at the University of Glasgow. He is author of *A Spenser Chronology* (1994), and *Salvaging Spenser: Colonialism, Culture and Identity* (1997), and co-editor of *Representing Ireland: Literature and the Origins of Conflict, 1534–1660* (1993), *Postcolonial Criticism* (1997) and *A View of the State of Ireland: From the First Published Edition* (1997).

MARGARET TUDEAU-CLAYTON teaches English Literature at the University of Zürich, Switzerland. She is co-editor of *Addressing Frank Kermode* (1991) and author of *Jonson, Shakespeare and Early Modern Virgil* (1998) as well as various articles, mainly on English Renaissance literature. She is currently working on Shakespeare and the ideology of linguistic practices in early modern England.

SUSAN WISEMAN is Reader in English Literature at Birkbeck College, University of London. She is author of *Drama and Politics in the English Civil War* (1998).

—introduction—

PHILIPPA BERRY &
MARGARET TUDEAU-CLAYTON

TODAY, at the opening of the twenty-first century, our conception of knowledge is undergoing an extraordinary process of redefinition. Postmodern theory may have reopened knowledge as a site of intellectual struggle through its unsettling of our formerly unexamined adherence to the grand intellectual 'metanarratives' of the Enlightenment and of modernity, yet ironically it seems now to be not *theoria* but *techne* (or technology) that is producing the most radical and far-reaching restructuring of conventional, 'modern' paradigms of knowledge. And technology is producing this transformation, of course, not by any direct intellectual challenge to the empiricism or consistency of our previous knowledge systems but instead by providing us with the ability to enter cyberspace, in order both to store and to access diverse forms or bodies of knowledge. Through its relocation in hyperreality, established or authoritative knowledge has acquired new qualities of fluidity (or 'virtuality') and multiplicity, along with a strange kind of autonomy, as different information networks, whose particular empirical truth-value is no longer subject to specialist legitimation, can now be instantly accessed and their data variously combined by any individual web-browser, in a playful process that additionally unsettles any authorial claims to ownership of individual ideas.

In his influential analysis of the rapid globalization and seemingly limitless proliferation of knowledge which began in the late twentieth century, Jean-François Lyotard observed ironically, but also accurately, that 'knowledge is [now] a matter for TV games', concluding that 'The nature of knowledge cannot survive unchanged within this context of general transformation'.[1] Yet it is not only the nature of knowledge but also previous conceptions of the putatively knowing subject that are being called into question by this process of transformation. It is notable, certainly, that our feelings of delight and empowerment in relation to the seemingly infinite intellectual resources now available to us are beginning to be tempered by anxiety, as we experience the *angst* not of doubt, or of not knowing, but rather of knowing too much. While postmodernism may have celebrated the fragmentation of former models of knowledge, the surfeit of facts currently available to our electronic age also seems to be producing subtle changes in our conception of the human subject, as we experience acute feelings of multiplicity, disloca-tion or alienation together with an incipient sense of intellectual chaos, or information overload.

In the context of this far-reaching epistemological and ontological shift, it is hardly surprising that scholarly engagement with previous paradigms of Western knowledge is itself in the midst of a significant process of re-evaluation and revision; in particular, the ineluctable erosion of a 'modern' paradigm of knowledge is enabling us to reassess and reinterrogate the intellectual conditions which preceded and gave birth to that paradigm. The late sixteenth and early seventeenth cen-turies have long been viewed as a turning point in the intellectual history of Western Europe. But from our contemporary late modern or postmodern situation of rapid intellectual change, many formerly neglected aspects of that earlier moment of extraordinary intellectual ferment, which is now described alternatively as Renaissance or early modern, are being foregrounded. To take one specific instance, the digital age's transformation of the ways in which knowledge is organ-ized, stored and transmitted has recently been compared to the revolu-tionary and destabilizing effects of the advent of print culture after 1455, producing a recognition, in the work of a new generation of biblio-graphers, that 'there is no last word in textual matters'.[2] In this volume our concern is, more generally, with the re-examination of the particular epistemic *texture* or rather *textures* of that historical moment. Central to this project is the recognition that the knowledge systems of Renais-sance or early modern culture are multiple, unstable, complex and over-lapping, sometimes contradictory and frequently strange. In consequence, we need to develop new interpretative skills, most importantly perhaps new practices of reading, in order to elucidate the subtle imbrication of different knowledges within this richly textured cultural context. It is to such textures that the contributors to this volume have addressed them-selves, taking diverse innovative approaches to a broad range of 'non-literary' and 'literary' texts as well as to textualized spaces and material artefacts such as paintings, monuments and sculptures from Western European cultures of the early sixteenth to the mid-seventeenth centuries. What emerges is a renewed sense of the difference or otherness of that moment as well as an awareness of the intriguing parallels it affords to our own moment of epistemological crisis. These parallels go beyond merely technological innovation to encompass anxieties about the co-existence of incompatible knowledge systems; uncertainties about the status of subjects of knowledge and the nature and limits of agency; and about the relation between quasi-scientific and textural or literary modes of knowledge. Perceived in these terms the time-frame of the Renaissance or early modern can be revisited as a moment of profound epistemological uncertainty.

More specifically, the essays here recurrently illustrate how the constitution of subjects and objects of knowledge entailed denial or negation of a disturbing epistemic difference or alterity. This difference may be of gender (as in Elizabeth Guild's essay on Montaigne), race (as in Willy Maley's essay on Spenser) or class (as in Margaret Tudeau-Clayton's essay on Jonson), and in the attention to these differences our volume registers continuity with the concerns of the revisionary critical movements of new historicism and cultural materialism. But attention is also focused on knowledges or aspects of knowledge which these movements neglected or marginalized: the alterity of the ancient pagan past (as in David Colclough's essay on Bacon and Philippa Berry's essay on Spenser), or of the material particularity of verbal or visual textures (as in the essays by Marie Garnier-Giamarchi and Ann Lecercle). These forms or modes of difference frequently overlap: social and gender differences, for instance, are interwoven with disturbing aural 'matter' in the Shakespearean text analysed by Garnier-Giamarchi, and with the disturbing 'matter' of the body in the playtext by Jonson examined by Tudeau-Clayton. The disturbing epistemic difference of the past is similarly interwoven with the (equally unsettling) difference of gender in the texts studied by Berry. Our aim has been to foreground at once hitherto neglected forms of difference and, more generally, those aspects of Renaissance culture which, as we have indicated, are currently receiving attention in what we perceive as an important shift of critical focus.

The revisionary critical movements in Renaissance or early modern studies which came to prominence in the late 1970s, notably new historicism and cultural materialism, put into question key epistemic assumptions: about the discrete and bounded character of the literary text, and about the kinds of knowledge that might be elicited not only from literary texts but also from 'history', reconceived as 'co-text' rather than as context, background or source. As they foregrounded the complex exchanges or negotiations between 'literary' and 'non-literary' discourses, these movements emphasized the extent to which all cultural representations are informed by relations of power, whether in the sphere of politics or religion, or, especially, in the sphere of sexuality and gender. More recently, however, the continuing interest in relating Renaissance textuality to questions of power and gender/sexuality has been supplemented by a developing awareness among scholars that there are other critical questions and other areas of study that need to be addressed if we are to engage more adequately with the epoch's epistemic and cultural particularity in ways which at once recognize its difference and respond to the changing concerns of our own moment.

The criticism which is emerging in the wake of these revisionary movements thus draws its theoretical insights not only from Marxism and anthropology but also from post-structuralist and postmodern thought, from psychoanalysis and phenomenology. And it calls attention at once to a broader range of cultural forms, and equally to material and immaterial aspects of Renaissance or early modern knowledge, addressing not merely the semiotic instability of the literary text but other important questions, such as: the material localization of knowledge; the changing cultural significance of things (including manuscripts and books) as variously implicated in specific systems of gift-giving and economic exchange; the ambiguous and changing status of the author; and the unsettling effect of pre-modern concepts of the sacred or spiritual on the elaboration of a proto-'modern' paradigm of knowledge. Thus, at the same time as new critical strategies are being devised to re-examine the importance within this culture of its diverse conceptions of the immaterial or unrepresentable, a more wide-ranging and finely nuanced view of Renaissance material culture is being developed in a new materialist criticism that underscores the instability of both subjects and objects of knowledge as these are interwoven in the intricate textures of particular texts or cultural artefacts.

When for instance Bruce R. Smith reasserts the importance of orality and the resonance of voice in early modern culture, he invites his readers to reflect upon 'the difference between *ontology*, which assumes a detached, objective spectator who can see the whole, and *phenomenology*, which assumes a subject who is immersed in the experience she is trying to describe'.[3] A comparable interpretative shift has been signalled by the editors of *Subject and Object in Renaissance Culture*, who ask: 'What new configurations [of cultural knowledge] will emerge when subject and object are kept in relation?'[4] In their heightened sense of the sometimes uncanny mutability and the diverse textures associated with cultural materiality at this historical moment, such critical interventions indicate that we need to reconsider at once the unstable status of the objects scrutinized by human subjects of knowledge and the fragile constitution of those 'knowing' subjects within and by their own texts and artefacts. Indeed, Michel Jeanneret has drawn a suggestive parallel to the radical fluidity of our current knowledge system(s) by arguing that a Lucretian or atomistic model of constant mobility and mutability within nature (which influenced not only natural philosophers but other key thinkers, such as Montaigne) is more characteristic of the aesthetic and epistemological structures of the Renaissance than stability and closure.[5] This conception of knowledge(s) in flux unsettles 'early modern' as well as modern aspirations to an 'objective' knowledge system. But Jeanneret also reminds us of the epoch's cultural and intellectual habit of analepsis: the pervasive influence of the heterodox knowledge systems of the pagan past, which characteristically focus on process and mutation. His work thus illustrates in exemplary fashion the delicate balance which more recent criticism seeks between perceptions of likeness to our own moment and the recognition of the difference and otherness of the earlier moment.

It is this difference – the otherness of the Renaissance – that we feel still needs to be emphasized today, because of its virtual erasure by the reclassification of the period as 'early modern'.[6] Though undoubtedly useful in reconnecting the past to the present in newly informed ways, this privileging of continuity with the 'modern' effectively elides epistemic differences or discontinuities and their 'strangeness'. At the same time the reclassification of this cultural epoch tends to imply rupture with prior eras, whether ancient or medieval. Both aspects of the reclassification are explicitly or implicitly put into question by contributors to this volume.

In questioning our epochal sense of early modernity, for instance, Stephen Clucas points out how it is informed by a progressivist, teleological model of knowledge as a process of increased secularization, mechanization and operative agency and autonomy, and, more specifically, as a narrative of the development of science from magic and religion. This narrative is critiqued by Clucas, who focuses on 'the will to perform' as articulated in a complex of religious and magical discourses in a range of 'non-literary' texts. He points out how in texts on magic by Reginald Scot and John Dee, for instance, subjective agency is circumscribed by the terms of religious discourse, and its associated *techne* of self-regulation, while in religious texts by the Calvinist divine William Perkins efficacious faith, again attended by pietistic self-regulation, replaces magical agency as the enabling and legitimizing ground of the will to perform – the shared 'intellectual horizon' of both magical and religious practitioners. The discursive economy of subjective agency in the production of knowledge is thus more complex – variegated and unstable – than post-Enlightenment narratives of the 'early modern' emergence of 'science' suggest. In the place of such overarching, linear narratives, Clucas argues, we should seek to plot an epistemic map of 'local discontinuities', rather as Timothy Reiss has recently done in pointing up 'the complex interweavings of continuity and change' in the period.[7]

David Colclough's essay on the textual strategies of Francis Bacon – a figure who has always occupied the foreground of discussions of knowledge in the period – underscores the point that cultural beginnings (and for that matter ends) are, like natural births, messy and complex rather than neat and linear. Like Clucas, Colclough engages closely with the discursive forms of 'non-literary' texts, again to interrogate a prevalent narrative, here of Bacon as an 'early modern' and as an inaugurator of 'modern science'. Specifically, he shows how Bacon's texts do not break with the ancients so much as perform intertextual negotiations with them in order to transmit a form of knowledge at once 'authoritative and insinuative' to a community of readers which Bacon seeks to constitute through his 'probative' discursive strategies. Both the objects of knowledge and their putatively knowing subjects are thus shown by Colclough as well as by Clucas to be embedded in and delimited by historically specific discursive environments in which the 'early modern' and the 'premodern' may be disentangled only at the cost of understanding what Clucas calls 'the patterns of intelligibility' which informed and determined practice.

Epochal definitions as well as prevalent critical narratives are put into question too by Willy Maley, who argues for the value of applying the critical vocabulary of postcolonial theory to Renaissance texts, and in particular to a text which has been taken as a key 'early modern' text on racial difference, Edmund Spenser's A View of the State of Ireland. Pointing out the myopic and reductionist character of responses by critics who in their obsessive focus on anti-Irish racism 'have let England – and others – escape examination', he goes on to show how, in its multiple, complex and layered mappings of place and identities, Spenser's text exhibits the hybridity and ambivalence usually regarded as the defining characteristics of postcolonial writing. Rather then defacing or demonizing the Irish, as critics have claimed, this complex texture works, he argues, to efface or dematerialize them, erasing them strategically from a picture or map which has other objects of knowledge in view, namely the 'refiguring' of (English) 'metropolitan identities' and the immediate political issue of competing territorial claims on Ireland. The critical vocabulary of a postcolonial critical discourse thus permits what Maley provocatively calls a 'more properly historical' reading of Spenser's text. Like several of the contributions Maley's essay thus illustrates what might be gained from looking at Renaissance texts from within modes of thought and critical discourses which have come 'after' the modern and which permit more nuanced styles of analysis appropriate to the complexities of Renaissance textures of knowledge.

Postmodern thought has in particular privileged figural and material aspects of language as sites of significant other knowledge as psychoanalytic discourse since Freud has always done.[8] The fertility of such 'post'-modern approaches to the textures of Renaissance knowledge is demonstrated here by the contributions of two distinguished French critics of Renaissance culture, Ann Lecercle and Marie Garnier-Giamarchi. Drawing on Lacanian psychoanalysis and post-structuralist thought Ann Lecercle explores the shared logic of representation in two Renaissance artefacts, an Italian painting and an English frieze, each of which attests to the uncanny disturbance of aesthetic order by the material particularity of the detail. The logic of these artefacts, Lecercle argues, is a logic of castration, an inscription of the Law on the senses of sight and hearing and the curtailment of the fleeting access they afford to a pleasure that is both epistemic and erotic. At the same time the interdiction of the Law tends to 'whet the edge of desire' for a forbidden knowledge of what she calls, following Bataille, the 'accursed part' (la part maudite). In the painting by Mazzolino it is the detail of two series or planes of white folds (which Lecercle, citing Deleuze, calls the folds of matter and the folds of the soul) that evokes this desire for 'the place of a jouissance forbidden to man'. In the English frieze a similar logic of castration evokes through the detail the very desire which it forbids, or curtails: as Lecercle points out, 'cur-tailing and de-tailing' are 'the two complementary faces' of this logic. While the painting is a male realization of this logic in relation to sight, the frieze is a 'feminine realization' in relation to hearing, the 'cutting edge' of the frieze serving to divide the mermaids' songs (carmen) from their sexual magic (charm). Lecercle situates this logic in relation to the iconoclasm of the Reformation, which highlighted the act of looking even as it installed the Law as an 'instrument of separation'. Inasmuch as this instrument worked to separate subject and object it facilitated the emergence of Western Europe's modern, 'objective' model of knowledge, which is arguably founded on a logic of castration.

While Lecercle points out the unsettling even 'subversive' effects of 'forbidden knowledge' in the detail, Marie Garnier-Giamarchi argues that it is the sensible or material aurality of words – their pounding in the ear – which carries the effect of 'other' (whether supernatural, magical or subconscious) knowledge in Mercutio's Queen Mab speech in Shakespeare's *Romeo and Juliet*. As she shows, this speech has been notoriously intractable to previous reading practices, requiring as it does a different reading practice: one which is lateral and mobile, sensitive to the 'uncouth' drumming of sound declensions. Drawing on Jean-François Lyotard as well as Jacques Derrida, Garnier-Giamarchi's essay demonstrates the interpretative difference which a postmodern focus on the sensible or material excess of the signifier can introduce into the reading both of a canonical literary text and of an equally canonical scientific or philosophical text.[9] In an exemplary, if provocative move she juxtaposes Shakespeare's Queen Mab speech with an extract from Descartes' *Treatise on Man*, not, as she says, 'in order to attract the Shakespearian text on to the proper path of modernity but to show traces of Shakespearian "mobility" in the philosophical text'. On the one hand, then, a speech traditionally placed as marginal or redundant to knowledge of the literary text is put at its centre, and the material excess of its mobile signifiers privileged as a site of 'other' knowledge; on the other hand, this different or other form of knowledge is shown to inhabit not only a canonical Shakespearian text but also the canonical 'scientific' writing of a figure traditionally regarded, like and with Bacon, as a founding father of Western Europe's 'modern' mechanistic and objective model of knowledge. The writing of Descartes is disturbed, that is, by 'des écarts insuppressibles avec le sensé' (to modify a quotation from Lyotard cited by Garnier-Giamarchi), disclosing a disturbing madness, or magic, in the Cartesian method, on which its founding subject/object divide founders.

In Shakespeare's Queen Mab speech the excess which traverses and confounds foundational divisions of modern forms of knowledge is associated with the feminine (if also with those on the other side of social and geographical boundaries – the mob 'below' and the Welsh). It is likewise a figure of the feminine – Venus – in another Shakespearian text, *Venus and Adonis*, that is shown by Dympna Callaghan to transgress and expose as artificial, other similarly foundational binary divisions: between nature and culture, human and animal. Anxiously insisted upon in contemporary discourses on bestiality, Callaghan argues that these divisions were at the same time perversely traversed by a historical figure of feminine power, Elizabeth I, who habitually treated her courtiers as pets, just as Venus treats Adonis. Here too a conception of the 'liminal' or 'in-between' character of the feminine is allied with poetic practices of figuration which metamorphose or undo familiar and foundational categories of knowledge. Here, however, it is not so much figures of sound (as in the Queen Mab speech) but figures of sense, notably metaphor. The human is joined to the animal, or vegetable, by these transgressive copulations, which have their narrative correlative in the penetration of Adonis by the boar and his subsequent metamorphosis into a flower. More specifically still, as Callaghan points out, the 'commonplace trope' of masculine hunter and feminine hunted is reversed, a back-to-fronting at the level of figuration which doubles the poem's explicit or implied 'unnatural' acts of loving. In contemporary discourses on bestiality such 'unnatural' acts of 'carnal knowledge' are said to generate monstrous offspring. Such an outcome, or 'issue', may be glanced at in the poet's acknowledgement, in his dedicatory address, that this, the 'first heir of [his] invention', may, similarly, 'prove deformed'.[10] The comment may be read too, however, as an oblique acknowledgement of the subversive power of poetic figuration, which, by traversing foundational dichotomies, deforms, and transforms, given forms of knowledge.

As Philippa Berry points out, it is similarly as 'monstrous shapes' that Edmund Spenser represents the epistemic disturbance generated by traversing or transgressing the boundaries of proper or correct forms of knowledge. Her essay explores the troubling epistemic surplus that the texts of pagan antiquity represented – an excess that, once identified, might be either abjected or celebrated in non-literary or literary texts of this epoch. Spenser's depiction of a paradigmatic figure of misrecognition or not-knowledge, Error, offers an especially vivid emblem of this problematic cultural residue or excess. Predictably personified as a woman, Error is also associated metonymically with a non-European cultural origin through an Ovidian allusion to the flooding of the Nile. Yet Berry points out that through Spenser's allusive use of Ovid in this passage a seeming intellectual waste is troped as a process that is also uniquely, if disturbingly fertile. The analogy suggests that, like the material origins of the grotesque maternal body with which they are conflated, the effects of an alien or officially 'false' knowledge will always exceed the containment attempted by their intellectual negation as Error. The ambivalence towards pagan culture which Berry traces in this essay puts into question the prevalent view that the relation of the Renaissance to antiquity should be interpreted primarily in terms of resemblance; at the same time, it unsettles the teleological forms of historical narrative that are implied in the revisionary reclassification of this epoch as 'early modern' by reasserting its backwards or analeptic orientation towards ideas of origin and the epistemic difference of archaic cultures.

'Against the idea of a universe which flows on while we are in it', Montaigne comments, 'how puny and stunted is the knowledge of the most inquisitive men.'[11] Despite this expressed scepticism, the negation as not-knowledge (ignorance or error) of knowledge associated with an 'other' is one of the moves of dismissal made by Montaigne in his textual 'commerce' with women analysed by Elizabeth Guild. Dismissive at worst, the mood of these negotiations with the problem of sex/gender difference is at best 'edgy'. Guild uses this adjective of a local textual effect, but it is more generally applicable to Montaigne's intertextual relations with 'the margin of unknowableness' represented by feminine alterity. To be edgy is to withdraw spasmically, instinctually, from that which is apprehended as an edge or limit *that may not be one*, but rather an abyss or 'vanishing point'. In Montaigne's case, which Guild twins pointedly with the case of Jacques Lacan, this withdrawal takes the form of mastering moves including the negation of the difference of the feminine as ignorance. Such moves tend to curtail epistemic negotiations in a precipitate coming to terms with, in order not to know, the otherness of the other sex, which, Guild suggests, may also represent an otherness within the authorial or analytic subject of knowledge. Women and the feminine consequently constitute a limit to the open, apparently limitless explorations that have marked Montaigne out as the exemplar of the (early) modern writing and desiring subject in quest of a self that is fashioned, and known, at least in part, through textual exchanges or 'commerce' with others.

Difference is again negated as ignorance in the exclusionary humanism of the topography of self-knowledge which Margaret Tudeau-Clayton traces in the printed version of Ben Jonson's *Bartholomew Fair*. This topography, she argues, encodes the playtext for educated readers as an allegory of the conditions of its production as performance in the Hope public theatre. Like and with the fair, the theatre is identified by 'learned and poetical' textual *loci* (places) mapped over it as an 'underworld', a place of negation or lack inhabited by spectators who are represented, through their 'play fellow' Bartholomew Cokes, as ignorant, childlike 'asses' without the privileged (and privileging) form of knowledge – self-knowledge – acquired by reading learned and poetical discourse. The difference here is not of gender or race but of a community and culture mapped by the terms of a bourgeois discourse as its own contrary or negation. Indeed, as Tudeau-Clayton shows, this hierarchical opposition is reproduced by the representation of women, which at the same time suggests how the topography of political exclusion also represents a topography of the psychic repression constitutive of the unified, transcendent bourgeois humanist subject. On the one hand, the material, multiple heterogeneity of the 'underworld' of the fair or public theatre is metonymically figured in the vast, sweating body of Ursula–Eve, who is identified with the *mater–materia* of embodied existence; on the other hand, the disembodied, homogeneous community of educated readers is metonymically figured in the (virtually bodiless and certainly sweatless) Grace Well-Born, who is identifed with a transcendent, unified essence (or soul) and who exhibits a 'self-possession' and detachment indicative of the model of self-knowledge she represents. As his loss of her during the play/fair signals, this is a self-knowledge that her betrothed Bartholomew Cokes is without, immersed as he is in the material objects and spectacles of his immediate environment, which are what he 'knows' and which are confused with his 'self'. If this negation by the playtext of embodied forms of knowledge and participatory forms of culture renders performance problematic, it is precisely theatrical performance that will expose as literally utopic – and subvert – the playtext's project of a bourgeois, politically exclusionary and psychically repressive topography of self-knowledge.

This problematic opposition of readers' abstract playtext and embodied performance or existence is underscored by the figure of Grace, inasmuch as abstract self-possession is the only mode of possession she enjoys. As ward of Justice Overdo, that is, in the historically embedded material conditions of her social place, she is an object of exchange in the system governing property relations. Her status in this respect together with the abstract model of self-knowledge with which she is associated in the playtext calls for comparison with Sue Wiseman's contrasting historical case study of Anne Clifford, a woman at once well born and well educated.

Clifford's aspirations went well beyond the limits of abstract self-knowledge to possession at once of place (her father's lands to which she was heir but dispossessed) and of an identity bound up with, or woven into, the (re)possession of place. The diverse modes and media of cultural production deployed by Clifford in the service of this aspiration imply, Wiseman argues, an elite woman's self-definition and knowledge as political subject. She shows how this knowledge is conveyed in Clifford's diaries as well as in the textualized places and spaces of buildings, monuments and self-portraiture, all designed to carry political as well as personal meanings. Clifford's output indicates the broad range of discursive possibilities for a privileged woman to insinuate herself into the political sphere, possibilities not allowed for by such ideologically overdetermined representations as Grace Well-Born. Clifford's case offers, moreover, an alternative to Jonson's male, bourgeois humanist model of self-knowledge. For her feminine, aristocratic model privileges the local, and a selfhood constructed in relations of possession to regionally specific textualized places. As such, Wiseman argues, it carried a potential for resistance to a centralised absolute political authority. In contrast, Jonson's model privileges withdrawal or abstraction from the local, and a detached, unified and transcendent selfhood constructed through the reading of learned and poetical texts, which are non-locally defined possessions of an ideal, indeed utopic, community of educated, bourgeois humanist readers. Further, although its bourgeois ideology works to replace the hierarchy according to birth with a hierarchy according to what is acquired through education, Jonson's playtext contains its subversive potential by an explicit endorsement of the centralized structure of absolute political authority – 'the King' – which Clifford's model of self-knowledge tends to resist.

Jonson's is only one of several texts discussed in this volume which seek through specific textual strategies to call upon a reader or community of readers to participate in the production of knowledge. In the case of Jonson these strategies include the epigraph to the printed book and intertextual allusions to learned and poetical discourse, which work to create, even as they assume, a community of learned readers. Similarly, as David Colclough shows, Bacon's textual strategies, notably his practice of self-citation as well as his citation of classical authors, work at once to create a constituency of readers and to weave or insinuate into it Bacon's own authority. In the case of Clifford, Sue Wiseman draws attention to the way the reader – hostile or sympathetic – is 'consistently imagined' in her writings, and, specifically, how marginal notes in the diaries work to draw from the reader sympathetic recognition of her self-definition as rightful owner of her father's lands.

There are no such obvious specific textual strategies in the writing of Montaigne, who would appear to have no overt designs on his reader(s), except, Guild suggests, when the reader is a woman. The textual negotiations at once become more complicated or (k)notted as Montaigne seeks in turn to flirt, seduce and master, just as, in representation, he seeks to deal with the problem of feminine alterity through mastering moves including the dismissal of women as lacking knowledge, especially self-knowledge. For Montaigne, as for Jonson, this self-knowledge was acquired above all through dialogic reading – textual intercourse or commerce – with other men's learned and poetical writing. As Sue Wiseman points out, Ann Clifford was herself a reader of Montaigne, and, although her responses are not recorded, one is justified in wondering whether, even as she drew on his writing as a model of self-discovery and definition, she chose not to hear his strategic attempts to seduce or master women readers and his dismissals of them as without self-knowledge.

If a mode or measure of ignorance may well be a condition of knowledge – and, for Socrates, famously, the highest form of knowledge lies in knowledge of one's ignorance – the essays in this volume draw attention to the epistemic disturbance produced when subjects and objects of knowledge are constituted by denying or negating the knots of alterity: whether these be of gender, class, race, materiality or history. At the same time they foreground the multiple complexities of Renaissance or early modern textures of knowledge, highlighting the alterities *of* as well as *in* these textures. What is to be gained from attending to such textures as these essays do is, moreover, not only a renewed awareness of the difference of the past. As Marie Garnier-Giamarchi suggests, to attend to the otherness of a singular texture from the past may enable us to engage differently with other forms of alterity in the present. It may, in other words, enable us to negotiate our own moment of epistemological crisis. Shakespeare's Queen Mab, she comments, is a mid-wife, a being-in-the-middle who invites us to effect a radical revision – a figurative mobilization – of our current models of identity and knowledge. Attending differently to the textures of Renaissance knowledge may thus enable us not simply to reimagine our intellectual and cultural past but also to imagine a different present, and, perhaps most importantly, a different future.

Notes

1 Jean-François Lyotard, *The Postmodern Condition: A Report on Knowledge*, trans. Geoff Bennington and Brian Massumi (Manchester: Manchester University Press, 1986), pp. 76, 4.

2 Neil Rhodes and Jonathan Sawday (eds), *The Renaissance Computer: Knowledge Technology in the First Age of Print* (London: Routledge, 2000), p. 11.

3 Bruce R. Smith, *The Acoustic World of Early Modern England: Attending to the O-factor* (Chicago: University of Chicago Press, 1999), p. 10.

4 Margreta de Grazia, Peter Stallybrass and Maureen Quilligan (eds), *Subject and Object in Renaissance Culture* (Cambridge: Cambridge University Press, 1996), p. 2.

5 Michel Jeanneret, *Perpetuum mobile: métamorphoses des corps et des oeuvres de Vinci à Montaigne* (Paris: Macula, 1997), translated as *Perpetual Motion: Transforming*

Shapes in the Renaissance from da Vinci to Montaigne (Baltimore: Johns Hopkins University Press, 2001).

6 The *locus classicus* for the use of 'early modern' is Leah S. Marcus, 'Renaissance/ Early Modern Studies', in Stephen Greenblatt and Giles Gunn (eds), *Redrawing the Boundaries: The Transformation of English and American Literary Studies* (New York: The Modern language Association of America, 1992), pp. 41–63. In a lucid intervention Heather Dubrow has argued that it is more helpful to think in terms of 'both and' rather than 'either or', a flexibility which has, as she points out, pedagogical as well as ideological value. See Heather Dubrow, 'The Term Early Modern', *PMLA* 109:5 (1994), 1025–1026. The resistance to 'early modern' by Renaissance scholars in continental Europe was highlighted at a recent international conference of the FISIER (Fédération Internationale des Sociétés et Instituts pour l'Etude de la Renaissance): 'Les études sur la Renaissance aujourd'hui; actualité et perspectives d'avenir' (Geneva, 27–29 September 2001). The term 'early modern' was used, if at all, untranslated, and in quotation marks, as it were, Renaissance being the preferred term throughout. The alterity of the Renaissance is underscored in the work of French scholars such as Frank Lestringant, who provide a valuable counterpoint to Anglo-American scholars whose use of 'early modern' has emphasized continuity and likeness.

7 Timothy J. Reiss, *Knowledge, Discovery and Imagination in Early Modern Europe* (Cambridge: Cambridge University Press, 1997), p. xiii.

8 See Jonathan Culler, 'The Call of the Phoneme: Introduction', in Jonathan Culler (ed.), *On Puns: The Foundation of Letters* (Oxford: Basil Blackwell, 1988), especially pp. 10–12. In his essay on Derrida in the same volume Gregory Ulmer argues that Derrida 'refunctions the pun into the philosopheme of a new cognition', which Ulmer calls the puncept. See Gregory Ulmer, 'The Puncept in Grammatology', in *ibid.*, pp. 164–189 (p. 165). He also suggests that 'how one feels about puns' serves as a measure of where one is situated in relation to postmodern sensibility. According to this test much 'premodern' writing anticipates this sensibility.

9 We use 'sensible' here as meaning perceptible to the senses, a use which the *OED* states as rare in contemporary English, but which has recently been remotivated under the impact of the French theorists and their use of the French word *sensible*.

10 William Shakespeare, *The Poems*, ed. John Roe (Cambridge: Cambridge University Press, 1992), p. 78.

11 Michel de Montaigne, 'Of Coaches', *The Complete Essays*, trans. M. A. Screech (London: Penguin, 1987), III, 6, p. 1028.

—part one—

Knowledge, nature, history

1

Renewing the concept of Renaissance:
the cultural influence of paganism reconsidered

PHILIPPA BERRY

> sic ubi deseruit madidos septemfluus agros
> Nilus ut antiquo sua flumina reddidit alveo
> aetherioque recens exarsit sidere limus,
> plurima cultores versis animalia glaebis
> inveniunt et in his quaedam modo coepta per ipsum
> nascendi spatium, quaedam imperfecta suisque
> trunca vident numeris, et eodem in corpore saepe
> altera pars vivit, rudis est pars altera tellus . . .
> ergo ubi diluvio tellus lutulenta recenti
> solibus aetheriis altoque recanduit aestu,
> edidit innumeras species; partimque figuras
> rettulit antiquas, partim nova monstra creavit.

So when the seven-mouthed Nile has receded from the drenched fields and has returned again to its former bed, and the fresh slime has been heated by the sun's rays, farmers as they turn over lumps of earth find many animate things; and among these some, but now begun, are upon the very verge of life, some are unfinished and lacking in their proper parts, and oft-times in the same body one part is alive and the other still nothing but raw earth . . . When, therefore, the earth, covered with mud from the recent flood, became heated up by the hot ethereal rays of the sun, she brought forth innumerable forms of life; in part she restored the ancient shapes, and in part she created creatures new and strange.[1]

D AVID HUME was disapprovingly to observe that 'Learning on its revival [in the early Renaissance] was attired in the same unnatural garb which it wore at the time of its decay among the Greeks and Romans'.[2] And the evident distaste felt by a representative of the Enlightenment for what he perceived as an earlier cultural inclination to decadence, or to 'unnatural' ideas, was shared by several of Hume's contemporaries, including Voltaire. It was subsequently to become a common theme in late nineteenth-century accounts of the Italian Renaissance, all of which were indebted to Jacob Burckhardt's *The Civilisation of the Renaissance in Italy*, in its potent combination of post-Hegelianism with an implicit religiosity. With a pejorative horror that was also, of course, invested with an intense fascination, Burckhardt characterized early Renaissance humanism as dangerously infected by paganism: in its superstition, its fatalism and above all in its elevation of philosophy above religion: 'This humanism was, in fact, pagan, and became more so as its sphere widened in the fifteenth century . . . Nor could they speak of Christianity without paganizing it.'[3]

There was certainly much contemporary evidence to support the Burckhardtian view. The widespread fear, frequently expressed between the fifteenth and seventeenth centuries, that the *renovatio* of Western culture within the crucible of ancient beliefs might be engendering a potent mixture of paganism with other, radically new ideas is given typical expression in a comment made by the Catholic theologian Gabriel de Puy Herbault in 1549, when he warned his contemporaries that coming out of Italy was 'A new paganism, a modern paganism, occasionally nourished by Greek and Latin sources and sometimes confused with that paganism bequeathed by the ancients, but emboldened by its own novelty, and vivified by an optimistic conception of man'.[4] Such evidence was reinterpreted, however, in a mid-twentieth-century reaction against the unbalanced but highly influential idea of 'Renaissance paganism' which Burckhardt had disseminated. The change of viewpoint was led by a group of scholars the secularizing character of whose work Warren Boutcher has persuasively related (in spite of some important differences of viewpoint) to their precarious identity as Jewish immigrants in postwar America.[5] The most notable member of this group was Paul Oskar Kristeller, who, observing that 'there were few, if any, [Renaissance or early modern] thinkers who seriously thought of reviving ancient pagan cults', redefined 'Renaissance paganism' in terms of a quasi-modern rationalism:

> The real core of the tradition concerning Renaissance paganism is something quite different [from the accounts of nineteenth-century historiographers]: it is the steady and irresistible growth of nonreligious intellectual interests which were not so much opposed to the content of religious doctrine as rather competing with it for individual and public attention.[6]

Along with other leading cultural historians of the postwar generation, Kristeller reconfigured the period in a guise that was consistent with the more rational and secular attitudes of his era; indeed, he described his work as specifically influenced by a Kantian notion of reason.[7] Yet Kristeller's increasing interest in Renaissance Platonism also contributed significantly to this reformulation of the debt of Renaissance humanism to antiquity. For in an echo of Plato's tightly organized analogical universe, both Kristeller and his contemporaries implicitly perceived this relationship rather as an intellectual recognition of resemblance than as a potentially disruptive encounter with cultural difference. The continuing influence of such a view is apparent in the still widely held assumption that premodern culture in general and premodern mimesis in particular were founded primarily on the perception of similitudes. This viewpoint informs even the seminal post-structuralist analysis of Renaissance or early modern practices of representation in Michel Foucault's *The Order of Things*:

> The relation of emulation [*aemulatio*] enables things to imitate one another from one end of the universe to the other without connection or proximity: by duplicating itself in a mirror the world abolishes the distance proper to it; in this way it overcomes the place allotted to each thing.[8]

Much of the huge volume of detailed research on humanist philosophy and scholarship that has been produced over the last few decades has been indebted, directly or indirectly, to Kristeller's reforming influence. But what was sacrificed by his brilliant account of the period's relationship to antiquity, and what in consequence has been largely absent from recent scholarly studies of its intellectual history, is the eighteenth- and nineteenth-century sense – exaggerated although it may have been – of the potential alterity or dissonance of classical influence within this epoch. (An important exception to this trend is obviously represented by those works which explore the topic of magic; it is my contention, however, that such studies occupy an implicitly marginal position in relation to the more rational and secular focus of mainstream Renaissance or early modern studies; indeed, this supplementary interest in the specific question of 'magic' seems ironically to have contributed to the neglect of the wider issue of the alterity of classical culture as a whole.) As a result of the change of scholarly perspective inaugurated by Kristeller, and in contrast to the excesses of the Burckhartian view, critics and scholars are now inclined to see the period in largely teleological terms: as a diachronic narrative which progresses towards a putative triumph of reason; at the same time, its tendency is still to efface the alterity of the period's self-declared reassessment of a cultural origin, representing the influence of antiquity instead in terms of a 'classicism' (defined as a perfection of style and form) which corresponds to the highest values of modern, post-Enlightenment culture.[9]

Kristeller's contribution to changing perceptions of intellectual history of Europe in the fifteenth and early sixteenth centuries is beyond question; yet one might have expected his somewhat sanitized and historically determined reinterpretation of the epoch's debt to antiquity to have been interrogated during the last two decades, if only because one highly vocal branch of research into Renaissance or early modern culture – that of new historicism – has declared itself to be especially attentive to questions of cultural difference, and suspicious of the hegemonic or anti-dialogical tendencies which have informed modern historical methodologies. But the ambiguity of 'early modern' specialists about the exact boundaries of their intellectual terrain, and about its relationship to modern culture in particular, suggests that the issue which is explicitly presented by the term 'Renaissance' – the problem of a return to archaic cultural origins – is still engendering some discomfort and uncertainty. In an intriguing exploration of the increasing preference of critics writing after new historicism for the period label of 'early modern' rather than 'Renaissance', Leah S. Marcus has argued that:

> We are moving away from interpreting the period as a time of re-naissance, cultural rebirth, the awakening of an earlier era conceived of as (in some sense) classic; we are coming to view the period more in terms of elements repeated thereafter, those features of the age that appear to us precursors of our own twentieth century, the modern, the postmodern.[10]

Marcus confirms that new historicist critics of the 'early modern' cultural moment assume (not unlike Kristeller) there to be 'pronounced elements of continuity' between early modern and modern culture; while she argues that contemporary critics recognize in this period elements of not only modern but also postmodern culture, she acknowledges that 'in the field of history, early modern leads directly into the modern era'. But as Margreta de Grazia has recently pointed out, 'the imperative to see the Renaissance as precipitating the modern' may have pressured critics into perceiving many of the details of Renaissance or early modern culture as 'modern before their time'.[11] And certainly, in focusing primarily upon those motifs of sexuality, race or politics which resonate with the cultures of late modernity, a majority of the many critics influenced by new historicism has preferred to avoid the wider cultural, philosophical, and religious questions posed by the compulsive mimesis of classical exempla which characterized this epoch.

Yet if contemporary Renaissance or early modern criticism is gradually to redefine itself as postmodern rather than late modern, and so begin to question some of the 'modern' methods and values which continue implicitly to influence its interpretative project, it will have to give more attention to the diverse ways in which its object of study not only differs from the rational modern era which succeeded it, but is also internally fissured, by its often problematic incorporation of fragments of classical culture. While his work is overtly concerned with contemporary aspects of cultural colonialism, Homi Bhabha has lucidly summarized the interpretative tendency which needs to be interrogated:

> However impeccably the content of an 'other' culture may be known, however anti-ethnocentrically it is represented, it is its *location* as the closure of grand theories, the demand that in analytic terms, it must always be the good object of knowledge, the docile body of difference, that reproduces a relation of domination.[12]

and Dominic LaCapra has articulated a similar viewpoint in relation to intellectual history:

> Even if one accepts the metaphor that presents interpretation as the 'voice' of the historical reader in the 'dialogue' with the past, it must be actively recognized that the past has its own voices that must be respected, especially when they resist or qualify the interpretations we would like to place on them. A text is a network of resistances, and a dialogue is a two-way affair; a good reader is also an attentive and patient listener.[13]

In order to remind ourselves that the Renaissance or early modern project of cultural renewal was also, in a very important sense, a process of defamiliarization or estrangement, I would suggest that, taking its figurative cue from the idea of Renaissance, a new generation of critics and cultural historians should direct its gaze away from the putative unity of a cultural ending, to reinterrogate instead that emblematic preoccupation with the redefinition of *beginnings* or origins which is announced by the word 'Renaissance' and its cognates (*rinascimento, renovatio*) – some of whose wider implications have yet, I believe, to be understood. Marcus notes that 'Scholars of the early modern period have devoted relatively little energy to the contestation of points of origin, much more to the issue of defining a terminus'.[14] Yet I will argue in the second part of this essay that it is paradoxically in this very cultural context, and specifically in England in the late 1590s, that a preoccupation with antiquity's own explorations of the disturbing mutability of origins assumes an increasing urgency and complexity.

By discarding the formalist assumptions which covertly inform modern definitions of the cultural influence of antiquity as 'classic', we shall hopefully be able to replace this perspective with a more developed sense of the inherent strangeness, as well as the problematic incompleteness, of those remnants of antique civilization that were embedded so deeply within the culture which flowered on the threshold of the modern. Such a reassessment should also enable us to elucidate more fully two aspects of Renaissance or early modern culture which are currently receiving renewed attention, and which, as I shall show in the second part of this essay, become intimately related, via the use of classical myth by some English literary texts, *not only* to ideas of classical origins *but also* to classical ideas of origin. These are: firstly, its practices of literary mimesis; and secondly, its discourses on the subject of matter or nature.

In the wake of deconstruction, a heightened interest in the polysemous textuality of this historical moment, and in its diverse cultural implications, has been articulated by several critics, including Terence Cave, Patricia Parker and Derek Attridge.[15] These critics have stressed that the epoch's pervasive interest in linguistic play is vitally indebted to its imitation of classical exempla, and that, as Judith M. Anderson has recently reiterated, '*copia* is implicated in fiction, in verbal constructs that do not simply mirror things, material *res*'.[16] Further investigation of these stylistic practices seems likely to require a fuller exploration of the classical fondness for rhetorical copiousness and semantic polyvalence which was imitated so extensively by Renaissance or early modern texts.[17] At the same time, at a moment when our contemporary scientific and ecological debates are stimulating renewed interest in premodern debates about nature, the literary interweaving of the subject matter of classical myth with diverse speculations about physical matter and the origins of the cosmos can afford new insights into the heterodox character of natural philosophy on the verge of the modern era.[18] The 'vitalist' or 'animist materialist' assumptions which inform Milton's *Paradise Lost*, nearly a century later, have now begun to receive considerable attention, while Michel Jeanneret has recently pointed out that similar attitudes were widely disseminated in sixteenth-century Europe.[19] It seems plausible, therefore, that comparable views are being adumbrated in English literature as early as the 1590s, albeit with some considerable ambivalence.[20]

In fact, just such an ambivalence or inconsistency appears to have been a distinguishing feature of the reception of ancient culture by early humanist thinkers. Hans Baron argued, for example, that the quattrocento humanist Coluccio Salutati gradually changed his view of ancient culture and its religious meanings in the course of his intellectual career, moving away from a quasi-medieval, religiously orthodox perspective towards a developing enthusisiam for a more pagan intellectual position, which he termed the theology of the poets (*theologia poetarum*).[21] A century later, while the neo-Platonist Marsilio Ficino typically stressed the resemblances, rather than the differences, between important strands of classical thought and Christian religion, he could also advocate the use of what D. P. Walker called 'spiritual magic', in musical invocations of the planetary deities.[22] Similarly, his younger contemporary Pico della Mirandola combined an intellectual disdain for the astrological fatalism of the ancients with a passionate enthusiasm for what he described in *De hominis dignitate* as the exotic strangeness of antique philosophy:

> In Porphyry you will enjoy the copiousness of his matter and the multiformity of religion; in Iamblichus you will revere an occult philosophy and strange foreign mysteries [*barbarorum mysteria*] . . . not to mention Proclus, who abounds in Asiatic richness, and those stemming from him, Hermias, Damascius, Olympiodorus, . . . in all of whom there ever gleams . . . 'the Divine', which is the distinctive mark of the Platonists.[23]

Pico's remarks suggestively conjoin a familiar humanist emphasis upon the stylistic copiousness or abundance of ancient literary material (as *res*, or matter) with less orthodox allusions to the multiformity of pagan religion; the intellectual and religious tradition which he evokes is evidently perceived as one of metamorphic strangeness, whose *barbarorum mysteria* incorporate a distinctive strand of racial difference, in the form of 'Asiatic richness'. Another century later, a similarly contradictory relationship to the classical tradition can be traced in the writings of Michel de Montaigne. Montaigne is now typically read as an exemplary precursor of the rational scepticism of the modern age; however, Daniel Martin has pointed out that the first edition of his *Essais* was closely examined by the Roman Curia, because of its extensive references to the pagan idea of Fortune. Martin demonstrates that even in subsequent editions of the *Essais* this unequivocally pagan concept, derived from the Roman thinkers whom Montaigne most sincerely admired, remains a central *leitmotif*.[24] If Montaigne is a privileged representative of that 'new paganism' which was feared by orthodox Christians during this epoch, then Martin's elucidation of his literary cult of Fortune appears to contradict Kristeller's influential argument that a Renaissance or early modern paganism is merely the precursor of modern scepticism.

It was through his literary cult of a personified Fortune that Montaigne embraced the inherent disorderliness and mutability of human affairs; it was likewise in their literary explorations of classical myth, now freed from the straitjacket of medieval allegory, that English writers of the sixteenth and seventeenth centuries were best able to explore the polymorphous difference of the classical tradition. The disturbing polysemy of this central element of the classical inheritance is now frequently elided by contemporary critics who stress its allegorical assimilation into Christian doctrine. Yet the conflict between classical myth and Christian faith was often acknowledged during the Renaissance or early modern period, and is explicitly recognized in a virulent attack on the disturbing and 'heathen' strangeness of classical myth, published by a zealous 'student in Divinity' just as English literature was beginning to rediscover the aesthetic attractions of mythological material.

Stephen Batman's *The Golden Booke of the Leaden Gods*, published in 1577, is the first English mythography. Although a very inferior contribution to the mythographic genre, its chief interest resides in its polemical exposition of the religious and cultural strangeness represented by classical myth and philosophy. The exaggerated tropes of Batman's prefatory comments are an eloquent testimony to contemporary anxiety concerning interest in this archaic cultural origin, which is here suggestively identified with the 'filthiness' of an originary matter:

> [In] this final treatise of the putative & imagined Gods of the Gentiles ... we Christians, now lyvinge in the cleare light of the Gospel, may evidently see, with what erroneous trumperies, Antiquitie hath bene nozzeled: in what foggy mystes, they have long wandered: in what filthye puddles they have bene myered: under what masking visors of clouted religions, they have been bewytched; what traditions they have of theyr owne phantastical braynes to themselves forged: & finallye into what Apostacye, Atheisme, Blasphemye, Idolatrye, and Heresie, they have plunged their Soules, & affiaunced their beleeves. Whose miserable captivitie, so long and so many yeres, under the grevous yoake, and thraldome of oure deadlye Enemie, and capital foe Sathan, as wee are most pitifullye to bewayle: so are we most humblye, and incessauntlye to prayse God for oure owne deliveraunce from the lyke slaverye.[25]

Batman's attack on the classical gods is most recognizably Puritan in its identification of paganism with the 'trumperies' or idols of 'clouted religions', whose fragmentary or patched character Batman implicitly contrasts with the unified doctrine of the Reformed religion. Yet by defining pagan belief as a work of the imagination, or of 'phantastical braynes', Batman obliquely acknowledges its potential attractions to writers and dramatists; indeed, his troping of pagan religion as a 'masquerade', involving the use of 'masking visors', allies it not only with dramatic performance and playing but specifically with courtly entertainments or masques, which were almost wholly peopled with the classical gods. Combined with this imagery of disguise, however, is a figurative mesh that additionally identifies the aberrations of paganism with the disorderliness of an abjected material origin, on which Batman imagines the ancients to have 'nozzled': to have fed, nursed or been nurtured.[26] Pagan myth and belief is thereby accorded a suggestively bodily and material character, defined as an infantile dependence upon a figuratively maternal, yet intrinsically deceitful source of knowledge. The theme is more fully expressed when (using the pejorative epithet of 'filthy' which was especially favoured by anti-theatrical Puritan polemicists) Batman identifies paganism with the disorderly waste or 'myre' of nature, as ordure and/or urine: 'filthye puddles' suggests both kinds of human waste. Finally, in a half-explicit equation of paganism with a diffuse fluidity that runs through the passage, the ancients' excessive immersion in the degrading physicality of a material origin is further troped as a 'plunging' into sin. Here the wateriness associated in Genesis with an originary nature or primal chaos is elided with that material or maternal substance on which the ancients 'nozzled', as the 'foggy mystes' wherein this heathen wateriness was apparently condensed are opposed to the clear and immaterial light of the Gospel.[27]

For Batman, it is evidently Christianity, rather than pagan culture, which is synonymous with the visual objectivity of reason. Yet ironically, his tropes simultaneously accord an increased substantiality – or materiality – to that obscure cultural 'origin' upon which Renaissance or early modern culture was still fixing its gaze. Batman's vituperative rhetoric consequently affords an unexpected insight into an aspect of the contemporary mimesis of classical myth which becomes especially marked in England during the 1590s, whereby the literary use of mythic materials frequently interweaves exploration of the disturbing grossness and mutability of the matter, or *materia*, of representation, with meditations upon the inherent disorderliness of origins. It seems not to be coincidental that these literary recognitions of the fundamental alterity of classical culture coincide with the emergence, in late sixteenth-century natural philosophy, of a new animist materialism (shaped to an important extent by interest in non-Aristotelian strands of ancient science, from Parmenides to the Stoics and Epicureans), whose view of matter differs both from the Aristotelianism of the medieval schoolmen and also from the mechanical philosophy of the seventeenth century. However, the chief impetus behind these literary meditations upon originary matter appears to have been the changing reception of Ovid's *Metamorphoses*.[28]

In Christopher Marlowe's narrative poem *Hero and Leander*, the bewildering copiousness of classical subject matter assumes human form in the protean and highly erotic materiality of the classical gods, who simultaneously emblematize the metamorphic fertility of matter or nature itself. Charles Martindale has recently observed that the poem implies a particularly sophisticated reading of the *Metamorphoses*, its chief classical influence, as a text 'in which genres and personalities are denaturalized, polarities and categories formed and broken down, closure both offered and denied, in dizzyingly vertiginous fashion'.[29] In Marlowe's inspired *ekphrasis* of the 'discloured', or multicoloured, temple of Venus at Sestos, the classical deities are represented as a semiotic excess that is almost indistinguishable from the substance or *materia* of representation – here, the crystalline materials from which the temple is fashioned:

> So faire a church as this, had *Venus* none,
> The wals were of discoloured *Jasper* stone,
> Wherein was *Proteus* carved, and o'rehead,
> A livelie vine of green sea agget spread:
> Where by one hand, light headed *Bacchus* hoong,
> And with the other, wine from grapes out wroong.
> Of Christall shining faire, the pavement was,
> The towne of *Sestos*, cal'd it *Venus* glasse,
> There might you see the gods in sundrie shapes,
> Committing headdie ryots, incest, rapes.[30]

Far from limiting or enframing their mythological potency, the diverse 'discoloured' materials of the building – the agate walls, the jasper ceiling, the crystal pavement – appear to participate in those mutable processes of nature which the classical gods personify, in an uncanny reabsorption of art into nature. Thus the allusion to the 'livelie' vine of 'sea agget' hints that the stone of the ceiling may be on the point of mutating into that seawater which will ultimately consume Leander; while a worshipper standing on the temple's mirror-like floor of 'crystal' would presumably see their own reflection disturbingly entwined with the figures of the gods. In its fluid and metamorphic character, the material frame or structure of Marlowe's temple appears to equate the mimesis of the classical gods not with perfection of form but rather with the incipient dissolution of form.

In Marlowe's temple, the polysemic abundance or copiousness of the world of classical myth is implicated not only in an incipient reversion of matter into an originary chaos but simultaneously in the covert dissolution of orthodox religious forms, as spirit (in the form of the gods) is shown to be intimately interwoven with matter. What the temple appears to invite the worshipper to contemplate, in other words, is the formlessness of prime matter; and Marlowe's syntax reinforces this impression, by observing that: 'So faire a church as this, had Venus *none*' [my emphasis]. The passage consequently has suggestive implications for the ambiguous centrality of the temple's absent tutelary goddess, Venus, to many contemporary redactions of classical myth; although her association with love of a transcendent or immaterial beauty was a central motif in the Platonizing love poetry of the period, it was the goddess's less idealized connection with the flux and fecundity of nature – as a Venus Genetrix who sometimes has an implicitly Lucretian significance – that was frequently privileged in English literary representations of the inherent disorderliness of origins.

The wider implication of Marlowe's *ekphrasis* appears to be that any cultural structure which attempts to incorporate such mutable materials will itself be transformed by them. This subtle poetic comment can consequently provide us with an interesting insight into the status of classical myth in the major poetic publication of the 1590s, Spenser's *The Faerie Queene*. For Spenser's developing awareness of the richness and polyvalency of classical culture – and his debt to the *Metamorphoses* in particular – appears to be increasingly at odds with his Protestant desire to fix this disturbingly protean material in a doctrinally orthodox allegorical frame (albeit one in which Christian belief is infused with Platonic philosophy). One way in which we can chart the gradual change in Spenser's attitude to this question is in the multiple textual traces within his epic of an abjected originary matter – as 'filth', 'slime' or 'mud'. Functioning as a recurring metonym for the dangers of pagan cultural influence, these 'mires' within the Spenserian text are typically associated with an abjected female genetrix or janitrix who emblematizes the disorderly multiplicity of origins.

The first female genetrix to be encountered in the poem appears in Book I's canto i. This is the serpentine yet grotesquely fecund figure of Error, of whom 'there bred / A thousand yong ones, which she dayly fed, / Sucking upon her poisonous dugs, each one / Of sundry shapes, yet all ill favored'. Although this figure is derived from Hesiod's serpent Echidna, what Spenser articulates in the succeeding stanzas is a Protestant allegory of the lines from *Metamorphoses* Book I which are printed as the epigraph to this essay; this is Ovid's comparison of the effects of the flood to the seasonal flooding of the Nile.[31] When she is gripped around the throat by the Redcrosse knight, the connections between Error's disgusting bodily emissions and what is here implied to be the almost unstoppable flood of pagan intellectual influence are made explicit, as (in an extended simile which is putatively inspired by Ovid's use of the verb 'edidit', to describe the Nile's paradoxical process of engendering) Spenser equates the textual content of Error's 'parbreake' or vomit with the material effects of the flooding Nile:

> Therewith she spewed out of her filthy maw
> A floud of poyson horrible and black,
> Full of great lumpes of flesh and gobbets raw,
> Which stunck so vildly, that it forst him slacke
> His grasping hold, and from her turn him backe:
> Her vomit full of bookes and papers was,
> With loathly frogs and toades, which eyes did lacke,
> And creeping sought way in the weedy gras:
> Her filthy parbreake all the place defiled has.
>
> As when old father *Nilus* gins to swell
> With timely pride above the *Aegyptian* vale,
> His fattie waves do fertile slime outwell,
> And overflow each plaine and lowly dale:
> But when his later spring gins to avale,
> Huge heapes of mudd he leaves, wherein there breed
> Ten thousand kindes of creatures, partly male
> And partly female of his fruitfull seed;
> Such ugly monstrous shapes elsewhere may no man reed.
>
> (I.i.20–21)

Since 'reed' had the archaic meaning of 'imagine' or 'guess at', this final line seems to combine an assertion of the unimaginable, unique character of Error with an interdiction against the reading of strange or monstrous matter (given the specific reference to the Nile, this appears to include the texts of antiquity as well as more contemporary heretical publications). But although Redcrosse kills Error, Spenser is not so easily to banish the disturbing materiality and copiousness of Western cultural origins from his text, for, by a process of metonymic association, the mud of Error's pagan flood is promptly transferred to the far more important character of Duessa, who is the female tempter of Redcrosse from his elected path of holiness. James Nohrnberg has connected Duessa's inherent doubleness 'with the processes of fiction, and especially the secondariness of an imitative production'.[32] Through Duessa's capacity for disguise, Error's 'filth' becomes more closely, albeit obliquely, allied with the inherent mutability of poetic mimesis. But at the same time, Duessa's association with the chthonic and maternal darkness of classical myths of origin amplifies Spenser's preliminary demonizing of the sphere of prime matter, through a figurative movement from Error's originary cave to the classical underworld into which Duessa briefly descends.

Duessa's related affinity, like Error, with a distorted and hidden birth-realm is further implied by Spenser's emphasis upon the grotesque yet partly hidden character of her 'neather partes'. In canto ii of Book I, Fradubio tells Redcrosse that 'Her neather partes misshapen, monstruous, / Were hidd in water, that I could not see, / But they did seeme more foule and hideous, / Than woman's shape man would beleeve to bee' (I.ii.41). When, on Duessa's exposure by Arthur in canto viii, this description is amplified, it is striking that her grotesque body (especially her breasts and her anus) is revealed to be further disfigured with 'secret filth', 'filthy matter' and 'dong' (I.viii.46–48). Her shaming through this iconoclastic striptease appears to be the end of Duessa; but, far from being eradicated, the 'secret filth' which she conceals on her body acquires an ever-greater importance in subsequent books, as, like the Egyptian Nile, the copious 'matter' of Spenser's text begins to overflow the limits or banks imposed by his Protestant allegory. This process appears to coincide with the poet's reluctant acceptance of that copious fecundity and mutability of matter or nature which pagan literature and thought had endlessly explored, and which the Protestant poet had initially coded as inherently negative. And the connections betwen the gross materiality of an orginary 'slime' and the polysemic, Babel-like, properties of language are once again implied in Spenser's representation of the wall of Alma's House of Temperance:

> First she them led up to the Castle wall,
>> That was so high, as foe might not it clime,
>> And all so faire, and fensible withall,
>> Not built of bricke, ne yet of stone and lime,
>> But of thing like to that *Ægyptian* slime,
>> Whereof king *Nine* whilome built *Babell* towre;
>> But O great pitty, that no lenger time
>> So goodly workmanship should not endure:
> Soone it must turne to earth: no earthly thing is sure.
>
> (II.ix.21)

In his subsequent dilations of this polysemic pagan 'matter', Spenser repeatedly echoes both the passage from Ovid's *Metamorphoses* I and the speech of Pythagoras in Book XV.

In canto vi of Book III the miraculous birth of the twin sisters Belphoebe and Amoret is compared to the after-effects of the Nile flood as descrived by Ovid: 'So after Nilus inundation, / Infinite shapes of creatures men do fynd, / Informed in the mud, on which the Sunne hath shyned' (III.vi.8). A process of creation or 'information' that similarly owes much to Ovid occurs in the Garden of Adonis, where 'Infinite shapes of creatures there are bred, / And uncouth formes, which none yet ever knew' (III.vi.35, ll. 1–2). Not only does this vital cycle of growth and decay encompass the Pythagorean doctrine of *metempsychosis*, it is now reluctantly recognized by Spenser to be dependent on that principle of Chaos or prime matter which in Book I he had troped as unequivocally evil:

> Daily they grow, and daily forth are sent
>   Into the world, it to replenish more;
>   Yet is the stocke not lessened, nor spent,
>   But still remaines in everlasting store,
>   As it at first created was of yore.
>   For in the wide wombe of the world there lyes,
>   In hatefull darkenesse and in deepe horrore,
>   An huge eternall *Chaos*, which supplyes
> The substances of natures fruitfull progenyes.
>
> (III.vi.36)

In this passage, Spenser's invocation of primal matter is still clouded by fear and disgust, but it seems that he has come to a recognition of its cosmological and creative importance: this admission, made half-way through his poem, is an important prelude to his final, albeit reluctant, admission, in his *Mutabilitie Cantos*, of an equilibrium between the material mutability of 'earthlie slime' and an immaterial eternity. For while she is refused a seat in heaven, the goddess Mutability's rule over the sublunar world is not ultimately contested. In the *declamatio* of her claims to universal rule, there is a final resounding echo of the Ovidian passages, as Mutability asserts the regenerative potential of 'earthly slime':

> And first, the Earth (great mother of us all)
>   That only seems unmov'd and permanent,
>   And unto *Mutability* not thrall;
> Yet is she chang'd in part, and eeke in generall.

> For, all that from her springs, and is ybredde,
>   How-ever fayre it flourish for a time,
>   Yet see we soone decay; and, being dead,
>   To turne again unto their earthly slime:
>   Yet, out of their decay and mortall crime,
>   We daily see new creatures to arize;
>   And of their Winter spring another Prime,
>   Unlike in forme, and chang'd by strange disguise:
> So turne they still about, and change in restlesse wise.
>
> (VII.vii.17–18)

One way in which we can read this 'final' *discordia concors* is as an admission of the different yet complementary truths of pagan and Christian thought, since Mutability's delivery of the speech which Ovid attributed to Pythagoras in the last book of the *Metamorphoses* makes her a potent personification of the alterity of classical as well as material origins. A detailed consideration of the intertextual effects of this Spenserian motif of a grotesque yet regenerative material origin is outside the scope of this essay; none the less, its influence reverberates in several texts of the early seventeenth century – notably, in Shakespeare's Jacobean tragedies and in the early Jonsonian masque – and survives as an important textual trace within Milton's *Paradise Lost*.[33]

John Hollander has argued that the relationship of this cultural epoch to antiquity is one of *metalepsis* or transumption, in which the messiness of origins is as it were sublated:

> The whole Renaissance is in a sense a transumption of antique culture, and the very concept of being reborn (*gennethê anôthen*, in the words of Jesus to Nicodemus, *John* 3: 3–8) is a partial misconstruction of the Greek. It gives 'born again' instead of 'born from above' – born from wind and water instead of from the unmentioned earth of the old Adam and the old birth. Rebirth is a revision of the original birth. The process of taking hold of something poetically in order to revise it upward, as it were, canceling and transforming (Hegel seems to use *Aufhebung* in such a constellation of ways) is a metaleptic act in the broadest sense.[34]

Yet Hollander's account seems ironically to perform a repetition of those scholarly and critical responses to Renaissance or early modern culture which I began by critiquing. For his persuasive interpretation of its mimesis of classical exempla appears to be contradicted by an increasing poetic interest in English literature of the late sixteenth and early seventeenth centuries, in the combined materiality and mutability of origins – of the 'old Adam'. As Spenser acknowledges in the *Mutabilitie*

Cantos, such a focus was intrinsically alien to the structures of Christian belief. And while it affords a striking literary parallel to some late Renaissance assertions of the vitality of prime matter, this aesthetic focus was also inherently opposed to what has been described by Susan Bordo as the seventeenth-century flight towards scientific 'objectivity', and away from identification with nature and the body.

It therefore seems that at the very moment when European culture is now understood as hovering on the brink of modernity, in quasi-prophetic anticipation of a new cultural future, it was in fact intensely preoccupied with the radical alterity of those classical origins through which it had recently sought to recreate Western culture. Perhaps a slight adjustment of the Ovidian passage which I read as echoing within *The Faerie Queene* may provide an apt redescription of this pivotal, yet very complex, historical moment. For among the innumerable forms engendered in this cultural crucible, I would suggest, are not only shapes that are strange in their newness, but other 'antique shapes' (*figurae antiquae*): shapes which only gradually reveal themselves to be equally strange and monstrous, precisely *because* of their antiquity.

Notes

1 Ovid, *Metamorphoses*, trans. Frank Justus Miller (London: Heinemann, 1916), 2 vols, I, ll. 416–437.

2 Cited in Edgar Wind, *Pagan Mysteries in the Renaissance* (London: Faber and Faber, 1966), p. 10.

3 *The Civilisation of the Renaisance in Italy*, trans. S. Middlemore, eds P. Burke and P. Murray (Harmondsworth: Penguin, 1990), pp. 479–483. For a detailed account of the prevalence of this view in Burckhardtian-influenced interpretations of the Renaissance see Wallace K. Ferguson, *The Renaissance in Historical Thought: Five Centuries of Interpretation* (Cambridge, Mass.: Houghton Mifflin, 1948).

4 R. Pintard, *Le libertinage érudit dans la première moitié du XVIIe siècle*, 2 vols (Paris: Boivin, 1943), I, p. 58.

5 Warren Boutcher, 'The North Atlantic Renaissance Organisation, c. 1940–c.1980', unpublished paper given as part of *Renaissance Careers*, a colloquium held at Birkbeck College, University of London, 8 June 1996.

6 Paul Oskar Kristeller, *Renaissance Thought: The Classic, Scholastic, and Humanistic Strains* (New York: Harper, 1961), p. 72.

7 Kristeller, *A Life of Learning*, Charles Homer Haskins Lecture, New York 1990.

8 Michel Foucault, *The Order of Things*, trans. A Sheridan (London: Tavistock, 1970), cited in James Nohrnberg, *The Analogy of 'The Faerie Queene'* (Princeton: Princeton University Press, 1976), p. 779. This 'Platonic and hermetic' view of the Renaissance or early modern episteme has been critiqued by Ian Maclean in 'Foucault's Renaissance Episteme: An Aristotelian Counterblast', *Journal of the History of Ideas*

59:1 (January 1988), 149–166. In 'Nietzsche, Genealogy, History', however, Foucault acknowledged that 'we must dismiss those tendencies that encourage the consoling play of recognitions' (*Language, Counter-memory, Practice: Selected Essays and Interviews*, ed. Donald F. Bouchard (Ithaca: Cornell University Press, 1977), p. 153).

9 For this reason I am uneasy about the use of 'classicism' to denote Greek and Roman cultural influence during this period.

10 Leah S. Marcus, 'Renaissance/Early Modern Studies', in Stephen Greenblatt and Giles Gunn (eds), *Redrawing the Boundaries: The Transformation of English and American Literary Studies* (New York: Modern Language Association of America, 1992), pp. 41–63.

11 Margreta de Grazia, 'Soliloquies and Wages in the Age of Emergent Consciousness', *Textual Practice* 9:1 (Spring 1995), pp. 67–92.

12 Homi Bhabha, 'The Commitment to Theory,' in Jim Pines and Paul Willemen (eds), *Questions of Third Cinema* (London: British Film Institute, 1989), p. 124.

13 Dominic LaCapra, *Rethinking Intellectual History: Texts, Contexts, Language* (Ithaca: Cornell University Press, 1983), p. 64.

14 *Ibid.*, p. 42.

15 Terence Cave, *The Cornucopian Text* (Oxford: Clarendon Press, 1979); Patricia Parker, *Literary Fat Ladies* (New York: Methuen, 1987) and *Shakespeare from the Margins* (Chicago: University of Chicago Press, 1996); Derek Attridge, *Peculiar Language: Literature and Difference from the Renaissance to James Joyce* (London: Methuen, 1988).

16 Judith M. Anderson, *Words that Matter: Linguistic Perception in the Renaissance* (Stanford: Stanford University Press, 1996), p. 131.

17 Frederick Ahl's *Metaformations: Soundplay and Wordplay in Ovid and Other Classical Poets* (Ithaca: Cornell University Press, 1985) has helped to disseminate a new awareness of the complex polyvalency of classical texts, while Charles Martindale has recently foregrounded the complexity of both Renaissance and modern mimesis of classical texts in *Redeeming the Text: Latin Poetry and the Hermeneutics of Reception* (Cambridge: Cambridge University Press, 1993).

18 The heterodox character of some strands of late Renaissance or early modern natural philosophy is lucidly summarized in Brian P. Copenhaver and Charles B. Schmitt (eds) *Renaissance Philosophy* (Oxford: Oxford University Press, 1992), chapter 5.

19 See Stephen M. Fallon, *Milton among the Philosophers: Poetry and Materialism in Seventeenth-century England* (Ithaca: Cornell University Press, 1991); John Rogers, *The Matter of Revolution: Science, Poetry and Politics in the Age of Milton* (Ithaca: Cornell University Press, 1996); Michel Jeanneret, *Perpetuum mobile: métamorphoses des corps et des oeuvres de Vinci à Montaigne* (Paris: Macula, 1997).

20 I discuss the likely influence of vitalist ideas upon Shakespeare in *Shakespeare's Feminine Endings: Disfiguring Death in the Tragedies* (London: Routledge, 1999), chapter 1.

21 The change in Salutati's reception of classical culture is explored in Hans Baron, *The Crisis of the Early Italian Renaissance: Civic Humanism and Republican Liberty in an Age of Classicism and Tyranny* (Princeton: Princeton University Press, 1966), pp. 296–300.

22 D. P. Walker, *Spiritual Magic from Ficino to Campanella* (London: Warburg Institute, 1958).

23 Pico della Mirandola, *De hominis dignitate*, cited and trans. in Wind, *Pagan Mysteries*, p. 8, n. 25.

24 Daniel Martin, *Montaigne et la Fortune: essai sur le hasard* (Geneva: Librairie Slatkine, 1977). Martin sees Montaigne's thought as oscillating between ideas of fortune and fate, just as his writing combines citation of biblical texts with that of pagan verses.

25 Stephen Batman, *The Golden Booke of the Leaden Gods* (London: 1577).

26 Batman's archaic diction here appears to give a variant spelling of 'nuzzel', whose meanings in the late sixteenth century, according to the *Oxford English Dictionary*, included 'to burrow or dig with the nose' (like a pig rooting for truffles), 'to train, educate, nurture', 'to nurse'.

27 In his *History of the World* (London: 1687, originally published 1614) Sir Walter Ralegh fuses Batman's metaphors of 'filth' and 'mist' in a similar contrast between paganism and Christianity: 'when that true light, which never had beginning of brightness, brake through the clouds of a virgin's body, shining upon the earth, which had long been obscured by idolatry, all these foul and stinking vapours vanished' (II.xv.2).

28 For changing attitudes to Ovid in these years see Ann Moss, *Ovid in Renaissance France: A Survey of the Latin Editions and Commentaries Printed in France Before 1660* (London: Warburg Institute, 1982), pp. 48–53, and Jonathan Bate, *Shakespeare and Ovid* (Oxford: Clarendon Press, 1993), chapter 1.

29 Martindale, *Redeeming the Text*, p. 60.

30 *Hero and Leander*, I, ll. 135–144.

31 In 'Monster-spawning Mud in Spenser', *Modern Language Review* XLI.3 (March 1926), 234–238, C. W. Lemmi suggests a range of classical sources for this passage, in particular Diodorus Siculus, in addition to the 'Nilus' passage from Ovid, although it is the Ovidian source with which Spenser would have been most familiar.

32 Nohrnberg, *The Analogy of 'The Faerie Queene'*, p. 132.

33 See Philippa Berry, 'Hamlet's Ear', *Shakespeare Survey* 50 (1997), 57–64, and *Shakespeare's Feminine Endings*, chapter 3.

34 John Hollander, *The Figure of Echo: A Mode of Allusion in Milton and After* (Berkeley: University of California Press, 1981), p. 147.

2

'Wondrous force and operation': magic, science and religion in the Renaissance

STEPHEN CLUCAS

O PERATIVE or instrumental practice has long been seen as a vital component of our historical sense of the rise of modern science, and in many accounts Francis Bacon's division of the field of knowledge into operative and speculative spheres, and his polemical pleas for an empirical, experience-based, operative orientation of natural philosophy has been given a privileged position in histories of science since the nineteenth century.[1] Following the publication of influential studies by Lynn Thorndike, Eugenio Garin, D. P. Walker and Frances Yates in the 1950s and 1960s,[2] intellectual historians have tended to shift the fulcrum of this account into the fifteenth and sixteenth century, by taking into account the operativity involved in magical practices or occult sciences, without seriously undermining the basic progressivist narrative of the transition from religious to scientific worldview. Frances Yates's view of the birth of science out of magic, in particular, has remained a potent historiographical model of the emergence of the scientific spirit. Yates saw the importance of Renaissance magic as connected to 'the sense of operational power' possessed by the magus or magical operator.[3] This operational power is seen by Yates as a nascent form of scientific operativity: 'Renaissance magic was turning towards number as a possible key of operations, and the subsequent history of man's achievements in applied science has shown that number is indeed a master-key, or one of the master keys, to operations by which the forces of the cosmos are made to work in man's service.'[4] The 'will to operate', she says, 'stimulated by Renaissance magic, could pass into, and stimulate, the will to operate in genuine applied science.'[5] Taking her lead from Lynn Thorndike, Yates situates magic in a progressivist narrative (i.e, magic as 'proto-science') partly in order to counteract the neglect of magic's role in intellectual history, and partly out of a real conviction that the instrumental, operative worldview of modern rationalism derived from this particular form of the 'will to operate'. Although Yates's view was a decided advance on whiggish historians of science who saw Francis Bacon as the decisive figure, in his role as revolutionary initiator of a new 'rational and scientific' inductive method, she shares their view that this 'will to operate' was a radical, innovative break with the past,[6] part of an ascendent secular spirit of action which was to leave passive 'superstition' and religion behind – 'crossing the bridge between the theoretical and the practical . . . going all out to apply knowledge to produce operations'.[7] While religion had glorified nature as God's creation, science would control and dominate it. Magic was merely an early, nascent form of this secular desire for control. Whereas religion had taught that 'the true end of man is contemplation, [and] any wish to operate was inspired by the devil', magic 'changed the will' of Western man, teaching him that it was 'dignified and important for man to operate'.[8]

Like Yates, Wayne Shumaker has argued in his work on occult sciences, most notably in his *Natural Magic and Modern Science*, that the Renaissance and the seventeenth century was a period of 'transition from pre-science to proto-science',[9] and emphasized the importance of the role of magic in this process: 'What the Renaissance called magic', he argued, 'was a more nearly direct ancestor of true science than either of the dominant philosophies, Aristotelianism and Platonism . . . [because] magic aimed . . . at producing changes in the physical environment desired by the operator'. The practitioner of magic, in Shumaker's view was 'better motivated . . . to experiment' than his scholastic contemporary.[10] Nicholas Clulee's work on John Dee,[11] which has radically remodelled our understanding of the occult sciences in the Renaissance, emphasizes the disciplinary diversity (or *per*versity) of Renaissance practitioners like Dee,[12] and complicated the magic-into-science question by stressing the syncretic complexity of the magical traditions which the Renaissance inherited from the Middle Ages,[13] and noting that these 'different traditions of magic available in the Renaissance had different implications for science'.[14] Thus he considers the astrological magic of Dee's *Propædeumata aphoristica* (1558), which was based on medieval optical theories and concerned the 'pattern of the propagation of force and the relations among quantitative measurements,'[15] as an occult science which was a 'stimulus to . . . mathematical work and the exploration of the practical uses of lenses and mirrors',[16] while he considered the cabalistic alchemy of the *Monas hieroglyphica* (1564) to be concerned primarily with 'the spiritual transformation of the soul and its mystical ascent from material to the supercelestial realm'.[17] While, like Yates, he considered magical philosophy to have had a formative role in the science of the seventeenth century, he disagreed with her emphasis on the importance of the 'Hermetic tradition':

> If a sense of operational power, a curiosity to test the secrets of the occult tradition, a willingness to consider the occult as intelligible, and a confidence in finding explanations for insensible agents were ways Renaissance magic prepared the ground for seventeenth-century science, these were more a central feature of natural magic independent of Hermetism, Neoplatonism and kabbalah than of the more religiously motivated ideas of magic.[18]

Alongside these fruitful and continuing historical investigations of the occult sciences, there have been a number of recent attempts by historians of science to reinscribe the scientific outside of the occult, including interventions by J. E. McGuire, Robert Westman, Mary Hesse and Brian Vickers.[19] Although Vickers is not anatagonistic to the study of the occult sciences per se,[20] he insists on the radical distinctness of the occult and scientific worldviews, describing them as 'two traditions each having its own thought processes, its own mental categories, which determine its whole approach to life, mind [. . . and] physical reality.'[21] Even as he acknowledges the 'frequently hybrid nature of much of seventeenth century science' (citing the example of John Webster, 'Baconian and anti-Aristotelian while simultaneously Fluddean and Boehmian'), he dismisses the idea of an osmosis or cross-fertilization between occult and scientific elements, presenting hybridity instead as the 'coexistence of incompatibles'.[22]

Even scholars sympathetic to the idea of occult scientific influence on thinkers of the scientific revolution such as Paolo Rossi, have reacted against the Yates thesis. Rossi has argued that 'The intellectual stance of magicians, alchemists, Paracelsians and hermeticists played a not indifferent role in the gradual acceptance of the new way of considering "experience" and "doing"', and he has emphasized Francis Bacon's 'profound indebtedness to the magico-alchemical tradition and to the Renaissance concept of magic'.[23] Yet he has resisted Yates's version of the importance of the occult philosophy. Deeply critical of what he calls Yates's 'retrospective form of historiography' with its insistence on the 'continuity between the hermetic tradition and modern science',[24] Rossi is an adherent of the idea of the scientific revolution as a radical break. Whilst he acknowledges the emergence of the scientific worldview out of a matrix of 'myths . . . religious and metaphysical ideas' he argues that the 'hidden presences' of magic and religion could not sanction the reduction of 'the whole structure of scientific knowledge [in]to these elements', the religious and metaphysical elements having been rather 'dissolve[d] into science in such a way as to defy philosophical interpretation'.[25] Despite Rossi's belief that these 'hidden presences' are inaccessible to philosophical consideration, there have been some recent attempts at tracing the religious genealogy of sixteenth- and seventeenth-century science. Amos Funkenstein, Richard Hookyas and Eugene Klaaren have all stressed the importance of theology in shaping scientific thought, but have tended to map theological concepts directly on to 'corresponding' scientific concepts and have largely ignored the role of magic and the occult sciences.[26] Funkenstein looks at the medieval roots of seventeenth-century 'secular theology' – the Thomist acceptance of God's *existentia in rebus*, and 'nominalistic revolution' leading to a 're-examination of . . . God's omnipresence in physical terms' as precursors of the unified mathematical universe.[27] Hookyas examines the rise of empiricism and rationalism in the Middle Ages and Renaissance as a product of mediaeval religious moves toward nominalism and theological voluntarism, and looks at religious predispositions towards certain kinds of scientific activity,[28] while Klaaren looks at voluntarist theological Creation theories as a source for Boyle's and Newton's concepts of the physical universe and natural laws. While all three make important cases for the importance of understanding the religious imperatives behind the scientific advances of the seventeenth century, their aetiologies tend toward a retrospective production of religion and theology as teleological stages on the road to scientific thought, rather than as intellectual formations in their own right, and by ignoring the liminal role of occult sciences suggest a rather unproblematic transition between secularized theology and secular science.

What has seemed increasingly imperative to me, however, is the need to examine the history (or genealogy) of the instrumental or the operative across a range of practices and disciplines, so that appeal to potentially misleading (or anachronistic) modern distinctions (between 'magic' and 'religion' for example) are delayed or postponed – perhaps indefinitely – while we re-examine the self-defining categories of the historical actors themselves. It seems possible to me that a study of operativity as an object of enquiry in its own right might help us make sense of the peculiarly unresolved suspensions between 'religion' and 'science' to be found in theurgy, divination, Lullism, alchemy, practical cabala, the *ars mnemonica* and other characteristic intellectual formations of the late-medieval and Renaissance period. Studied in the light of religious conceptions of practice, use, instrument and agency, perhaps these disciplines, previously categorized as proto-scientific or unscientific, may be seen in new epistemological terms – terms not predicated upon the discursive separability and incompatability of their elements. My primary objective here is to sketch out a prolusory approach to instrumentalism and operation in the sixteenth century, which rather than opposing categories such as magic and science, or science and religion (or contemplation and operation), will attempt to consider the manifestations of the 'will to perform' as an object of study in its own right, by examining its role or function in a diversity of practices, some of which render the categories of 'magic', 'science' and 'religion' unhelpful, or even obstructive.

Reginald Scot's *Discoverie of Witchcraft* (1584): operativity and the 'embezzlement of God'

In his critique of the craze for 'witchmongering' written in 1584, the *Discoverie of Witchcraft*, Reginald Scot addressed himself to the whole issue of the 'will to performe' or operating on nature, and its relation to God's power. Scot, who addressed his book to representatives of the magistracy and the universities as well as the Church, was an orthodox Calvinist, although, unlike William Perkins, and other theological contemporaries, he does not acknowledge the real existence of the magical powers of witches or conjurors. Belief in these powers was as blasphemous as claiming to possess those powers, Scot believed. His work is an attack on 'two sorts of most arrogant and wicked people, the first challenging to themselves, the second attributing unto others, that power which onelie apperteineth to God ... who neither giveth nor lendeth his glorie to anie creature'.[29] As a Calvinist, Scot denies that human agency is possible without God, and further that God would 'never performe the will and commandement' of a mortal. The source of the witch's power is debated: is the witch the devil's instrument, or vice versa? If the witch is the devil's 'instrument' ('to execute his pleasure in anie thing'), Scot says, it is harsh to execute the witch: 'for actions are not judged by instrumentall causes'. Others, however, argue that the witch 'hath a will to performe that which the divell committeth', 'to bring her purposes and practises to passe',[30] and so deserves to die. Scot refuses to acknowledge this instrumental power – whether it is the witch's or the devil's. For to allow this is 'to embezill the title of [God's] immortal glorie',[31] 'yielding to creatures such infinit power as is wrested out of God's hand'.[32] Instead he views witchcraft and magic – citing Calvin's authority – as 'cousenage, fraud, knaverie and deceipt'.[33]

Scot's objection to the 'arrogancie of those which take upon them to worke wonders'[34] is a characteristic articulation of the 'doctrine of means', which forbade man to glory in his own powers but compelled him instead to attribute them to God's grace. Belief in man's own instrumental powers was to 'abridge' or 'abase' God's power.[35] What is interesting about Scot's account, however, is precisely the *amount* of agency which he is prepared to concede as legitimate for man, rather than his proscriptive measures. Divination, for example, by which Scot means 'To fortell things to come upon probable conjectures' is 'not unlawfull', 'so as therein we reach no further than becommeth human capacitie'. Indeed such practices are a 'commendable manifestation' of the 'good gifts and notable blessings' bestowed upon us by God, while the discovery of nature's secrets is a form of 'praise and honour' in that through it we reveal 'the noble order which he hath appointed in nature'.[36] God does not wish to withold from us the 'true knowledge of the workmanship of his hands', and we may pray for him to 'lighten our hearts' with this knowledge. The point at issue is *how much* or *what kind* of knowledge '*becommeth* human capacitie'.

In this partial concession to human agency, one can trace the influence of Augustine, who was one of the key figures in shaping medieval and post-medieval praxiological conceptions. Augustine (whom Hans Blumenberg has credited with the 'instrumentalization of the world') separated hermeneutic and ethical labour into 'use' and 'delight'.[37] Only use was lawful and that use had to be well-intentioned: 'the law is good to edify if a man use it lawfully [*legitime utatur*] so that the end of it is charity, out of a pure heart and good conscience and faith unfeigned'.[38] It is precisely the *pious intention* of Scot's notional operator which renders his operations lawful. The virtuous soul, Scot says, is 'a good instrument raised up for this purpose by God'.[39] An example of 'unlawfull' divination was Colebrasus who believed 'all man's life was governed by the seven planets' and so 'abased' rather than praised the glory of God.

Essentially lawful practice, for Scot, is that practice which glorifies God, whereas unlawful practice is that which pretends to usurp powers to its own agency. That is to say claims to *mediated* power are looked on more favourably than claims to *unmediated* power, albeit in both cases instrumental agency is employed. The limits of man's unaided power are carefully proscribed: 'neither anie ... humane nor yet diabolicall cunning,' Scot says, 'can adde anie such strength to God's workemanship, as to make anie thing anew, or else to exchange one thing into another. New qualities may be added by humane art, but no substance can be created by man.'[40] The limit of *techne* is creation, which is the province of God. And yet Scot does not proceed from here to an outright condemnation of all pretension to magical agency.

Natural magic, for example, is considered as a potentially legitimate and acceptable form of human agency, with certain provisos. The fashioning of 'amulets' from 'hearbs, roots, stones or . . . metall' may have 'medicinable operations', but only 'by the vertue given to them by God in their creation'. Which is to say it is a *natural* rather than a *human* agency. 'To imput this virtue to anie other matter' – by which Scot probably intends astral demons or intelligences – 'is witchcraft'.[41] It is when 'deceit and diabolicall words' are 'coupled' with the 'woonderful graces' which God has endowed on bodies that 'conjuration' begins. Natural magic itself, Scot believed, was 'the verie absolute perfection of naturall philosophie . . . shewing forth the *active part* thereof'.[42] The 'convenient *applieng*' of this knowledge is, however, performed 'not so much by art, as by nature'. To construe human agency as a mediation of god-given operation is to free magic from its agentive stigma. It is not man's work but God's work *through* nature, by *means* of man as a 'good instrument'. Seen in this way, 'God's glorie is magnified therein', and art can be praised for the 'necessarie and sober things' which it contains. Human industry is construed as the 'manifestation of [God's] works' which, if 'skillfullie' applied, can tend to the 'use and service . . . [of the] commonwealth'.[43]

What is significant about Scot's account of magic is that the practices he records are presented as *mediated operations*, ritualized practices which draw heavily on pre-existent ascetic, religious practices for their legitimacy. In his book he describes a number of theurgical 'experiments' in which operators invoke the aid of spirits to procure visions. In 'An experiment for the dead',[44] for example, a spirit called Sibylia ('blessed virgin of the faeries') is requested to 'shew . . . true visions' in a 'christall stone'.[45] The preparations for this transaction are important – resembling as they do the ascetic practices of 'godly regiment'. The operator here must 'first fast and praie three daies, and absteine . . . from all filthinesse'.[46] These 'observations of clenlinesse, abstinence and devotion'[47] are common to all of the spiritual 'experiments' which Scot describes, as are the invocation of God, Jesus, Mary and the Angels in whose names the operators call for obedience to their requests. It is precisely this combination of the call on higher powers and the will to possess a magnified *personal* power which is to be noted. If personal agency is severely circumscribed by theologians, the claims to power *mediated through Christ* seems less clearly and unequivocally forbidden. When the operator invokes Sibylia, for example, he demands

41

that 'thou doo *obey to my words*', but '*by* the resurrection of our Lord'. Although the 'instrument' of this practice is a 'berill stone' or 'christall glass', it could be argued that the objectified power of Christ is also playing an instrumental role here. In another experiment we find the same instrumental mediation – the operator demands that 'you obeie unto me, *in the part of* the living sonne of God', he desires to 'binde and constreine' the spirit to his 'will and power', but this personal power is claimed 'by all the forsaid vertues and powers' of Christ and the angels.[48] Just as Augustine saw legitimate use as a gift of the pious practitioner so Scot's theurgists claim their warrant through elaborate purifying practices and general moral worthiness. Despite his scepticism towards these theurgical 'cousenors', even Scot notes 'with what vices the cousenor . . . must not be polluted: therefore he must be no knave'. This includes the operator abstaining from 'lecherousnes and dronkenesse and from all false swearing'[49] and penitential preparations: 'being clothed with all new and fresh and cleane araie, and shaven, and that day to fast with bread and water, and . . . confessed, saie[ing] the seaven psalmes and the letanie'.[50] 'Psaulmes and praiers' form an integral part of this invocatory magic and are as important as the chanting of divine names and the 'figures', 'seales' and 'periapts' which accompany them.

These practices described by Scot in the late sixteenth century are part of a long tradition of theurgical magic which stretches back to the thirteenth century and probably beyond, known as the *ars notoria*. Attributed to Solomon these magical operations involve the invocation of angels, the use of mystical figures (pentagons, seals, rings etc.) and magical prayers which promise the operator knowledge *direct* from God so that 'in a short time [one can] acquire all the liberal and mechanical arts'.[51] The *Liber sacer*, for example, teaches that, by observing purificatory rites, and using the appropriate seals and prayers, the Christian operator can:

> obteyne his will by every angell . . . to obteyne all syences . . . to know the power of dethe . . . to know all thinges present and to comme . . . to alter or chaunge ye influence of the planetts and sterres . . . to change the daye in to nighte and the nighte into ye daye [etc].[52]

This medieval tradition has many, if not all, of the features of the practices of Renaissance magicians which Yates saw as vital to the birth of science in the seventeenth century. I shall consider the case of one of Yates's exemplary magi, John Dee, before looking at the works of a contemporary Puritan divine, William Perkins, with a view to considering the instrumental and agentive dimensions of theological discourse.

'Instruments to a mightie honour':
John Dee's 'Heptarchicall Art'

Like Scot's theurgical operators, and those of the pseudo-Solomonic manuscripts, John Dee in his celebrated 'angelic conversations' in the late sixteenth and early seventeenth centuries laid claim to miraculous agency and exalted powers through the medium of God and his angels, although in Dee's case this instrumental mediation has an apocalyptic colouring and a sense of special election which differentiates his practice from that of his predecessors.[53] Beginning in his house in Mortlake in the 1570s, and continuing later (after 1583) in a variety of locations in continental Europe, Dee held a series of visionary 'conversations', in which a 'skryer' (a person able to see and speak to spirits) would report angelic communications obtained by means of a mirror or crystal globe. Dee would act as amanuensis on this occasions, meticulously noting down the angelic pronouncements and details of the numerous related mystical visions or scenes which would appear in the 'shewstone'. In addition to the principal angels of the Christian tradition (including Michael, Raphael and Gabriel), appearances of a variety of minor angels and spiritual beings of various kinds were also recorded. Many offered their services to Dee, promising to perform anything which he desired of them. Whilst freely drawing on a wide range of neo-Platonic and cabalistic elements Dee's angel magic was firmly in the tradition of the pseudo-Solomonic *ars notoria*.[54] The angels with whom he deals claim to have been in the service of Solomon before him,[55] and in one of the visionary meetings he is given a magical ring which, it was claimed, 'was never revealed since the death of Solomon ... wherewith all [his] Miracles, and divine works and wonders were wrought'.[56] These Solomonic rings were the subject of medieval treatises such as the *De quatuor annulis* condemned as diabolic by Albertus Magnus in his *Speculum astronomiae*.[57] Dee also used crystal stones or mirrors (described in the *Liber sacer* of Pseudo-Solomon, and other medieval magical sources),[58] a magical table decorated with 'seals' or 'lamines' (see the *Liber de Almandal qui dicitur tabula vel ara Salomonis*)[59] and a talismanic 'Seal of God' (*Sigillum Dei* or *Æmeth*), whose construction seems generically very close to similar pentagonal constructions adorned with angelic names described in various versions of the *Liber sacer*.[60] These, together with the Angelic or 'Enochian' alphabet, are the instruments of Dee's art, transmitted to him via his medium Edward Kelley. Dee believed that the 'heptarchicall art' – so named because of its reliance on the numerological significance of multiples of seven – would grant him untold powers over the natural and political worlds, and give him supreme knowledge of God's mysteries. He would be able, he believed, to receive 'immediate powre' from God – a blessing which was not enjoyed by the Apostles who 'liued with him, eat and dranke with him, [and] were instructed by him' but were 'hearers only'.[61]

These 'immediate powres' promised to fulfil Dee's and Kelley's mortal longings: the 'heavenly doctrine' they are taught is promised to be 'the ende and consummation of all thy desired thirst'.[62] 'All wants shalbe opened unto you', the angel Raphael tells them.[63] The angel Bynepor, who governs 'the generall state and condition of all things', promises Dee that he 'shall work mervaylous mervaylously by my workeman[ship] in the highest'. Blisdon, who possesses the 'keyes of the mysteries of the earth', exhorts him to 'use them, they are . . . at thy commandement'.[64] 'Thow shalt prevayle', he is told, 'with kings, and all the creatures of the world'.[65] The 49 parts of the book being dictated to Dee are '49 voyces whereunto the so many powres . . . shalbe obedient'.[66]

'Thou desyrest use', Dee is told, 'I teache use'.[67] But if Dee's angelic instructors teach use, and promise him limitless powers, this use and power is not uncircumscribed, and is qualified by certain provisos. The angel Uriel, for example, reminds Dee of his duty to practise piously: 'Yf you use me like worldlings I will suerly stretch out my arme uppon you, and that hevily.'[68] When the angel Babalel exhorts him to use the angels who control the seas and their hidden treasures, he adds the qualification 'use them, to the glory, prayse, and honor of him, which created them, to the Laude and prayse of his Majestie'.[69] Dee himself framed his agency in these terms. The angels promise him only such things as 'god can performe, and is for his servyse and glory to performe'. It is not 'unmete' for him to hope for these powers because his action is not tainted by 'any ambition, hypocrisie, or disorderly longing, but onely is bent and settled in awayting the Lord his helping hand to make me wise for his servyce'. If the promised powers are to grant Dee control of the whole world, it is a control which itself is dedicated to God, and not to human agency: 'I make no accownt of all this worlds possessing', Dee protests, 'unleast I might enioye his favor, his mercies and graces'.[70] If Dee and Kelley are continually interrogating the angels for practical details of how to *use* and *practise* the art which they are promised, they are also exhorted to circumscribe their actions and operations according to the dictates of the divine will. They are told to 'use humility' and 'prepare themselves'[71] – as operators they must restrain their 'disorderly longings' for agency and subordinate their actions to God's providential scheme. This exigency is figured into Dee's practices eschatalogically: the art they were being taught was to have *one operation only*: it was to be an instrument of apocalypse. Dee's *Liber mysteriorum* was to be a second Book of Revelation – the outcome of their actions would be the advent of the Last Days – scheduled initially for 1 August 1583.[72] The 'things' which must be 'put in practise' are those that 'knitteth up all'.[73] Human agency and divine agency become one – Dee will 'see and performe the tyme of God his Abridgeme[n]t'.[74] In this special election, the human dream of unlimited agency is subsumed harmlessly in an eschatalogical horizon – as prophets of the last days the miraculous powers of Dee and Kelley makes them 'instruments to a mightie honour.'[75] As such, Dee's magic is strictly within the scope of Augustine's concept of legitimate use – actions performed for the glorification of God.

In preparing themselves for their momentous single operation, Dee and Kelley literally '*use* humilitie', modelling their behaviour on pre-existent ideals of priestly or ministerial virtue.[76] Like the theurgists of the *ars notoria*, they prefaced their divinatory practice with acts of ceremonial and corporeal purification: fumigation with sulphur,[77] the use of clean linen, pure oil and wax,[78] washing, and abstinence from food and sexual intercourse.[79] The actions are structured around prayers of invocation and psalms in Dee's 'oratorie'.[80] These pietistic preparations (together with a continued certification of salvation) ensure the piety and legitimacy of their actions. Without this piety, Raphael tells Dee, nothing can be performed: '[no]thing [can] be browght to pas in me, without a perfect sight and a perfect mynde'.[81] As in alchemy (where a similar requirement of personal piety on the part of the operator is frequently required as a gurantee of success) the character of *agency itself* in this form of magic requires an instrumental *techne* of self-government as much as an instrumental view of the creation.

If, as Yates claims, it is the 'sense of operative power' which was the crucial element in the Renaissance magical worldview, it would none the less seem that this power was not conceived outside of strictly religious parameters of agency – it rose and stooped in a single motion, circumscribed at the moment when it seemed to promise most. Rather than radically separate from the preceding religious worldview, the instrumentalism of magic seems to have taken its original stimulus from religious imperatives, and continued to be shaped by the fideistic and pietistic motives of magical practitioners. The fact that the magical practices of European scholars should be so coloured by their Christian beliefs as to blur the distinction between religious and magical practices in this way is, perhaps, not very surprising. But I wish to propose a further, more unsettling question: are religious practices in this period so radically different from these operative, magical regimes? Is religion itself, in the sixteenth century, an operative or instrumental practice? Keith Thomas and Valerie Flint[82] have shown that there were aspects of medieval Catholicism which can be deemed 'magical': the quasi-talismanic use of scripture and Christian symbols such as the *agnus dei* and instrumental uses of sacramental substances, for example. But I would like to argue – unlike Thomas – that the Protestant Reformation was not necessarily detrimental to a magical instrumentalist worldview,[83] but merely to particular forms of magical or instrumental agency. In many ways, Protestant theology and its attendant practices became a privileged domain of instrumentalism, in which the elect sought (and found) legitimate warrant for their operative desires.

Theology, practical divinity and the 'will to performe'

In every religion that deserves the name, there is in fact an essential dimension reserved for something operational, known as a sacrament . . . if it is a sacrament, if it operates, it operates on something.[84]

If we look at the works of the influential Calvinist theologian William Perkins, for example, we find theology presented as a metadiscourse subordinating an array of instrumental practices. In his *Golden Chaine: or the Description of Theologie*, Perkins construes theology as a universal science of human conduct, founded on the Bible, which is 'distinguished into sacred sciences'. The 'principall' science of theology itself, 'a science of living well and blessedly for ever' and the 'attendant' sciences or 'handmaides' are a series of *practical techniques* for the government of various aspects of human life: '*Ethiques*, a doctrine of living honestly and civilly, *Oeconomickes*, a doctrine of governing a family . . . *Ecclesiastical Discipline*, a doctrine of wel ordering of the Church' etc.[85] These 'holy sciences'[86] constitute a body of instrumental practices for the fashioning of human individuals and their social institutions – a practical theology or divinity.[87]

If Dee's 'heptarchicall art' foregrounds 'use' and 'practise', both in its discourse and in its glossatory apparatus, this same concern is evident also in the works of Perkins. In his consideration of the nature of the sacraments, for example, Perkins attacks the Catholic belief in the 'force or efficacy' of these 'externall signes' in 'making us holy'.[88] Unlike the Catholics who preached the doctrine of transubstantiation, and who believed that the elements of the sacrament had an independent power *ex opere operato*,[89] Perkins claims that there is no change in the 'substance' of the sacramental sign, but a 'respective' alteration by means of *use*. In communion the natural substance is 'severed from a common to an *holy use*'.[90] Calvin likewise had derided the Catholics who 'pretend there is a magical force in the sacraments, independent of efficacious faith'.[91] Two things are to be noted here. Firstly, the proscription of magical agency, but secondly (and perhaps more importantly) the *transference* of this 'force' or 'use' to 'efficacious faith' itself. Faith for Perkins (as for Paracelsus) is seen as the legitimating basis of all human agency or operation. Perkins sees the sacrament as merely the outward signs of 'Actions spirituall and inward' – which are willed and agentive. The believer must '*consecrate himselfe* to God ... *forsake* flesh, divell and world' and '*feele* the inward washing of the spirit'.[92] This spiritual agency also shaped and transformed the devotant's understanding of outward actions and physical agency. In the Protestant extension of the theological concept of religious calling or vocation, the believer's daily existence and temporal labours were sacramentalized, so that various forms of secular activity and profession were seen with reference to faith and its duties:

> we must doe the offices and works of our callings in good manner. For this cause first of all, they must bee done in obedience to God, that is, with a minde and intention to please and obey God. Secondly they must bee done in the name of Christ, that is with prayer and thanksgiving in the name of Christ. Thirdly they must be done in faith, because we must alwaies by our faith depend on God for the blessing & good successe of our labours. Fourthly they must be in love to God and man, yea all the religion we have, all the grace and goodnesse of our hearts, must shew it selfe in the workes of our particular callings.[93]

If one's 'particular calling & practise of the duties thereof' was 'severed from ... generall calling', Perkins believed, it was 'nothing else but a practise of injustice and profanenes'.[94] As in Augustine's concept of legitimate use, it was the *intention* of human actions which transformed their nature:

> in the substance of any duty ... there be two things, the act to be done, and the manner of doing it: & that is to doe it in faith, with a mind to obey God, and to intend his honour thereby. And this manner of doing a worke is the forme of every worke, that makes it to be good indeede: and without it, works commanded in the law, are but as body without life or soule, or as matter without forme.[95]

While all labour was defined with reference to faith, faith itself was construed as labour. In *Of the Nature and Practise of Repentance*, for example, Perkins stresses that Repentance is a 'work' or 'practise' for man as well as a gift from God:

> Repentance is a *worke* of grace, arising out of godly sorrow; whereby a man turns from all sins unto God and *bringeth forth fruites* worthy amendment of life. I cal Repentance a *work*, because it seems not to be a qualitie or vertue, or habit, but an *action* of a repentant sinner.[96]

Far from Yates's view of a passive, theoretical and contemplative religion, Calvinist theology construed salvation as practical, active and operative – a form of agency, albeit proscribed and limited by man's natural depravity. Repentance, Perkins suggests, is *'performed*, when as any one by the instinct of the holy Ghost, doth *purpose, will, desire, and indeavour to relinquish* his former sinnes'.[97]

Although Perkins accepts the Calvinist creed that human agency is essentially vain and depraved – that '[no] works of ours are meritorious' – he also believes (citing the authority of Ephesians 2:10) that we are 'created in Jesus to do good workes'.[98] These quasi-meritorious works are part of the 'right applying' of the doctrine of predestination, the *'use* of it'* in the life of the believer.[99] Christian warfare and metaphors of medicinal operativity (so common in salvation literature) are two forms in which Protestant theology conceptualizes legitimate use of human agency. The practice of Repentance requires 'resistance', or 'an action, whereby the souldier doth *withstand* temptation',[100] and the use of 'preservatiues' or 'spirituall remedies'. These preservatives include forms of abstinence and restraint, but also positive willing and desiring, such as 'premeditation of the power and use of the word', 'Diligent attention of the mind', 'An hungring desire of the heart', the 'casting away of evill affections' and 'Inward consent . . . with the word preached'. The believer is exhorted to *'subdue* the lesser sins', to *'apply* thyself to thy appointed calling' and to *'oppose* the law . . . against the rebellion and loosenesse of the flesh'. Perkins provides scriptural remedies or 'directions' for the various temptations which beset the believer. The scriptures thus become *instruments* of a spiritual medicine (in medieval Latin usage scriptural texts were, in fact, often described as *instrumenta*).[101] If resistance and preservatives are seen as 'wrought by the spirit of God'[102] and the penitential processes of mortification and vivification by 'the force of Christ's death [. . . and] resurrection',[103] Perkins none the less sees human agency as central to penitential practice: 'An endeavour or purpose to doe well according to . . . God's word', it is a willed 'turning' or conversion, which is the 'very essence or nature of repentance', a 'purpose and resolution in mind' as well as 'indeavour in life and conversation'.[104]

The proscribed or partial admittance of human agency is clear in Perkins's treatment of mortification, which he likens to the operative agency of the surgeon. As surgeons 'lay plaisters to [. . . the body] to mortifie it', so the believer must 'use all helpes and remedies prescribed in the word . . . to weaken or kill sinne'.[105] At this point Perkins partially recoils from his own prescription of operative remedies:

> it must not seem strange, that I say we must *use meanes* to mortifie our own sinnes. For howsoever *by nature* we cannot *doe* anything acceptable to God, *yet*, being quickened and mooved by the holy Ghost, we stirre and *moove ourselues* to doe that which is truely good.[106]

The *techne* of self-conquest and self-government is affirmed by reference to Paul, who 'saith, *I beate down my bodie, and bring it into subjection*'.[107] This belief in the legitimacy of pious or inspired agency, which is close to Augustine's doctrine of legitimate use, confirms that the notion of operativity, albeit heavily circumscribed, was not absent from medieval and Renaissance religious culture, prior to Yates's magico-scientific 'operative' revolution. While on one level theologians such as Perkins attacked operative agency and instrumentalism as impiety towards God – Perkins, for example, attacks astrologers, 'wizzards', 'Patrons of charmes' and 'implicite and Close Magique'[108] on much the same grounds as Scot (i.e. that faith in non-divine natural causes 'withdraweth mens mindes from the contemplation of God's providence')[109] – at another level they present a legitimate form of will, purpose and desire, whose magical force is that of efficacious faith, and whose outcome is salvation. This is not to say that such operative agency is seen as restricted to the soul, and removed from agency in nature: Perkins saw one of the concomitant blessings of 'adoption' by God as 'dominion over all creatures' and 'angels as ministring spirits attending upon them for their good'. The use of the natural world is a privilege of the elect: 'The faithful alone have the true use of the lord's goods.'[110] This belief had continued credence in the seventeenth century amongst, for example, the Protestant 'Baconian reformers'.[111]

The difficulty of disentangling religious, magical and scientific attitudes in early modern practices can be seen clearly in the work of the Polish Protestant alchemist Michael Sendivogius, whose *Novum lumen chymicum*, first published in 1604, was widely read in the seventeenth and eighteenth centuries.[112] In the preface to his influential work

Sendivogius outlines the character of the alchemist, and his discipline. Rejecting humanist argument by authority (the testimonies of 'Sage Authors' and 'divers honourable Ancients'), he stresses the empirical nature of his work – 'those things which are manifest by ocular experiment, need no further proof', he says, his findings are 'taken out of manuall experience'. But these practical experiences are described as having been 'vouchsafed' to him, by God, as a 'singular Philosophicall blessing'. The alchemist pursues the 'higher secrets' through experience, but he needs the 'blessing of God to obtain them':

> For it is the gift of God, and truly it is not attained to, but by the alone favor of God, enlightening the understanding together wth a patient and devout humility (or by an ocular demonstration from some experienced Master:) wherefore God justly thrusts them far from his secrets that are strangers to him.[113]

Thus empiricism and experimentalism are subordinated to (and underwritten by) providentialism and pietism. The occult scientist makes practical trials, but his success is dependent upon his ethical character and God's permission. The conception of the occult scientist as both a pious operator and an empirical student of nature is clear from Sendivogius' characterization of the true alchemist in the opening chapter of his treatise:

> The searchers of nature ought to be such as nature her selfe is, true, plaine, patient, constant, &c. and that which is chiefest of all, religious, fearing God, not injurious to their neighbour.[114]

The alchemist relies on nature's 'clear example', but also on his Christian charity and religious awe. The dual nature of this mode of truth production is clearly shaped by Protestant ideas regarding vocation and the sacramental nature of labour and daily experience,[115] as is also apparent in the concluding prayer to nature:

> he which is desirous of the art, and feares God, may the more easily understand all things, which through Gods blessing, with my eyes I have seen, with my mine own hands have made without any deceit of sophistication: for without the light, and knowledge of Nature, it is impossible to attain to this Art, unlesse it come to any by Gods speciall revelation, or some speciall friend doth privately shew it.[116]

The simultaneous stress on observational experience and manual operation and divine sanction and providentialism, 'speciall revelation' and experimental demonstration, makes Sendivogius's preface a *locus vertiginosus* of epistemological complexity for the modern reader. Such internal complexity is not restricted to alchemy and the occult sciences, I would suggest, but is characteristic of a wide range of early modern knowledges. Consider the variety of styles of argumentation at work in Copernicus's *De revolutionibus* or Kepler's *De nive sexangula*, for example, where observational, empirical and mathematical arguments coexist with a variety of theological, metaphysical and aesthetic modes of argument.[117]

Conclusions: agency and its limits

When one considers Sendivogius' sense of 'singular Philosophicall blessing', or Copernicus's stress on the philosopher's 'endeavour to seek the truth in all things to the extent permitted to human reason by God',[118] it is not difficult to see how Dee's sense of election could lead him to a sense of agency in the natural domain which was both ecstatically exalted and carefully proscribed. To distinguish between the various kinds of operativity underlying the practices of natural philosophers like Kepler or Copernicus, alchemists like Sendivogius, Calvinist theologians such as Perkins, and magicians or occult philosophers such as Agrippa, Paracelsus or Dee, is perhaps not only a difficult but in many ways an artificial task for modern historians. This is not to deny the distinctness and autonomy of their various practices, but merely to recognize a common horizon of instrumental agency among early modern practitioners, a shared sense of the theological intelligibility of action. All of them considered human agency and human knowledge to be subordinate to divine grace and providence, and were obligated (in varying degrees) to piety, ascesis and self-government in their personal and professional conduct. The insistence on pious operation and legitimate use was by no means abandoned with the advent of the scientific revolution – scientific discovery continued to be represented as a species of revelation or a form of worship, and the ethical character of the scientist could still be seen as a warrant of scientific truth as late as Newton, and probably beyond.[119] If, as Hans Blumenberg has argued, post-Enlightenment modernity has maintained an 'innocent ignorance' of its own origins[120] – assuming secular modernity as a germinal norm embedded in a superfluous pre-Enlightenment husk of myth, dogma and superstition, which was shed in a revolutionary moment, part of this innocence has involved a variety of tendentious differentiations of the components of early modern practices and disciplines (characterizing certain elements as proto-modern and others as premodern), rather than attempting to characterize them within early modern patterns of intelligibility. Not only are early modern practices artificially divided up between historians with specialized disciplinary interests, but many early modern disciplines are excluded and unregistered by virtue of their incommensurability with modern categories. A fully interdisciplinary account of the will to operate (an examination of the nature and limits of human agency) in the four hundred years between 1300 and 1700 would be compelled to rewrite enlightenment narratives of revolutionary progress from passive, speculative theology to active, operative science and create instead a series of local discontinuities in our present epistemic map. The grand narratives of the genetic transformation of religion (or magic) into science will need to be replaced with dedicated accounts of praxiological localities, in which practices are situated in a far more complex understanding of the 'instrumentalization of the world' than has yet been envisaged by intellectual historians.

Notes

An earlier version of this paper was presented at *Rethinking the Middle Ages and Renaissance*, a conference held at the Arizona Center for Mediaeval and Renaissance Studies, Tempe, Arizona, in February 1995.

1 Francis Bacon, *The Advancement of Learning*, ed. Arthur Johnston (Oxford: Clarendon Press, 1974), II.vii.1, p. 88.: 'it were good to divide natural philosophy into the mine and the furnace, and to make two professions or occupations of natural philosophers, some to be pioneers and some smiths; some to dig and some to refine and hammer. And surely I do best allow of a division of that kind, though in more familiar and scholastical terms; namely that these be the two parts of natural philsophy, the inquisition of causes, and the production of effects; speculative and operative.' But see also II.viii.3, p. 97, where he divides the 'part operative of natural philosophy' into the 'experimental, philosophical and magical'. Quotations throughout with modernised *u/v, i/j*.

2 For succinct accounts of the 'occult' turn in intellectual history see Brian Vickers, *Occult and Scientific Mentalities in the Renaissance* (Cambridge: Cambridge University Press, 1984), pp. 1–5, and Wayne Shumaker, *Natural Magic and Modern Science: Four Treatises 1590–1657* (Binghamton, New York: Mediaeval and Renaissance Texts and Studies, 1989), pp. 14–17.

3 Frances A. Yates, *Giordano Bruno and the Hermetic Tradition* (London: Routledge Kegan Paul, 1964, reprinted 1978), p. 150.

4 *Ibid.*, p. 146.

5 *Ibid.*, p. 150.

6 See for example *Ibid.*, p. 155, where Yates claims that the idea of 'Renaissance magic as a factor in bringing about fundamental changes in the human outlook' is 'a theme . . . of absolutely basic importance for the history of thought'.

7 *Ibid.*, p. 155.

8 *Ibid.*, p. 156.

9 Shumaker, *Natural Magic*, p. 4.

10 *Ibid.*, p. 3.

11 Nicholas Clulee, *John Dee's Natural Philosophy: Between Science and Religion* (London: Routledge, 1988). See also his 'At the Crossroads of Magic and Science: John Dee's Archemasterie', in Brian Vickers (ed.), *Occult and Scientific Mentalities in the Renaissance* (Cambridge: Cambridge University Press, 1984), pp. 57–71.

12 Clulee, *John Dee*, p. 119: 'Not only does Dee transgress normal disciplinary boundaries, but the constellation of disciplines he creates shatters even the most flexible Aristotelian classification of the sciences.' Cf. also p. 115.

13 *Ibid.*, pp. 129–142.

14 *Ibid.*, p. 240.

15 *Ibid.*, p. 117.

16 *Ibid.*, p. 69.

17 *Ibid.*, p. 127.

18 *Ibid.*, p. 241.

19 Robert S. Westman and J. E. McGuire, *Hermeticism and the Scientific Revolution* (Los Angeles: William Andrews Clark Memorial Library, University of California, 1977); Mary Hesse, 'Hermeticism and Historiography: An Apology for the Internal History of Science', in R. H. Stuewer (ed.), *Historical and Philosophical Perspectives of Science* (Minneapolis: University of Minnesota Press 1970), pp. 136–160; Vickers, *Occult and Scientific Mentalities*, and 'On the Function of Analogy in the Occult', in Ingrid Merkel and Allen G. Debus (eds), *Hermeticism and the Renaissance: Intellectual History and the Occult in Early Modern Europe* (Washington: Folger Books, 1988), pp. 265–292, and 'Frances Yates and the Writing of History', *Journal of Modern History* 51 (1979), 287–316.

20 See, for example, his critical remarks about Mary Hesse's 'internalist' history of science, *Occult and Scientific Mentalities*, p. 46 n. 10, and his outline of social anthropological approaches to magical belief systems, pp. 30–44.

21 Vickers, *Occult and Scientific Mentalities*, p. 6.

22 *Ibid.*, p. 29. Cf. his characterization of Van Helmont's 'amphibious nature' (p. 16) and the 'radical incoherence' and 'simultaneous acceptance of incompatibles' in the worldviews of Bacon and Newton (p. 20).

23 Paolo Rossi, 'Hermeticism, Rationality and the Scientific Revolution', in M. L. Righini Bonelli and William R. Shea (eds), *Reason, Experiment and Mysticism in the Scientific Revolution* (New York: Science History Publications, 1975), pp. 247–273 (p. 256).

24 *Ibid.*, pp. 257, 264–265.

25 *Ibid.*, p. 269.

26 Amos Funkenstein, *Theology and the Scientific Imagination: from the Middle Ages to the Seventeenth Century* (Princeton: Princeton University Press, 1986), Richard Hookyas, *Religion and the Rise of Modern Science* (Edinburgh and London: The Scottish Academic Press, 1972), Eugene M. Klaaren, *Religious Origins of Modern Science: Belief in Creation in Seventeenth-century Thought* (London and New York: University Press of America, 1985).

27 See Funkenstein, *Theology and the Scientific Imagination*, pp. 3–5, 26–28, 49–51, and 70–72.

28 See Hookyas, *Religion and the Rise of Modern Science*, pp. 29–53, 88–97 and 101–106.

29 Reginald Scot, *The Discoverie of Witchcraft* (London: 1584), sig. A2r.

30 *Ibid.*, sig. A3r.

31 *Ibid.*, sig. A4r.

32 *Ibid.*, sig. Aa2.

33 *Ibid.*, sig. A3v.

34 *Ibid.*, sig. B2r.

35 *Ibid.*, sig. B2r.

36 *Ibid.*, p. 167.

37 Hans Blumenberg, *The Genesis of the Copernican World*, trans. Robert M. Wallace (Cambridge, Mass.: MIT Press, 1987), p. 179.

38 Augustine, *Confessions*, XII, 28.

39 Scot, *Discoverie*, sig. Avr.

40 *Ibid.*, p. 218.

41 *Ibid.*, p. 218.

42 Cf. Pico della Mirandola, *Conclusiones magicae*, 9:3–4, in Steven A. Farmer, *Syncretism in the West: Pico's 900 Theses (1486): The Evolution of Traditional Religious and Philosophical Systems* (Tempe, Arizona: Mediaeval and Renaissance Texts and Studies, 1998), pp. 494–495.

43 Scot, *Discoverie*, p. 291.

44 *Ibid.*, pp. 401–407.

45 *Ibid.*, p. 404.

46 *Ibid.*, p. 401.

47 *Ibid.*, marginal gloss, p. 411.

48 *Ibid.*, p. 412.

49 *Ibid.*, p. 415.

50 *Ibid.*, p. 411.

51 See, for example, *Ars notoria*, British Library, Harleian MS 181, fol. 18r. On the *Ars notoria* see Lynn Thorndike, 'Solomon and the Ars Notoria', in *A History of Magic and Experimental Science*, 8 vols (London and New York: Macmillan & Co., 1923–58), II, 279–289, Richard Kieckhefer, *Magic in the Middle Ages* (Cambridge: Cambridge University Press, 1989, repr. 1993), pp. 151–172, and Frank Klaasen, 'English Manuscripts of Magic, 1300–1500: A Preliminary Survey', in Claire Fanger (ed.), *Conjuring Spirits: Texts and Traditions of Mediaeval Ritual Magic* (Stroud: Sutton Publishing, 1998), pp. 3–31 (pp. 14–20).

52 Honorius of Thebes, *Liber sacer*, British Library, Royal MS 17.A.XLII (fifteenth century), fol. 5r.

53 On Dee's angelic conversations see Nicholas H. Clulee, *John Dee's Natural Philosophy: Between Science and Religion* (London and New York: Routledge, 1988), pp. 203–230, and Deborah E. Harkness, *John Dee's Conversations with Angels: Cabala, Alchemy and the End of Nature* (Cambridge: Cambridge University Press, 1999).

54 See Stephen Clucas, 'John Dee's *Liber Mysteriorum* and the *ars notoria*: Renaissance Magic and Mediaeval Theurgy', in Stephen Clucas (ed.), *John Dee: Interdisciplinary Essays in English Renaissance Thought* (Dordrecht: Kluwer Academic Publishers, forthcoming).

55 John Dee, *Liber mysteriorum*, British Library, MS Sloane 3188, fol. 55r.

56 *Ibid.*, fol. 11r.

57 Paola Zambelli, *The Speculum astronomiae and its Enigma: Astrology, Theology and Science in Albertus Magnus and his Contemporaries* (Dordrecht: Kluwer Academic Press, 1992), XI, pp. 240–241.

58 See Christopher Whitby, 'John Dee and Renaissance Scrying', *Bulletin of the Society for Renaissance Studies* 3:2 (1985), 25–37.

59 Thorndike, *History of Magic*, II, 280.

60 Stephen Clucas, '*Non est legendum sed inspicendum solum*: Inspectival Knowledge and the Visual Logic of John Dee's *Liber Mysteriorum*', in Alison Adams and Stanton J. Linden (eds), *Emblems and Alchemy* (Glasgow: Glasgow Emblem Studies, 1998), pp. 109–132 (pp. 122–124).

61 Dee, *Liber mysteriorum*, fol. 66r.

62 *Ibid.*, fol. 68r.

63 *Ibid.*, fol. 75r.

64 *Ibid.*, fol. 56r–v.

65 *Ibid.*, fol. 59v.

66 *Ibid.*, fol. 70v.

67 *Ibid.*, fol. 51r.

68 *Ibid.*, fol. 92r.

69 *Ibid.*, fol. 55v.

70 *Ibid.*, fol. 91r.

71 *Ibid.*, fol. 66r–v.

72 *Ibid.*, fol. 101r: 'This boke, and holy key, *which unlocketh the secrets of god his determination, as concerning the begynning, present being, and ende of this world, is so reverend and holy* ... This boke (I say) shall, to morrow, be finished: One thing excepted: which is <u>the Use thereof</u>. Unto the which the Lord hath appointed a day ... see that all things are in redynes <u>agaynst the first day of August next</u>. ... The Lord *hath sent his angels allready to visit the earth, and to gather the synnes thereof to gither, that they may be wayed before him in the balance of Justice*: and <u>Then</u> is the tyme that the promise of God, shalbe fulfilled.'

73 *Ibid.*, fols. 79v–80r.

74 *Ibid.*, fol. 80r.

75 *Ibid.*, fol. 65r.

76 On models of ministerial virtue see Neal Enssle, '"Patterns of Godly Life": The Ideal Parish Minister in Sixteenth- and Seventeenth-century English Thought', *The Sixteenth Century Journal* 28:1 (1997), 3–27.

77 Dee, *Liber mysteriorum*, fol. 10v.

78 *Ibid.*, fol. 10r.

79 See, for example, this exhortation attributed to the angel Gabriel, 13 October 1583: 'Hereby you become Martyrs, for that you mortifie yourselves ... But great are the temptations of the flesh, and mighty is his strength where the spirit is weak ... But this is true abstinence, when contemning the world you fly the delight therein: refraining from the pleasures of the body, Temperating the flesh and making it weak, and that for the Lord his sake.' Meric Causabon, *A True and Faithful Relation of What passed for many Yeers Between Dr John Dee ... and Some Spirits* (London: 1659), pp. 39–40.

80 See especially Dee, *Liber mysteriorum*, fol. 9v: 'He [the angel] is to be invocated by certeyn of the Psalmes of David, and prayers.'

81 *Ibid.*, fol. 56v.

82 Keith Thomas, *Religion and the Decline of Magic: Studies in Popular Belief in Sixteenth- and Seventeenth-century England* (London: Weidenfeld and Nicolson, 1971, repr. Harmondsworth: Penguin Books, 1991), especially pp. 27–57; Valerie Flint, *The Rise of Magic in Early Mediaeval Europe* (Oxford: Clarendon Press, 1992), especially, pp. 254–328.

83 See Thomas, *Decline*, pp. 58–70, 78–80.

84 Jacques Lacan, *Four Fundamental Concepts of Psychoanalysis*, ed. Jacques-Alain Miller, trans. Alan Sheridan (Harmondsworth: Penguin Books, 1977), p. 265.

85 William Perkins, *A Golden Chaine: or the Description of Theologie containing the order of the causes of Salvation* in *The Workes of that Famous and Worthy Minister of Christ in the Universitie of Cambridge, Mr William Perkins*, 3 vols (London: John Legatt/John Haviland, 1626–31), I, Table attached to sig. B2v.

86 *Ibid.*, I, 11r.

87 On 'Practical divinity' in the Elizabethan period see Peter Lake, *Moderate Puritans and the Elizabethan Church* (Cambridge: Cambridge University Press, 1982), pp. 116–168.

88 Perkins, *Workes*, I, 71.

89 Thomas, *Decline*, p. 53.

90 Perkins, *Workes*, I, 71.

91 Jean Calvin, *Institutes of the Christian Religion*, cit. Thomas, *Decline*, p. 53.

92 Perkins, *Workes*, I, Table between pp. 72 and 73, 'The Sacramental Vision' (italics mine).

93 *Ibid.*, I, 716.

94 *Ibid.*, I, 756–757.

95 *Ibid.*, I, 733. Cf. Augustine, *De civitate Dei*, X, 6, which insists that our bodily powers be 'offered . . . to the service of God as the instruments of righteousness', rather than 'to the service of sin as the instruments of iniquity'.

96 Perkins, *Workes*, I, 85 (my emphasis).

97 *Ibid.*, (my emphasis).

98 *Ibid.*, I, 113.

99 *Ibid.*, I, 112

100 *Ibid.*, I, 85.

101 See 'Instrumentum' in J. F. Niermeyer, *Mediae Latinitatis lexicon minus* (Leiden: Brill, 1976), p. 547.

102 Perkins, *Workes*, I, 86.

103 *Ibid.*, I, table between pp. 72 and 73.

104 *Ibid.*, I, 89, 455, 456.

105 *Ibid.*, I, 457.

106 *Ibid.*, I, 457.

107 *Ibid.*, I, 457.

108 *Ibid.*, I, 43–44, 444, 459.

109 *Ibid.*, I, 43. On Perkins's antipathy to sorcery and magic see Leland L. Estes, 'Good Witches, Wise Men, Astrologers and Scientists: William Perkins and the Limits of

the European Witch-Hunts', in Merkel and Debus (eds), *Hermeticism and the Renaissance*, pp. 154–164.

110 Perkins, *Workes*, I, 82–83.

111 See Charles Webster, *The Great Instauration: Science, Medicine and Reform 1626–1660* (London: Duckworth, 1975), pp. 324–483.

112 On Sendivogius see Zbigniew Szydlo, *The Water Which Does Not Wet Hands: The Alchemy of Michael Sendivogius* (Warsaw: Polish Academy of Sciences, Institute for the History of Science, 1994).

113 Michael Sendivogius, *Novum lumen chymicum* (1604), trans. John French, *A New Light of Alchymie* (London, 1650), sig. Ar–A4v.

114 *Ibid.*, pp. 4–5.

115 On the sacramentalization of daily life and lay vocations, and its impact on early modern science, see Hookyas, *Religion and the Rise of Modern Science*, pp. 88–97.

116 Sendivogius, *New Light of Alchymie*, pp. 40–41.

117 On Copernicus's 'aesthetic' and rhetorical modes of argumentation see Robert S. Westman, 'Proof, Poetics and Patronage: Copernicus' Preface to *De revolutionibus*', in David C. Lindberg and Robert S. Westman (eds), *Reappraisals of the Scientific Revolution* (Cambridge: Cambridge University Press, 1990), pp. 167–205. On Kepler's humanist and metaphysical arguments see Anthony Grafton, 'Humanism and Science in Rudolphine Prague: Kepler in Context', in *Defenders of the Text: The Traditions of Scholarship in an Age of Science* (Cambridge, Mass.: Harvard University Press, 1991, repr. 1994), pp. 178–203; and Lancelot L. Whyte, 'Kepler's Unsolved Problem and the *Facultas Formatrix*', in Lancelot L. Whyte (ed.), *The Six Cornered Snowflake: Johannes Kepler* (Oxford: Clarendon Press, 1966), pp. 57–64.

118 Nicolaus Copernicus, *De revolutionibus orbium coelestium* (Nuremberg: 1543), trans. Edward Rosen, ed. Jerzy Dobrzycki, *The Complete Works of Copernicus On the Revolutions*, 3 vols, vol. 2: *On the Revolutions* (London: Macmillan, 1978), p. 3.

119 See, for example, the accounts of the interractions between ethical character and scientific credibility in the career of Robert Boyle in Steven Shapin, *A Social History of Truth: Civility and Science in Seventeenth-century England* (Chicago and London: Chicago University Press, 1994), esp. pp. 126–192 and 310–354, and Michael Hunter, 'Alchemy, Magic and Moralism in the Thought of Robert Boyle', *British Journal of the History of Science* 23 (1990), 387–410.

120 See Blumenberg, *Genesis of the Copernican World*, p. xix.

— 3 —

(Un)natural loving: swine, pets and flowers in *Venus and Adonis*

DYMPNA CALLAGHAN

THE HISTORY of the twentieth century is such that one is tempted to assume that it surpassed all previous eras in every form of depravity. Yet, one abuse, which much preoccupied the inhabitants of early modern England, 'buggery with beasts', has been either in sharp decline since the Renaissance or, at the very least, eclipsed by more comprehensively destructive rapes of nature.[1]

One can say with certainty, in any event, that attitudes towards bestiality (which are probably never fully coincident with practice) were markedly different in the early modern period from our own. For the Renaissance, sexual congress with brute creation transgressed the fundamental distinction between the human and the animal even as it served to articulate the notion of an absolute and inviolable distinction between them. Bestiality was the worst of sexual crimes according to one Stuart moralist because 'It turns man into a very beast, makes a man a member of a brute creature'.[2]

It was in 1534, at the beginning of the Reformation, that animal buggery – 'when a man or woman commiteth filthinesse with a beast'[3] – became a capital offence. This legislation, which proffers an unaccustomed view of rural life in Tudor England (one assumes, perhaps unjustly, that bestiality was less prevalent in towns), was renewed in 1536, 1540, 1548, 1553 and again by Elizabeth I. (Offenders could be hanged for this transgression up until 1861.[4]) Legal and moral anxiety about bestiality reveals the androcentric boundaries of certain foundational categories in the period's taxonomy – 'man' and beast, culture and nature – and in doing so brings the radical alterity of nascent modernity starkly into focus. This is important not because this particular past is usually remote and hidden, but rather because it is so familiar and proximate, everywhere so visibly embedded in the structures of the present that it is only with difficulty that we can see it as belonging to history at all. The system of distinctions around bestiality reveals, then, not so much the categories it takes such pains to detail, but rather exposes the difference between the past and the present, the space of history itself.

In what follows, I want to address a series of related conceptual categories – humans and animals, culture and nature – which are largely the same as our own but whose demarcations and contents are irreducibly different. The textual focus of my analysis is Shakespeare's singularly Ovidian poem *Venus and Adonis* (1593), whose literary merit has hitherto been generally understood to reside in those moments closest to our modern sensibilities, namely, in its exquisite mimetic descriptions of the natural world.[5]

In Shakespeare's poem, the fundamental distinction between the human and the animal, whose articulation is undergirded by the ostensible sexual integrity of the human species, also depends on what threatens to undermine it, namely sex itself. Indeed, Renaissance Ovidian poetry with its emphasis on illicit sexual desire and 'unnatural' consummation, as well as metamorphosis, represents the disturbing capacity to 'turn man into a very beast', to effect, like bestiality, an 'unlawful conjunction', 'which is a most abominate confusion'.[6] That is, poetic metaphor contains the propensity to convert the human into the animal, or more radically, in the specific context of metamorphosis, to reduce it to the vegetative matter at the base of nature. Taking bestiality as a new figure for the demarcation between culture and nature, I propose that these categories are themselves produced along a spectrum of specifically sexual discriminations about 'kind'.[7]

Loving swine

> 'Tis true, 'tis true, thus was Adonis slain:
> He ran upon the boar with his sharp spear,
> Who did not whet his teeth at him again,
> But by a kiss thought to persuade him there;
> And nuzzling in his flank, the loving swine
> Sheath'd unaware the tusk in his soft groin.
>
> (1111–1116)

Consistent with the Ovidian world of forbidden wishes, the death of Adonis constitutes the fatal consummation of interspecies desire: ' "I know not love" quoth he, "nor will not know it, / Unless it be a boar, and then I chase it" ' (409–410). A painfully comic measure of Adonis's profound alienation from his own species,[8] 'the tusk in his soft groin' serves as a grotesque parody of the legal definition of bestiality, 'carnall knowledge' of a brute, as explained by Sir Edward Coke in *The Third Part of the Institutes of the Lawes of England* (1644): 'there must be *penetratio*, that is, *res in re*, either with beast, but the least penetration maketh it carnall knowledge'[9] Coke's solemn explication cannot fully anticipate a scenario, such as the one outlined by Venus, where the animal and not the human, 'the loving swine', is the active sexual partner. Like Coke, Peter Barker's *A Judicious and Painefull Exposition upon the ten commandments* (1624) envisages human culpability and bestial ingenuousness: 'Buggery with beasts is . . . a sinne so hated of God, that the innocent and harmless beast should dye as well as the party that committed the fact.'[10] William Gouge likewise denies animal agency claiming that beasts (*contra* Venus) never attempt sex with humans or other creatures outside their own species: 'bruit beasts content themselves with their own Kinde'.[11]

Certainly, the poem's comic imputations about bestiality had serious ramifications in a culture where, as Keith Thomas points out: 'The frequency with which bestiality was denounced by contemporary moralists suggests that the temptation could be a real one.'[12] Summarizing conventional wisdom on the matter of venturing outside one's own species for sexual satisfaction, Richard Capel's *Tentations* (1635) admonishes: 'It is a pit, out of which those few that do fall into it do hardly recover: it is like a winter Plague, some doe recover, but in comparison of those that perish, a poore few.'[13] Similarly, in the widely circulated *Domesticall Duties*, William Gouge finds it necessary to point out the importance of selecting as a marriage partner another human being, 'One of the same Kinde or nature':

> for among all the creatures which were made, *there was not found an helpe meet for man*: therefore God out of his bone and flesh made a woman of his owne nature and Kinde.
> Contrary to this is the detestable sinne of buggery with beasts, expressly forbidden by the law.[14]

Although there is a degree of cultural uncertainty – one made very much apparent in Shakespeare's poem – about the question of woman's 'kinde', Gouge constructs what amounts to a choice, not between, say, heterosexuality and homosexuality but between the love of women and the love of beasts.

Yet, Adonis is unequivocal in his election of the boar over Venus, a choice which the poem constructs within a specifically sexual context. Thomas Middleton's *A Mad World My Masters* (c. 1604), a play which explicitly references *Venus and Adonis* (I.ii.44), offers an interesting cultural reflection on the implications of such an erotic choice. In this play, 'The worst [creature] that ever breathes', 'a wild boar', is punningly extrapolated as and conflated with 'a vild whore, Sir' (IV.iii.71–75). Both sexual and species difference here articulate the contradictory, driving forces of attraction and repulsion that characterize heterosexual and misogynist male desire. This double nature of desire, however, is apparent not only in terms of men's conflicted feelings about female sexuality but also, astonishingly, in relation to pigs. For example, Gervase Babington in a commentary on Old Testament dietary prescriptions, demonstrates, rather like Zeal-of-the-land Busy in Ben Jonson's *Bartholomew Fair*, a deep-seated hatred of swine, matched only by his equally profound love of sausage:

> The Swine was uncleane, Because he parteth the hoofe, but cheweth not the cudde; and of their flesh they might not eate, nor touch their carkasse &cc. .... God would admonish the Jewes by this figure, and still we may learne by it, to be no Swine, no Hogges, no fylthie myrie creatures, wallowing in sinne and uncleannesse, withought regard and feeling, loving the earth, and looking ever on the earth and rooting in it all the day, and feeding the bellie with all greedinesse ... A knife therfore to the Hogge, that we may have Puddings.[15]

Babington's desire for 'Puddings' finds him in violation of the very injunction he is at pains to explicate and appears to run a very different course from that of Adonis's perilous pursuit of wild bacon. The latter, however, is curiously contiguous with the Biblical injunction against sodomy in Judges 5:7, defined as 'going after strange flesh'.[16] Since sodomy is in the period a figure for the reversal and dissolution of order, the risibly gruesome *ars verse* of Adonis's preposterous death carries inescapable (and ultimately tragic) imputations of human as well as bestial buggery, especially in the image of his feminized, castrated/ invaginated body: 'the wide wound that the boar had trenched / In his soft flank'.[17] From the chiastic formulation of the opening lines: 'Hunting he lov'd, but love he laugh'd to scorn' (1–2), the poem rhetorically anticipates the final transposition of categories – hunter and quarry against man and beast. In thus forging an alliance between comic inversion and sodomitical reversal, *Venus and Adonis* is undeniably, as Mario DiGangi has observed, 'a highly queer' poem.[18]

In fact, in legal and religious discourse of the period, bestiality and homosexuality were often contiguously positioned. In Gervase Babington's biblical commentary, bestiality and sodomy are near neighbours: 'Thou shalt not lye with the male, as one lyeth with a woman: for it is abhomination. Thou shalt not also lye with any beast to be defiled therewith.'[19] Sir Edward Coke's legal explication concurred:

> If any person shall commit buggery with mankind, or beast; by authority of parliament this offence is adjudged felony without benefit of Clergy . . . Buggery is a detestable, and abominable sin, amongst Christians not to be named, committed by carnall knowledge against the ordinance of the Creator, and order of nature, by mankind with mankind, or with bruite beast, or by woman-kind with bruite beast.[20]

Curiously, it is not so much object choice (man, woman or animal) that is a matter for condemnation here, but the somewhat undefined practice of 'buggery' itself.[21] Having ruled out a series of possible options for sexual encounter, intercourse between men and women presumably remains, like English Protestantism, the *via media*. This is, of course, the very middle path – woman not beast – that Adonis refuses to take. In this, he demonstrates obstinate indifference to received cultural wisdom on several fronts, including Edward Topsell's sage admonition that 'It behooveth the hunter of boars to be very wary'.[22]

The indistinction of boundaries between animal and human sexuality, on the one hand, and animal ferocity and divine vengeance on the other, is played out, most vividly in Venus's own identification of her lust for Adonis with that of the boar: 'Had I been tooth'd like him, I must confess / With kissing him I should have killed him first' (1117–1118) There is, indeed, a cultural consensus on the libidinous nature of boars. Andrew Willet emphasizes both the similarities between human coitus and the mating habits of boars in his commentary on Leviticus: 'This kinde of creature is prone unto lust, and more then commonly other are: for *at eight moneths* they begin to couple; and when they begin, they keepe not their seasons and times of the yeere, as other beasts doe, but *at all times*, and night and day they come together.'[23] Venus herself relates to Adonis the terrifying demeanor of the boar, 'a mortal butcher' whose back has 'a battle set / Of bristly pikes', whose 'snout digs sepulchers where're he goes,' and 'whom he strikes his crooked tushes slay' (619–624). Edward Topsell's natural history of the period paints a similarly vivid portrait not just of the boar's ferocity but also of his savage lust:

> being inflamed with venereal rage, he so fretteth upright the bristles of his neck, that you would take them to be the sharp fins of Dolphins; then champeth he with his mouth, grateth and gnasheth his teeth one against another, and breathing forth his boyling spirit, not only at

his eys, but at his foaming white mouth, he desireth nothing but copulation, and if his female endure him quietly, then doth She satisfie his lust, and kill all his anger; but if she refuse, then doth he either constrain her against her will or else layeth her dead upon the earth.[24]

Crucially, the boar's violent sexual aggression is connected by Topsell with a refusal of coitus. In this, the boar has a ferocious, vengeful, and specifically masculine energy: 'The males have upon that occasion deadly *and strange fights*, one with another, and the wilde Boares whet their tuskes against trees for the fight.'[25] While the boar has an inescapably masculine dimension, Venus's identification with this beast also resembles that between the goddess Diana and the boar of Calydon in Book VIII of the *Metamorphoses*, 'The which Diana for to wreake her wrath conceyvde', and 'In great Orithyas thigh a wound with hooked groyne he drew'.[26] Thus, Adonis's boar 'always has the double role of being both the Goddess, infernalized and enraged, and her infernal consort (Mars in boar form)'.[27]

In a story familiar in the Renaissance via both Euripides and Seneca, Hippolytus, son of Theseus, is dragged to his death by a monstrous sea bull who frightens the horses pulling his chariot along the strand. Crucially, this ferocious sea creature represents the slighted Aphrodite. Not only has Hippolytus rejected the goddess, however, but he has also spurned the incestuous advances of his stepmother, Phaedra: 'the rejected Goddess comes to emerge in her animal form, claiming in violence what she has been denied in love'.[28] The boar, then, has mythological connotations of taking vengeance on behalf of rejected yet powerful women. There is, in addition, a parallel notion current in the moral literature of the period that animals are capable of avenging themselves on humans who use them in acts of sexual perversity. In *The Theatre of Gods Judgements* (1597) Thomas Beard offers instances of precisely this phenomenon whereby nature retaliates on depraved human sexuality. A male goat avenges the buggery committed upon his mate by a shepherd by 'running at him so furiously with his hornes, that he left him dead upon the ground'.[29] Similarly a horse 'ran so furiously upon the keeper' who has compelled him to mate with his mother, that 'incontinently he tore him in pieces'.[30]

When the ironically named Elizabethan family of love declared that all men were brothers, and added 'whosoever is not of [our] sect, [we] account him as a beast that hath no soul',[31] they demonstrated that violence is the logical (and ideological) destination of difference, and that it is inherent in the absolute distinction to which difference is always continually propelled. The regimes of gender and species difference necessarily inhere not only in desire but also in violence. So it is that Adonis loves the ferocious boar and Venus 'murders with a kiss'.

The queasy, tragicomic violence of Adonis's end on the tusk of a loving swine follows in the wake of the most frothily humorous dimension of Shakespeare's *epyllion*, namely, the transposition of gender attributes between the lovers *manqués*. The exaggeratedly feminine, hefty, oversized goddess of love, saturated with corporeality and perspiration, figures both the fragile cultural membrane that separates the feminine from animal sexuality and the taxonomic confusion that ties them together.[32]

Pets

Although it is axiomatic that the only perfect companion has four feet, in Shakespeare's poem the only *sexual* companion has four feet. Animals, like the 'lusty courser' (31), are possessed of a sexuality which is happily confined within the bounds of 'natural' propriety. Here, nature is resolutely natural while human sexuality – although, strictly speaking, flinty Adonis is the only human (mortal) in the poem – is aberrant. Contemporary moralists such as Richard Capel argued that human beings are tempted to 'unnaturall sins' such as bestiality and incest because 'Sathan hath no naturality in him, for he lost all in his fall: the Law of Nature was not given to him'.[33] Even Venus in her sexual personae as Nature is given to perverse, and therefore 'unnatural', desire, signalled in the poem not only by Adonis's indifference to her but also by the uneasily semi-incestuous tenor of her designs upon him. Not only, says Capel, will the devil 'tempt on both sides of the hedge if he can' but also, as he points out, in a remark which is of considerable relevance to the psychosexual dynamics of the poem: 'It is our corrupt humor, to be strongest where we are denied.'[34] Indeed, the poem repeatedly engages the question of what, given the inherent perversity of desire, constitutes 'natural' sexual behavior – among human beings, among animals, as well as in that shady area, both literal and metaphoric, of relations between the species.

The blindly procreative aspect of her divinity represented by *Venus genetrix* together with her rapacity as *Venus vulgaris* offers a reminder that Venus's identity is essentially non-human, both bestial *and* immortal. Crucially, also, the poem signals her specifically *maternal* and feminine propinquity to the animal kingdom. Amid parodic[35] and overtly bestial variations on coitus, there is also some very heavy petting:

'Fondling,' she saith, 'since I have hemm'd thee here
Within the circuit of this ivory pale.
I'll be a park, and thou shalt be my deer:
Feed where thou wilt, on mountain or in dale;
Graze on my lips, and if those hills be dry,
Stray lower, where the pleasant fountains lie'.
(229–234)

Venus's outlandish imagery reverses the familiar poetic trope whereby the woman is the poet's hunted hind (as, for example in Sir Thomas Wyatt's Petrarchan 'Whoso List to Hunt') and Adonis as 'deer' is reminiscent of Mistress Ford's mockery of Falstaff's romantic rhetoric in *Merry Wives*: 'Sir John! Art thou my there, my deer, my male deer?' (V.v.14–15). 'Feed where thou wilt', an invitation to the breast (the 'mountain') and to cunnilingus ('lower where the pleasant fountains lie'), further positions Venus in a simultaneously maternal and sexual relation to Adonis. It is the liminal condition of femininity that signals Venus's alliance with nature. Within a single animal identity, she is possessed of an almost instinctive sexual voracity and maternal nurture: 'With blindfold fury she begins to forage' (554); 'glutton-like she feeds, but never filleth' (548). Venus's animal insatiability as a mother bears some resemblance to a phenomenon described by E. Fenton in *Certaine Secrete Wonders of Nature* (1569). In this account, the all-consuming powers of a pregnant woman are such that she turns not beast but cannibal, the terrifying embodiment of devouring femininity: 'lusting to eate the flesh of a faire boy'. Monstrosity in general, Fenton opines, is the result of animal sexuality, which, he argues, violates the laws of nature:

> It is moste certaine, that these monstrous creatures, for the most part do proceede of the judgement, justice, chastisement and curse of God, which suffreth the fathers and mothers bring forth these abominations, as a horrour of their sinne, suffering themselves to run headlong, as brute beastes without guide to the puddle or sink of their filthie appetites, having no respect or reggarde to the age, place, tyme or other lawes ordained of Nature.[36]

Her simultaneously amorous and motherly address to Adonis as 'Fondling' also connotes both pet and infant, and blurs the boundaries between sexual and non-sexual relations. Adonis becomes Venus's animal familiar, her protected game, a deer/dear within 'this ivory pale' (240). In petting the 'fondling' Adonis, Venus transgresses – and perhaps, transcends – both interspecies, intergenerational and intrafamilial distinctions.[37] Pet keeping is, inescapably, parental, making the beast part of the family, obscuring the division between kin and kind, from whence as moralists continually reminded their readers 'the change is easie, from naturall love to Carnall'.[38]

Of course, the relationship of pethood is precisely (or, rather, ideally) not sexual, though it is so as much on grounds of incest as of bestiality. Incest and bestiality constitute categories which are conceptually and antithetically related because they define with what or whom sexual congress is permitted or prohibited. Incest prohibits endogamy and finds its furthest exogamous reach in bestiality while bestiality, the cultural imperative against endogamy, discovers its logical destination in incest.[39] Incest and bestiality are, in fact, versions of one another, and neither prohibition is necessary or 'natural'. In a sense, Adonis finds himself caught between the suffocating passions of the maternal Venus and the ferocious embrace of a 'loving swine'. In this situation, connection between 'kin' and 'kind' (*Hamlet*, I.ii.65), or rather, the imperative to make the distinction between them, becomes critical. That is, at one level forced to chose between bestiality and incest, Adonis chooses bestiality. Pets, however, serve as transitional objects that conveniently defer the necessity of making such a drastic choice. If Venus can keep Adonis as a pet, she can possess him both as child and lover, human and animal.

While, as we have seen, bestiality was discursively if not actually rife in this period, the institution of pethood had yet to be fully instantiated. In a statement that be might intended to discourage a range of possible behaviours, from copulation with donkeys to fondness for kittens, Erasmus in *De civilitate morum puerilium* argued that 'Over-familiar usage of any brute creature is to be abhorred'.[40] He would surely have condemned Samuel Pepys who confessed the jealously he felt ('God forgive me') when a dog was brought to line with his little bitch.[41] A less disturbing instance of pet love, one is tempted to say, evidence of a more robust affection, was to be found in Sir John Harington's account (1608) of 'my rare dogge', 'my *Bungay*, (for so was he styled.)'.[42]

In a strategy which deftly demonstrated both condescension and affection, Elizabeth I had what Hamlet described as the distinctively feminine habit of giving her courtiers animal pet names: 'You jig and amble, and you lisp, you nickname God's creatures, and you make your wantoness your ignorance' (*Hamlet*, III.i.143–145). Elizabeth used the diminutive 'Robin' to refer to the Earl of Leicester, Ralegh was 'Fish' and 'Goose' (though he went mostly by the cognomen, 'Water') and the French envoy who wooed Elizabeth on Alençon's behalf she named 'monkey' because his last name was Simier. Alençon himself was nicknamed 'Froggy', and, during the marriage negotiations, Elizabeth accessorized her wardrobe in accordance with this thematic. Lady Margaret Norris was dubbed 'Crow', and in a letter of 1579 before his ascendancy to the office of Lord Chancellor, Sir Christopher Hatton sycophantically signed himself, 'your majesty's sheep'.[43] Anthony Petti observes:

> In giving beast nicknames to all her favourites, Elizabeth appears to have acted according to that strong mixture of sentimentality and cynicism in her personality which affected nearly all her love relationships as far as they can be ascertained. They are certainly strong marks of affection, but reduce their bearers considerably in stature, for they are highly dependent, incapable, or uncomely creatures. Such is likely to be the case for a pre-eminently queenly sovereign with subjects for lovers, some of them easily young enough to be her children or grandchildren.[44]

Like Venus, for whom, as Anthony Mortimer points out, 'incest is the only conclusion that can satisfy [her] desire to possess Adonis both as a child and as a lover',[45] Elizabeth's penchant for petting allows her to maintain power over her courtiers both as minions and as lovers. Not only is it that, as Jonathan Bate observes, 'the sexual dealings of partners of greatly unequal age are bound at some level to replicate the archetypal relationship based on an unequal power structure, incest between a parent and a child'[46] (such relationships are presumably not uncommon in love), but also, more specifically, that in a rigidly patriarchal society any form of female sovereignty could be represented as a form of overpowering maternal control. Certainly, these petting relationships – Venus with Adonis, and Elizabeth with her courtiers – violate the widespread belief that for sexual (i.e. conjugal) relations to be appropriate 'there should be some equality betwixt the parties ... in Age, Estate, Condition, Piety'.[47] Shakespeare's Venus unquestionably (although perhaps not intentionally) offers a satirical glance at Elizabeth herself.[48] There were solid political and literary precedents for such an incongruous identification as that between the virgin queen and the goddess of love. In a situation precisely the inverse of Elizabeth's, Diane de Poitiers styled herself after her virgin namesake despite being mistress to the King of France, while, in the more exalted literary context of Virgil's *Aeneid*, Venus-in-Virgo represented the union of chastity and love whose double nature was extrapolated with both frivolity and reverence throughout the Renaissance.[49] That the maternal relationship might be experienced as a kind of primal female sovereignty is emphasized when, in his struggle to escape, Adonis is described as being 'like the forward infant stilled with dandling' (562). Philippe Ariès has shown the astonishing sexual liberties early modern adults habitually took by way of public amusement with very young children (though not with children who had reached puberty). For example, adults would manipulate infant genitals in spite of children's protests, and engage children in lewd conversation. Astonishingly, none of this was regarded as remotely incestuous or paedophilic. In one incident from the court life of the three-year-old Louis XIII, the Marquise de Verneuil, a woman who 'often put her hand under his coat',

> wanted to play with him and took hold of his nipples; he pushed her away, saying, 'Let go, let go, go away.' He would not allow the Marquise to touch his nipples, because his nanny had told him: 'Monsieur, never let anybody touch your nipples, or your cock, or they will cut it off.' He remembered this.[50]

Admittedly, the conduct of the seventeenth-century French court was probably considerably less inhibited than that at the court of Elizabeth. Possibly, however, aristocratic French child-rearing practices were no less restrained than those reported by Juliet's Nurse in *Romeo and Juliet*. Further, both of these contexts may be significantly closer to the decadent pagan world of Shakespeare's poem. Like little Louis XIII, Adonis is child-like in relation to Venus: ' "Fie, fie" he says, "you crush me. Let me go. / You have no reason to withhold me so" ' (611–612). That his petulant protests also represent, symbolically at least, a proleptic response to castration is confirmed by the description of Adonis's ravaged corpse: 'In his soft flank, whose wonted lily-white / With purple tears that his wound wept was drenched' (1053–1054).

Shakespeare's Ovidian source for *Venus and Adonis*, *Metamorphoses* Book X, is narrated by an explicitly pederastic Orpheus who, in grief for Eurydice, has turned not just to homosexuality but specifically to 'boayes'. Orpheus 'did utterly eshcew'

> womankynde. Yit many a one desyrous were to match
> With him, but he them with repulse did all alike dispatch.
> He also taught the Thracian folke a stewes of Males to make
> And of the flowring pryme of boayes the pleasure for to take.[51]

On the one hand, Orpheus demonstrates a reluctance about women very like that of Adonis, but, on the other hand, his object choice, 'flowring ... boayes' resembles, though it does not exactly replicate,

Venus's parental passion for her flower-child. There is a further etymological connection between Venus and Orpheus in Richard Huloet's 1552
definition of a 'bugger' as a 'Lover of chyldren buggerly or dissolutely,
Paederastes'.[52]

The inequities of power inherent in 'petting' (the fondling of
both dependent animals and people, but especially children) are, then,
structurally speaking, indebted to both bestiality and incest. The incestuous aspects of Venus's pet love become quite explicit towards the
end of the poem in her frantic apprehension and when, in her grief, she
becomes the *mater dolorosa*:

> To grow unto himself was his desire,
> And so tis thine; but know it is as good
> To wither in my breast as in his blood.
> (1180–1182)

Adonis is now literally at Venus's maternal breast, and, given this
context, Adonis's desire to 'grow into himself' also suggests a symbolic
manifestation of inbreeding, namely a narcissistic insistence on physical
integrity. Adonis is himself, of course, in the Ovidian source literally the
product of an incestuous union, 'the cursed seede in [Myrrha's] wicked
wombe'.[53] 'A son [Adonis] that sucked an earthly [and incestuous]
mother [Myrrha]' (863–864) is now explicitly linked via an image which
returns the relation between Venus and Adonis not just to an incestuous paradigm but crucially also to an animal one, namely the anguished
'milch doe whose swelling dugs do ache' (875–876).

Adonis's mother bears in the poem an important connection with
the aberrant desires of Venus. As *Venus genetrix*, mother goddess of
omnipresent fecundity, Venus urges indiscriminate copulation: 'By law
of nature thou art bound to breed' (171),[54] and, crucially, she does so by
way of the poem's central reference to Myrrha:

> O, had thy mother borne so hard a mind,
> She had not brought forth thee, but died unkind
> (202–203)

Here, Venus represents Myrrha as being less self-enclosed ('incestuous'
in the broader sense) than her son. Myrrha would have 'died unkind' if
she hadn't loved a man and thus borne a child but 'it would have been
better if she had died untouched by her own kind'.[55] Yet, a recent critic
on the subject of incest argues: 'Incest is not "unnatural" in the same
sense that the mating of different species is unnatural.'[56] Presumably,
what McCabe means is that incest is, potentially at least, procreative,

and thus, in a sense, permitted by nature, in a way that, *contra naturum*, bestiality is not. Such distinctions, however, elide the fact that the prohibition against incest may, in fact, *produce* the prohibition against bestiality. Further, in the late sixteenth century and seventeenth centuries, bestiality was believed to be procreative, and the biological degeneration now adduced to incest was then routinely assigned to bestiality. As Gouge remonstrates: 'Monstrous it [bestiality] is in the kinde thereof: and a cause of abominable monsters.'[57] Deformity, or 'monstrosity' as it was often known, was defined by the likes of Fenton and Ambrose Paré primarily in terms of the way in which apparently physiologically animalistic characteristics adhered to the progeny of otherwise unremarkable, human parents. William Ramesey believed that copulation with animals might produce 'a monster, partly having the members of the body according to the man, and partly according to the beast'.[58] Outrageous tales about such phenomena abound. For example, a sheep allegedly violated by a youth gave birth to a half-human monster – a human/animal hybrid, which was nailed up by way of a warning to others in the local parish church at Birdham near Chichester in 1674.[59] At Shrewsbury in 1580 an eight-year-old boy was exhibited with 'both his feet cloven and his right hand also cloven like a sheep's feet'.[60]

Crucially, deformed children were often understood as signs of their mother's aggressive and unnatural sexual agency in relation to animals. Theologians explained that, like men, 'neither shall any Woman stand before a beast to lye downe thereto: for it is abhomination. Ye shall not defile yourselves in any of these things.'[61] Nor was legal clarification wanting. The Act prohibiting bestiality, Sir Edward Coke emphasized:

> extend[s] as well to a woman as to a man, and therefore if she commit buggery with a beast, she is a person that commits buggery with a beast, to which end this word [person] was used. And the rather for that some what before the making of this Act, a great Lady had committed buggery with a Baboon and conceived by it.[62]

Curiously, Coke implies that women might have claimed exemption from regulation in earlier acts. 'Buggery', which usually implies the act of penetration, comes under some pressure here because it seems to imply that the woman, like Venus, was the 'active' partner and the baboon the 'passive' one. The reverse is true in Anthony Wood's racist account of the generation of an Irishwoman's deformed child, in which the woman is clearly the passive and penetrated partner of both man and beast: 'originally begot by a man, but a mastiff dog or monkey gave the semen some sprinkling'.[63]

The culture is no doubt that the generation of hybrids is possible as a result of bestiality. What is in doubt is whether progeny belonging to only one of the two species which generated it can result from copulation with animals. Writes Willet *'Against the abominable sinne of bestiality'*:

1. This horrible wickednesse committed by the male, or female, by this Law is provided against: for such is the corruption of mans nature, that not onely men have companied with beasts, as Mares, Kine, Swine, and such other: but even uncleane women have prostituted themselves unto beasts as *Pasiphae* to a Bull, *Polyphontes* to a Beare, *Semiranus* to an Horse: the women of *Mendes* in Egypt, to Goats . . .
2. But whether any perfit kind may by such monstrous copulations be brought forth, it is a question. 1. Some thinke that beside monstrous births, which are usually fruits of such bestiall lust, there have been borne sometime perfit men: sometime beasts: as *Plutark* writeth of a boy begotten of a man, and a mare; and a girle, of a man, and an asse . . . *Galen* denyeth, that any such generation may bee of mankind, but *Porta* maintaineth it.[64]

Bizarre and unscientific as these accounts may seem to us, they offer none the less incontrovertible evidence of the way in which animals are understood as beings whose sexual desires physically and affectively bear a close affinity with those of humanity.

Beasts also figure regularly and significantly in early modern arguments against incest. Gervase Babington contends in his commentary on Leviticus: 'Yea the Camels (saith Aristotle) abhorre it [incest] by nature, and the Colt will not come neere in this sort to the Dam; God being pleased in bruit beasts to give us an example against this thing.'[65] A compelling counter-example of incest among the beasts is Myrrha'a articulation of her desire for her father, Cinyras, in the *Metamorphosis:*

For every other living wyght dame nature dooth permit
To match without offence of sin. The Heifer thinkes no shame
To beare her father on her backe: the horse bestrydes the same
Of whom he is the syre: the Gote dooth bucke the kid that hee
Himself begate: and birdes doo tread the selfsame birdes wee see
Of whom they hatched were before. In happye cace they are
That may doo so without offence. But mans malicious care
Hath made a brydle for it self, and spyghtfull lawes restreyne
The things that nature setteth free. [66]

Horses do it, cows do it, goats do it; yet human law forbids it. Myrrha's bizarre rationalizations of her lust for her father are not only reminiscent of Venus's tenderly ludicrous images of love, 'I'll be a park, and thou shalt be my deer' (231), but like Shakespeare's poem figure human sexual discriminations which constitute incest via species distinction, both as relations between beasts and the difference between humans and animals.

Critics of *Venus and Adonis* have long suggested that Shakespeare might have known Titian's painting of the reluctant Adonis, anxious to be on his way to the boar,[67] but a more appropriate visual analogue for my purposes (one whose relevance is in no way dependent upon Shakespeare having known it) is Bronzino's late sixteenth-century *Allegory of Venus and Cupid*, where mother and (adolescent rather than cherubic infant) son are 'locked in a peculiarly sensual embrace'.[68] Of course, Bronzino's Cupid is no reluctant Adonis, but the painting does suggest the incestuous overtones of even Venus's maternal aspect as mother of Cupid. Richard McCabe's remarks on this painting, whose figures strike him as 'reptilian' ('not merely in the contrived contortion of the limbs, but in the narrowed, mesmeric eyes and the thin wedge of tongue obscenely parting the goddess's lips'), are also remarkably apposite for Shakespeare's *Venus and Adonis*: 'It would appear that the ultimate expression of eroticism necessitates the ultimate confusion of animal and human nature, the ultimate desecration of kinship.'[69]

There is, however, a further sacred and sacrilegious dimension to the desecration of kinship here. Petting an infantalized Adonis not only replicates the relation between Venus and Cupid but also proffers the pagan and erotic equivalent of the Madonna and Child. Adonis as 'a son that sucked an earthly mother' (863–864) himself reflects the infant Christ, while Venus and Adonis, after the latter's death, form an erotic Pietà.[70] Religious forms and experiences are those which are normatively scandalous – eating bodies, drinking blood, crucifying gods, incest within the holy family (Mary is both mother of Jesus and daughter to his Godhead). Within the framework of religion, one is permitted to contemplate what Peter Barker says he will 'purposely pass over' in the course of his commentary on bestiality: 'Other sinnes of the like sort, which nature doth abhorre and chaste eares will not willingly heare, the very thought whereof woundeth the heart with horrour'.[71] Ultimately bestial and sacred, *Venus and Adonis* also represents the sublime eroticism of both pagan and Christian profanity.

Flowers

Whereas in early modern anxieties about the integrity of human identity, copulation with animals figured the fragile boundary between nature and culture, modern anthropology and psychoanalysis cite the incest taboo as the foundational distinction between them.[72] This prohibition, writes Juliet Mitchell, is 'the decisive break man makes with the beasts. It is definitional of humanity.'[73] In the poem's incestuous family, however, Adonis is, like Christ, both father and child whose fate it is to wither in Venus's distinctively maternal bosom. That is, the most incestuous moment in the poem represents a return to nature of the most extreme, but literary kind. 'Poor flower,' quoth she, 'this was thy father's guise, – / Sweet issue of a more sweet-smelling sire' (1177–1178), the anemone seems to be, like the flower in *A Midsummer Night's Dream*, which represents Elizabeth's virginity, an emblem of chastity:

> And in his blood that on the ground lay spill'd,
> A purple flower sprung up, checkere'd with white,
> Resembling well his pale cheeks and the blood
> Which in round drops upon their whiteness stood
> (1167–1170)

Always predisposed to rot rather than to reproduce, 'For flowers that are not gathered in their prime / Rot, and consume themselves in little time' (131–132), Adonis remains immured in the world of great creating nature, which has consumed and regenerated him according to its cycles:

> Here was thy father's bed, here in my breast.
> Thou art the next of blood, and 'tis thy right.
> Lo, in this hollow cradle take thy rest;
> My throbbing heart shall rock thee day and night,
> There shall not be one minute in an hour
> Wherein I will not kiss my sweet love's flower.
> (1183–1188)

Mythologically speaking, of course, Adonis has always been biodegradable. The anemone, into which Adonis is transformed in the *Metamorphosis*, is associated by Ovid with the fruit revealed when the rind of the pomegranate was removed. In a sense Adonis here returns to his Ovidian origins because he was born from the weeping cypress tree to which his mother was confined. Fissuring the bark or rind from which he emerges, Adonis comes to figure the permeability of the boundaries of 'kind'.

Rigorously self-cultivating even before he becomes a flower, Adonis argues: 'Who plucks the bud before one leaf put forth' (416); 'The mellow plum doth fall, the green sticks fast, / Or, being early plucked is sour to taste' (517–522). But now, in his final metamorphosis, he literally becomes an object of cultivation, a plant and a 'cult', namely the pagan cult of Adonis. Unlike the naturalistic depictions of the host of nature's creatures in the poem – the boar, the deer, the hare, the eagle, the horse, the jennet, the snail – the depiction of the flower is completely emblematic. This is because, as Leonard Barkan has so acutely observed, the artistic effect of metamorphosis is 'to transform human identities into images'.[74]

The emblematic status of flowers seems, oddly, to have intensified during the spectacular growth of domestic flower cultivation in Elizabethan England. One of the new flowers introduced was the wild anemone, and, at the same time, potted plants, known as 'Gardens of Adonis', also became popular. That is, the cultural understanding of flowers as signifiers is actually, though perhaps paradoxically, continuous with horticultural advances, which, as Polixenes points out in *The Winter's Tale*, had served only to complicate the distinctions between nature and culture: 'The art itself is nature' (IV.iv.97). Cultivation does not so much usurp the art of nature as erase the boundary between the natural and the artificial. Significantly, the 'art' to which Polixenes refers is constituted by the vegetative equivalent of the incest taboo: 'we *marry* / A gentle scion to the wildest stock / And *make conceive* a bark of baser kind / By a bud of nobler race' (IV.iv.92–95, emphasis mine). In this instance, inbreeding is antipathetic to cultivation, and thence to culture.

Demarcations between nature and culture have also been part of the poem's critical mythology, which has long maintained that Shakespeare made such an art of nature in *Venus and Adonis* that he may have composed the poem while he was still in Stratford and had not yet been inducted into the sophistication of metropolitan culture. In Muriel Bradbrook's (mistaken) verdict: 'Shakespeare still had some heavy provincial Warwickshire loam sticking to his boots.'[75]

Although distinctions between nature and culture are all too easily trivialized, it is worth remembering that, in essence, Reformation theology addressed itself to the question of how the animal aspects of human nature, the 'corrupt flesh',[76] estranged human beings from God, while the exultant spirit of the Renaissance celebrated humanity's divine potential as 'the paragon of the animals' (*Hamlet*, II.ii.297). As Golding put it in the preface to his translation of the *Metamorphoses*:

> Our soule is wee endewd by God with reason from above;
> Our bodie is but as our house, in which wee worke and move.
> T'one part is common to us all, with God of heaven himself;
> The tother common with the beastes, a vyle and stinking pelf.[77]

That Golding was the translator of both Ovid and Calvin exemplifies the irreconcilable contradictions of Renaissance humanism and radical Protestantism, which were being played out in relation to the status of poetry at the end of the sixteenth century. The *epyllion* in particular seemed dedicated to frivolity and delight, to what human beings have in 'common with the beastes, a vyle and stinking pelf' rather than to the more sober task of Protestant aesthetics.[78] In fact, Shakespeare's poem works over these contradictions in human nature, or rather the contradictions between the human and the natural. The poem's naturalistic images of wildlife at one end of the spectrum, the mythically voracious boar, and (ostensibly one of the most frivolous images of the poem) Venus's deer park at the other, bespeak the inherent perversity of desire and are precisely what lend the poem its tragiccomic quality. By repeatedly transgressing the discrete taxonomies of human and animal, nature and culture, the poem's images render them demonstrably artificial categories. In so doing, *Venus and Adonis* conveys with singular poignancy the (un)naturalness of loving where we should not love, or where we are not wanted.

Notes

1 Bruce Thomas Boehrer argues that 'the rhetoric of bestiality was in some basic ways more important than the crime itself' on the grounds that there were so few prosecutions and executions for the offence during the period. It was, he argues, 'a victimless crime' against 'a kind of abstract linguistic principle'. 'Bestial Buggery in *A Midsummer Night's Dream*,' in David Lee Miller, Sharon O'Dair and Harold Weber (eds), *The Production of English Renaissance Culture* (Ithaca: Cornell University Press, 1994), pp. 123–150 (p. 132). While this essay was in the press the following important volumes appeared: Tom Betteridge (ed.), *Sodomy in Early Modern Europe* (Manchester: Manchester University Press, 2002), and Bruce Boehrer, *Shakespeare Among the Animals: Nature and Society in the Drama of Early Modern England* (Basingstoke and New York: Palgrave, 2002). See too Bruce Bohrer, *Monarchy and Incest in Renaissance England: Literature, Culture, Kinship and Kingship* (Philadelphia: University of Pennsylvania Press, 1992).

2 Keith Thomas, *Man and the Natural World: A History of Modern Sensibility* (New York: Pantheon, 1983), p. 39.

3 James Usher, *A Body of Divinity* (London: 1645), p. 280.

4 Thomas, *Man and the Natural World*, p. 39. In sharp contrast, a recent commentator remarks: 'there is no satisfactory reason for retaining in the modern law a crime of buggery with animals . . . It has become pointless.' Tony Honoré, *Sex Law* (London: Duckworth, 1978), p. 176.

5 'Indeed, the reminiscences of the countryside, especially the hunting of the hare, have often been praised as the most "natural" parts of the poem.' M. C. Bradbrook, *Shakespeare and the Elizabethan Poets* (Cambridge: Cambridge University Press, 1951), p. 62. See also E. Berry, *Shakespeare and the Hunt: A Cultural and Social Study* (Cambridge: Cambridge University Press, 2001). Citations from and references to the poem will be taken from Stephen Greenblatt *et al.* (eds), *The Norton Shakespeare*

(New York: W. W. Norton, 1987), pp. 607–634. References to plays will also be from this edition.

6 Usher, *A Body of Divinity*, p. 280.

7 See Philippa Berry, 'Hamlet's Ear', *Shakespeare Survey* 50 (1997), 57–64.

8 Coppélia Kahn, *Man's Estate: Masculine Identity in Shakespeare* (Berkeley: University of California Press, 1981), p. 40.

9 Sir Edward Coke, *The Third Part of the Institutes of the Lawes of England* (London: 1644), p. 59. On the uniqueness of Shakespeare's treatment of this episode see William Keach, *Elizabethan Erotic Narratives: Irony and Pathos in the Ovidian Poetry of Shakespeare, Marlowe, and Their Contemporaries* (New Brunswick, NJ: Rutgers University Press, 1977), p. 80.

10 Peter Barker, *A Judicious and Painefull Exposition upon the ten commandments* (London: 1624), p. 270.

11 William Gouge, *Of Domesticall Duties* (London: 1634), p. 185.

12 Thomas, *Man and the Natural World*, p. 118.

13 Richard Capel, *Tentations: Their Nature, Danger, Cure* (London: 1635), pp. 356–358.

14 Gouge, *Of Domesticall Duties*, p. 185.

15 Gervase Babington, *The Works* (London: 1615), p. 461. Christian commentators found it expedient to allegorize biblical injunctions against eating pork. Intriguingly, Andrew Willet argues that 'the Jews abhorred Swinnes flesh . . . because *Adonis* whom *Bacchus* loved, who is worshipped of the Jewes, was slaine of a Boare'. Andrew Willet, *Hexapla In Leviticum that is, a six-fold Commentarie upon the third booke of Moses, Called Leviticus* (London: 1631), p. 224.

16 Capel, *Tentations*, p. 358.

17 See Jonathan Goldberg, *Sodometries: Renaissance Texts, Modern Sexualities* (Stanford: Stanford University Press, 1992); Patricia Parker, *Shakespeare from the Margins: Language, Culture, Context* (Chicago: University of Chicago Press, 1996), pp. 186–213. As Coppélia Kahn remarks 'The playful suggestion that . . . he would rather "know" or love the boar seems a kind of risqué joke at first, a glance at sodomy. But it carries the serious undertone that he is deeply alienated from his own kind determined not to love even at the expense of being perverse' (Kahn, *Man's Estate*, p. 40). C. L. Barber has argued that the boar is a figure of 'homosexual rape'. C. L. Barber and Richard Wheeler, *The Whole Journey: Shakespeare's Power of Development* (Berkeley: University of California Press, 1986), p. 147.

18 Mario DiGangi, *The Homoerotics of Early Modern Drama* (Cambridge: Cambridge University Press, 1997), pp. 136–137.

19 Babington, *The Works*, p. 480.

20 Coke, *The Third Part of the Institutes*, p. 59.

21 Even today, the *OED* opts for the vague but symptomatic 'Unnatural intercourse of a human being with a beast, or of men with one another, sodomy. Also used of unnatural intercourse of a man and a woman. Now mainly a technical term in criminal law.'

22 Edward Topsell, *The History of Foure-Footed Beasts* (London: 1607), p. 541.

23 Willet, *Hexapla In Leviticum*, p. 224.

24 Topsell, *The History of Foure-Footed Beasts*, p. 540.

25 Willet, *Hexapla In Leviticum*, p. 224.

26 *Ovid's Metamorphoses: The Arthur Golding Translation*, 1567, ed. John Frederick Nims (New York: Macmillan, 1965), Book 8, lines 360, 497.

27 Ted Hughes, *Shakespeare and the Goddess of Complete Being* (London: Faber and Faber, 1992), p. 73.

28 *Ibid.*, pp. 68–69.

29 As quoted in Boehrer, 'Bestial Buggery', p. 134.

30 *Ibid.*

31 John Rogers, *The Displaying of an Horrible Secte of Grosse and Wicked Heretiques, Naming Themselves the Family of Love* (1578), quoted in Marc Shell, 'The Family Pet', *Representations* 15 (1986), 121–153 (p. 138).

32 Katharine Mauss points out: 'Again and again, its [the poem's] metaphors and similes insist on the similarity of what seems different, the difference in what seems the same' (*The Norton Shakespeare*, p. 603).

33 Capel, *Tentations*, pp. 52, 53–54.

34 *Ibid.*, p. 408; p. 378.

35 Jonathan Bate, 'Sexual Perversity in *Venus and Adonis*', *The Yearbook of English Studies* 23 (1993), 80–92 (p. 92).

36 E. Fenton, *Certaine Secrete Wonders of Nature* (London: 1569), p. 13; p. 12.

37 '[P]et love traduces (or transcends) two practices we ordinarily think of as being taboo. One of these practices is besiality, or interspecies lovemaking, which is an effect of traducing the ordinary interspecies distinctions between human and non-human beings, or between kind and non-kind. The other practice is incest, or intrafamiliral lovemaking, which is an effect of traducing the ordinary distinction bewtween kin and non-kin.' Shell, 'The Family Pet', p. 123.

38 Capel, *Tentations*, p. 408.

39 Astonishingly, incest was not criminalized until 1908 although of course it was prohibited via the tables of consanguinity.

40 Quoted in Thomas, *Man and the Natural World*, p. 40.

41 *Ibid.*, p. 119.

42 Sir John Harington, *Nugae Antiquae*, 2 vols. (London: 1804), I, 390–394.

43 Thomas, *Man and The Natural World*, p. 99.

44 Anthony G. Petti, 'Beasts and Politics in Elizabethan Literature', *Essays and Studies* 16 (1963), 68–90 (p. 77).

45 Anthony Mortimer, 'The Ending of *Venus and Adonis*,' *English Studies* 78:4 (1997), 334–341 (p. 338).

46 Bate, 'Sexual Perversity', p. 92.

47 Gouge, *Of Domesticall Duties*, p. 188.

48 Heather Dubrow, *Captive Victors: Shakespeare's Narrative Poems and Sonnets* (Ithaca: Cornell University Press, 1987), p. 34. See also Peter Erickson, *Rewriting Shakespeare, Rewriting Ourselves* (Berkeley: University of California Press, 1991), p. 31.

49 'In view of the Italian sources of Elizabethan imagery, perhaps the question is not unjustified whether the worship of Queen Elizabeth as Diana was not also a cult of Venus in disguise.' Edgar Wind, *Pagan Mysteries in the Renaissance* (Oxford: Oxford University Press, 2nd edn, 1980), p. 77. See also p. 24; p. 75.

50 Philippe Ariès, *Centuries of Childhood*, trans. Robert Baldick (London: Pimlico, 2nd edn, 1996), p. 99.

51 *Ovid's Metamorphoses*, ed. Nims, Book 10, lines 87–93.
52 See *OED* s.v.
53 See Richard A. McCabe, *Incest, Drama and Nature's Law, 1550–1700* (Cambridge: Cambridge University Press, 1993), p. 19.
54 Kahn, *Man's Estate*, p. 34.
55 Bate, 'Sexual Perversity', pp. 84–85.
56 McCabe, *Incest, Drama and Nature's Law*, p. 21.
57 Gouge. *Of Domesticall Duties*, p. 185.
58 Thomas, *Man and the Natural World*, p. 135.
59 *Ibid.*, p. 145.
60 Vavasor Powell, *God the Father Glorified* (1649), as quoted Thomas, *Man and the Natural World*, p. 135.
61 Babington, *The Works*, p. 480.
62 Coke, *The Third Part*, p. 59.
63 Thomas, *Man and the Natural World*, p. 135.
64 Willet, *Hexapla in Leviticum*, p. 434.
65 Babington, *The Works*, p. 478.
66 *Ovid's Metamorphoses*, ed. Nims, pp. 258–259.
67 For a full discussion of the relations between Shakespeare's poem and the treatment of Venus and Adonis in painting see Clark Hulse, *Metamorphic Verse: The Elizabethan Minor Epic* (Princeton: University Press, 1981), pp. 141–194.
68 McCabe, *Incest, Drama and Nature's Law*, p. 28.
69 *Ibid.*
70 James Nohrnberg, *The Analogy of the Faerie Queene* (Princeton: Princeton University Press, 1976), p. 565. Edgar Wind observes: 'Renaissance art produced many images of Venus which resemble a Madonna or a Magdalen. An extreme instance is the Hyperotomachia, in which Venus is pictured as *mater dolorosa*, nourishing her infant son with tears.' Wind, *Pagan Mysteries*, p. 24.
71 Barker, *A Judicious and Painefull Exposition*, p. 270.
72 For Freud, Lévi-Strauss and others, the incest taboo is the cornerstone, the foundational moment of civilization, making the fundamental development from the state of nature to that of culture. McCabe, *Incest, Drama and Nature's Law*, p. 17.
73 Juliet Mitchell, *Feminism and Pschoanalysis* (New York: Pantheon Books, 1974), p. 374.
74 Leonard Barkan, *The Gods Made Flesh: Metamorphosis and the Pursuit of Paganism* (New Haven: Yale University Press, 1986), p. 26.
75 Bradbrook, *Shakespeare and the Elizabethan Poets*, p. 62.
76 Capel, *Tentations*, p. 408.
77 The preface 'To the Reader' in *Ovid's Metamorphoses*, ed. Nims, pp. 425–426.
78 'By and large the poems of the minor epic genre have no great ethical import and little redeeming social value. They are by turns artificial, frivolous, arcane.' Hulse, *Metamorphic Verse*, p. 3.

—part two—

Negotiating knowledge

4

'Non canimus surdis, respondent omnia sylvae': Francis Bacon and the transmission of knowledge

DAVID COLCLOUGH

FRANCIS BACON seems always to be standing on the threshold between premodernity and modernity; indeed, the difficult relationship, in his works and in their reception, between the past, the present and the future might seem to make him the archetypal 'early modern' writer. Categorized variously as the prophet of instrumental science and the covert pupil of his arch-enemy Aristotle, Bacon's status as honorary ancient or modern has dominated interpretation of his writings from the seventeenth century to the present day.[1] Bacon himself was firmly convinced that he was inaugurating a new mode of knowledge. In 1605, dedicating the second book of *The Advancement of Learning* to James I, he asked the king, 'why should a few received authors stand up like Hercules' columns, beyond which there should be no sailing or discovering, since we have so bright and benign a star as your Majesty to conduct and prosper us?'[2] The question was echoed by his conclusion in *Cogitata et visa* ('Thoughts and conclusions') that in the field of natural philosophy, 'Pillars have been erected beyond which progress is forbidden'.[3] Such forward-looking statements, which recall immediately the famous title page to the 1620 *Novum organum* ('New instrument') showing a ship sailing between the pillars of Hercules, present a picture of Bacon as looking towards the future, trapped within a society where 'the last thing anyone would be likely to entertain is an unfamiliar thought', and trying somehow to a find a way of thinking the unthinkable (*F*, p. 79). At the same time, the very novelty of his ideas could lead to a sense that his proper place was in the past rather than in the present: writing to Isaac Casaubon in 1609, Bacon claimed that the unresponsiveness of his readers had forced him into the company of those authors whose hold over the imagination of his contemporaries he so resented: 'I seem to have my conversation among the ancients more than among these with whom I live.'[4]

In this essay I will show, by reading three of Bacon's short Latin texts, how he imagined his place in the history and the future of philosophy. By attending to Bacon's interest in the possibilities and limitations of different textual forms for the discovery and transmission of knowledge, I will argue, we can come to a better understanding of what it was that made his philosophy new and its acceptance uncertain. A close reading of *Temporis partus masculus* ('The masculine birth of time'), *Cogitata et visa* and *Redargutio philosophiarum* ('The refutation of philosophies'), I suggest, sheds new light on Bacon's conception of his audience and of the nature of knowledge in the Renaissance.

A major obstacle to considering Bacon's texts in this way is that, as I shall argue below, the three manuscript works I discuss present a particularly anomalous case in relation to questions of audience. None the less, it is clear that each performs a different task; is, as it were, a different kind of textual intervention into a particular social, political, or 'scientific' debate.[5] Employing a commonplace of rhetorical theory, Bacon declared in the second book of *The Advancement of Learning* that 'the proofs and persuasions of rhetoric ought to differ according to the auditors', while Lisa Jardine has shown that in many of his texts Bacon sees the end of instruction less as the discovery of truth and more as 'securing assent'.[6] By examining Bacon's exploitation of different textual forms for the various purposes of those parts of the *Instauration* he did manage to complete, we are able to see them more clearly as part of a debate over the way that knowledge works in society. This in turn enhances our ability to uncover the ways in which early modern England generated criteria and arenas for judging or dealing with authority – both textual and temporal.

The texts I focus on were probably written between 1603 and 1609, and existed only in manuscript during Bacon's lifetime.[7] All three survive in unique copies – though there is also a draft in English of *Cogitata et visa* entitled *Filum labyrinthi, sive formula inquisitiones* ('The clue to the labyrinth, or the rule for enquiries') – and they are all in the hands of Bacon's amanuenses, with occasional autograph corrections and emendations. The extent of their dissemination in manuscript thus remains extremely obscure. After Bacon's death the three works were published, though not adjacently, in Isaac Gruter's collection *Francisci Baconi de Verulamio, scripta in naturali et vniversali philosophia* ('Francis Bacon of Verulam: writings on natural and universal philosophy') (Amsterdam: 1653).[8] In this discussion I will treat them as individual works 'recovered' by Spedding from the fragments found in Gruter and elsewhere, although given greater space it would be useful to analyse the *Scripta* and its organization in detail.[9] The texts are concerned not so much with the questions of what knowledge consists in (explored in *The Advancement of Learning* of 1605 and the *Novum organum* of 1620) or with offering natural philosophical 'facts' (also the intention of the *Novum organum*, and of the natural histories, such as *Historia ventorum* ('History of the wind') (1622), *Historia vitae et mortis* ('History of life and death') or *Historia densi et rari* ('History of dense and rare') (1658)) but rather with the question of how the acquisition of 'new' knowledge can be facilitated by the philosopher and how readers' minds can be prepared for this acquisition. Their preoccupations are primarily heuristic and propaedeutic rather than epistemological, that is to say, and they form an extended reflection on the best way of establishing and retaining textual authority while avoiding the deceptive or 'magistral' modes of instruction which Bacon deplores in the philosophy of the ancients.[10] In reading these texts I will consider the rhetorical strategies deployed by each, and then suggest how they fit in with Bacon's conception of his own purpose and skills as a writer and reader.

Although the texts contain many of the notions expounded in *The Advancement*, they also show Bacon experimenting with a range of textual forms, and it is the search for a range of authoritative textual strategies that most concerns him here. Bacon was beginning to sketch out in manuscript his plans for the *Instauratio magna* ('Great instauration'), and one of the most pressing parts of that plan was the *pars destruens*, or destructive part, necessary before the production of the *pars construens*, or constructive part. The foremost part in this destructive enterprise was, as Spedding says, given to the *redargutio philosophiarum*.[11] In the three manuscript works Bacon spends some time discussing whether new ideas can be absorbed before the old are dispensed with, and to what extent the inherited doctrines of philosophy could or should be rejected. It is this preparatory enterprise that he later included in the second section of the *Instauratio* in his *Distributio operis* ('Outline of the work'), as the *expurgatione intellectus* ('clearing of the mind').[12]

Temporis partus masculus, probably written around 1602–03, deals directly with the problem of finding a method of communication both authoritative and insinuative for the promulgation of the new philosophy. What philosophers lack, the speaker says, is 'any art or precepts to guide them in putting their knowledge before the public' (*F*, p. 61). The text is a monologue whose addressee is referred to as 'my son', and the latter's possible objections and thoughts are anticipated by the speaker – all of which sets up a highly 'magistral' and hierarchical situation. Yet rather than the speaker leading the addressee from a position of ignorance towards the light of truth, the 'son' is already a sympathizer to the new ideas. The reader is implicitly included in this community, and by this oblique mode of instruction Bacon is able to approach the removal of impediments preventing further development. He stresses the need for an insinuative pedagogy, since 'when all the entrances and approaches to men's minds are beset and blocked by the most obscure idols ... A new method must be found for quiet entry into minds so choked and overgrown' (F, p. 62). This method must have the dual properties of being able both gently to persuade and to select its readers, so that the unsullied continuation of knowledge in its reinvigorated form is assured:

> The method must be mild and afford no occasion of error. It must have in it an inherent power of winning support and a vital principle which will stand up against the ravages of time, so that the tradition of science may mature and spread like some lively vigorous vine. Then also science must be such as to select her followers, who must be worthy to be adopted into her family.
>
> (F, p. 62)

After laying out the importance of the new method, the speaker moves on to a name-by-name condemnation of the 'sham philosophers' of the past. Such a thorough *vituperatio* is necessary, he says, 'for their authority is great and if not named they may be thought to be excepted' (F, p. 63). The list mainly attacks its victims' concentration on words at the expense of experience, so that Aristotle is condemned for having 'composed an art or manual of madness and made us the slaves of words' (F, p. 63), while Ramus is reviled specifically for his supposed immersion in language and described as 'that pestilent book-worm, that begetter of handy manuals' (F, p. 64). Plato, Cicero, Seneca, Plutarch and Hippocrates are all summarily dealt with, as are Galen and all modern Galenic physicians (F, p. 64; pp. 67–68; pp. 64–65). Paracelsus' claims to base his theories on experience are rubbished in a general attack on the Alchemists; and though the speaker grudgingly praises Paracelsus' follower Peter Severinus, acknowledging that the Paracelsians have uncovered some isolated truths, he stresses that these are the products of chance and have no basis in an understanding of the principles of nature: 'a pig might print the letter A with its snout in the mud, but you would not on that account expect it to go on to compose a tragedy' (F, p. 71). The speaker is emphatic that knowledge 'is to be sought from the light of nature, not from the darkness of antiquity. It matters not what has been done; our business is to see what can be done' (F, p. 69).

The ultimate ambition of this new method is to marry 'things themselves' to the listener's mind, avoiding the distorting media cultivated by the ancients. While the preparatory project of *The Advancement* required a survey and even incorporation of the works of the ancients in order to suggest a way forward for learning, *Temporis partus masculus* suggests that they must be dispensed with entirely. This can only be achieved, however, in conjunction with the promulgation of the new philosophy – rather limiting the effectiveness of the text – since 'on waxen tablets you cannot write anything new until you rub out the old. With the mind it is not so; there you cannot rub out the old until you have written in the new' (*F*, p. 72).

Cogitata et visa and *Redargutio philosophiarum* share many of the key ideas of *Temporis partus masculus*, and often even reuse whole phrases or sentences, although they differ significantly in form. *Cogitata et visa*, written in or around 1607, is closest in form of the three to the aphoristic style that Bacon praised in *The Advancement* as best suited to the presentation of new knowledge, since by presenting the 'thoughts' as independent sections of text followed by 'conclusions' it goes some way towards representing the progress of thought – or at least argument. In personalizing these 'thoughts'– the text begins 'Franciscus Bacon sic cogitavit' ('Francis Bacon thought thus') and each subsequent section is prefaced 'cogitavit et illud' ('he thought also thus') – the work allows room for dissent, the fruits of which, Bacon emphasizes, have been stunted by the enslaving power of authority. He draws a distinction, as in *The Advancement*, between magistral and probative methods, saying that aphorisms

> gave a bare outline of their discoveries and left obvious blanks where no discoveries had been made. It was a stimulating method which made their readers think and judge for themselves . . . But nowadays the sciences are presented in such a way as to enslave belief instead of provoking criticism; the intervention of a blighting authority precludes fruitful research.
>
> (*F*, pp. 75–76)

The arguments against authority in *Cogitata et visa* are concentrated on the institutions of learning, which Bacon sees as producing, like the libraries on which they depend, 'infinite repetition, new in the manner but not in the substance' (*F*, p. 75). He distinguishes prudently between the world of politics, where innovation is justly suspect – 'for political control rests on authority, assent, reputation, opinion, not on demonstration and truth' – and that of the Academies, which represses the challenges of which it has need: 'in these places studies are confined to the works of certain authorities; and a man who disagrees with them or raises awkward questions is censured as a disturbing and revolutionary influence' (F, p. 79). These authorities are again censured for having conducted their inquiries at a level removed from nature itself, namely that of language – which, Bacon says, echoing his description of the Idols of the Market-Place, 'reflect[s] vulgar opinions and preferences' (F, p. 81).[13] Thus Aristotle's chief failing was that he 'left nature herself untouched and inviolate, and dissipated his energies comparing, contrasting and analysing popular notions about her' (F, p. 83). The problem that concerns Bacon is how one can pass beyond the analysis of popular notions to a direct encounter with nature, since subservience to the authority of tradition does not just impede progress by rendering it unrespectable; it actually hinders the ability to conceive of progress, exercizing a tyranny over the imagination so that 'Men's anticipations of the new are fashioned on the model of the old' (F, p. 96). The first step in even pointing towards change and new ideas, therefore, must be the attempt to make one's audience capable of *thinking* novelty; it is this epistemological gear-change, I would suggest, that the three texts are intended to provoke.

Cogitata et visa provides the clearest description in any of these works of what shape the new philosophy might take, describing how the gradual progression from axiom to axiom, based on a process of exclusion, provides a way of locating the 'Forms' of nature and defining them along the way. Understanding these basic principles would allow scientists to reproduce them, and thus to control nature. The delineation here of knowledge arrived at by representation mirrors Bacon's description of the 'probative' method of transmission, where the reader's understanding is facilitated by a reproduction of the writer's arrival at his conclusions, and it glosses his statement that 'Nature cannot be conquered but by obeying her' (F, p. 93).[14]

It is apparent here, as in the *Novum organum*, that despite Bacon's desire to evade the distorting influence of language, his method remains an extremely textual one. Bacon describes *Cogitata et visa* as a preface to his Tables of Discovery, which by arranging instances of the presence and absence of a Form in various different aspects of natural processes are intended to uncover the conditions of its operation. Particulars, and axioms, are seen in this part of Bacon's theory as the smallest particles of natural facts or of language that produce meaning; they are less susceptible to the influence of the Idols, and they leave space for engagement on the part of the reader. Rather than offering explicit

comment or exposition of the facts arranged, the Tables generate meaning in the very act of their arrangement, again allowing the space on the
surface for a resisting reading of the 'facts' but suggesting implicitly an
inescapable conclusion. This technique is similar to Bacon's description
of the value of commonplacing in the second book of *The Advancement*.[15]
Commonplacing and natural philosophy were not, however, incompatible at the time Bacon was writing. Ann Blair sees the commonplacing
technique as dominant in the work of several other contemporary natural
philosophers, including Jean Bodin, whose *Universae naturae theatrum*
(1596) 'gather[s] entries under a thematic heading to pursue a general
pattern of nature'.[16] She suggests that such methods treat 'each entry
independently of its source, as potentially useful knowledge equivalent to
every other entry'.[17] However, rather than being a specifically early modern development as Blair suggests, such textual tolerance of 'cognitive
dissonance' was inherited from the medieval encyclopædic tradition,
as displayed in the work of Vincent of Beauvais and even Gesner.
Certainly, while appearing to proffer the 'facts' about nature with only
an implicit authorial commentary and conclusion, the commonplacing
method used by Bacon in the Tables and the *Novum organum* could be
seen instead to be silently introducing the paradigms and assumptions
of the authorities of the past by relying on their criteria for the gathering
of such facts, and thus for the conditions that determine what makes
up 'knowledge'. This double bind is one that runs through Bacon's
writings, and is most apparent in the overt confrontation with textual
authority common to these preparatory texts.

Redargutio philosophiarum was written at about the same time as
Cogitata et visa and, like the other two manuscript works, it highlights
the problems of writing and transmitting texts that treat or prepare
for new ideas, beginning with a consideration of the difficulty of writing a refutation of philosophies. Bacon again compares the mind to a
palimpsest where the new is written over the old, rather than a wax
tablet which can be reduced to the state of a tabula rasa. He sees his
peaceable entry into the minds of his readers as similar to Pope Alexander
VI's description of the entry of Charles VIII's army into Italy, with chalk
to mark up their lodgings rather than weapons to destroy them.[18] The
direct address from writer to reader is deflected a short way in by an
anecdote about a friend of the writer's attendance at a lecture in Paris.
The remainder of the *Redargutio* is a record of that speech, but one that
has suffered in its transmission; we are informed at the outset that what
we read is 'very inferior to the original' (*F*, p. 104). Much as in the other
preparatory texts, authenticity and the 'real' are represented as deferred,

and as obscured by words and the distortion attendant on the transmission of texts.[19] While emphasizing the possibility that meaning may
drain from a text in the process of its transmission, its translation from
speech to writing, from one country to another, and from report to
incorporation in Bacon's text, this framing technique also allows room
for the development of thoughts expressed in that report. In suggesting
that the text facing the reader is neither final nor authoritative, it invites
participation in the acts of interpretation and in the 'plan for an honest
interpretation of nature' proposed by the speaker in his lecture (*F*,
p. 119). Once more Bacon is attempting to create a 'probative' pedagogy,
which artfully places the reader on the same level as the writer in the
path they follow through the text, rather as the speaker is said to deliver
his lecture from a position 'on level with the rest' (*F*, p. 104). And once
more, part of this 'probative' method consists in the appropriation of
the authorities that must be refuted in order for progress to be possible.
The *Redargutio* is itself a rhetorical refiguring of the process whereby a
text (or in this case an oral event) is accorded authority, then framed
by a commentary and a contextualizing preface only in order for it
ultimately to be superseded. On the one hand, depending on the ancients
simply in order to lend one's own text authority is condemned as the
fraudulent appropriation of reputation, and is compared to upsetting a
'natural' hierarchy by usurping its symbols:

> I could, by referring my present proposals to those ancient times,
> invest them with a certain solemnity, as self-made men do, who attach
> to themselves the nobility of some ancient stock by means of genea-
> logical hints and conjectures.
>
> (*F*, pp. 120–121)

But, on the other, Aristotle's refusal to acknowledge the authority of his
intellectual forebears is used as a means of denying him his own authority and refiguring him as Antichrist (Bacon is referring here to John
5:43):

> Christ says that he who comes in the name of the Father, which in a
> true and pious, if not a literal, sense is in the name of antiquity, will
> not be received; but he who, levelling and destroying all that went
> before, usurps authority to himself and comes in his own name, him
> men will follow.
>
> (*F*, p. 113)

By extension, Bacon suggests, one should engage with the ideas of the
ancients to provoke further thought, neither rejecting them out of hand

nor using them as respectable markers to stand in for the authority one's own writing lacks.

The *Redargutio* leads its readers through a complex set of positions towards the uses of the ancients and employs highly self-reflexive textual manoeuvres to generate a dual sense of at once undergoing (along with Bacon himself, the writer or reader) a learning process, and yet of having progressed only part of the way along a still rather uncertain route. Thus the description of the audience's dazzled reaction to what they have heard is implicitly equated with that of the reader. The text's final return to its framing narrative emphasizes the need faithfully to preserve and circulate such works. The friend entrusts his report to the writer, and once more the work acts out what Bacon expects of its reception: ' "Then," said he, "if, as you say, you like it, will you, when you write on these matters, find room to include my report and not suffer the fruit of my travels to perish." "A fair request," said I, "and I shall not forget"' (*F*, p. 133).

I have stressed above the lack of evidence for the circulation of these texts during Bacon's lifetime. There are, however, scattered references to them and to their fortunes in Bacon's letters, and, judging by what we can reconstruct from these comments, among sections of his selected audience they proved characteristically vulnerable to the vicissitudes of reception. In 1607 Bacon wrote reproachfully to Sir Thomas Bodley, who had taken his claims to some 'propriety' in Bacon's texts to extremes in retaining a copy of *Cogitata et visa*:

> In respect of my going down to my house in the country, I shall have miss of my papers; which I pray you therefore to return unto me. You are, I bear witness, slothful, and you help me nothing; so as I am in half conceit that you affect not the argument . . . I can say no more to you, but *non canimus surdis, respondent omnia sylvae* ['we do not sing to the deaf; the woods echo every note']. If you be not of the lodgings chalked up (whereof I speak in my preface) I am but to pass by your door.[20]

Bacon's use here of the hexameter from Virgil, *Eclogues* X, like all citations, participates in and articulates a struggle for textual authority. One of the first things to notice is that it is a quotation from *The Advancement of Learning*, as is the reference to the 'lodgings chalked up'.[21] Bacon is suggesting with the hexameter both that he will not carry on singing to the deaf (i.e. Bodley) – which is a somewhat strained reading of Virgil – and that he is not singing to the deaf because he has an audience elsewhere (which is closer to Virgil's meaning). It simply does not matter if Bodley will not listen or cannot hear, because something more important – Nature – is echoing and assenting. As Bacon writes in *The Advancement*,

> If it be truth,
>> Non canimus surdis, respondent omnia sylvae;
> the voice of nature will consent, whether the voice of man do or no
> . . . I like better that entry of truth which cometh peaceably with
> chalk to mark up those minds which are capable to lodge and harbour
> it, than that which cometh with pugnacity and contention.[22]

The use here and in the letter to Bodley of the echo topos interestingly reverses that found in Bacon's exposition of the myth of Pan, or Nature, in *De sapientia veterum* ('The wisdom of the ancients') (1609). There he writes that it is fitting that Pan should take Echo as his wife, since 'that alone is true philosophy, which doth faithfully render the very words of the world . . . not adding any thing of its owne, but onely iterates and resounds'.[23] Here it becomes clear that the echo works both ways.

In using this quotation Bacon appropriates it to his own purpose but wishes at the same time to retain the authority conferred by the absent name of Virgil. The citation both gathers Bodley into one community (that of the humanist gentleman) by assuming he will recognize it, and excludes him from another (that of the intellectual innovator or 'advancer') by suggesting that he is not 'of the lodgings chalked up'. In addition, Bacon makes himself part of the quotable community by multiple reference to his own texts, as if they had familiar currency.

The woods that echo Bacon's words also signify his subsequent textual authority; that is to say, the process of reading, quotation and appropriation that he initiates in this process of self-citation. He describes *The Advancement* as a 'preface', and he refers to the other texts I have discussed in the same way in several of his letters. In many of his works it is hard to see where the preface might end and the text 'proper' begin.[24] This anticipatory and suggestive rhetoric attempts to seek out and constitute networks of intellectual contact and textual communities of learning, in the absence of the sort of research institution Bacon referred to in the notebooks of 1608. There he writes of 'Layeng for a place to command wytts and pennes', and suggests as most likely or useful 'Westminster, Eton, Wynchester, Spec. Trinity College in Cambridg, St Jhons in Camb. Maudlin College in Oxford' – or, 'Foundac. of a college for Inventors past and spaces or Bases for Inventors to come And a Library and an Inginary'.[25] He goes on to outline some of the administrative details that would be involved in running such an

institution, including 'Qu. of the Maner and praescripts touching Sec-
recy, tradition, and publication'.[26] Bacon also amasses a heterogeneous
– and generally politically heterodox – list of likely (or perhaps unlikely)
participants, including the Earl of Northumberland, Sir Walter Ralegh,
Thomas Hariot, Archbishop Bancroft, Lancelot Andrewes and Prince
Henry. Of that number, two were imprisoned in the Tower of London
on treason charges at the time that Bacon was writing. In establishing
purely textual communities he seems equally happy to cross serious
political and religious divides, perhaps harking back to a humanist
republic of letters before confessional divisions across Europe hindered
the free passage of texts, individuals and ideas.[27] Anti-Catholic sentiment
in *The Advancement* was tempered for the *De augmentis*, and the popu-
larity of Bacon's ideas in Catholic France is attested to by the thirteen
translations of his texts that appeared between 1619 and 1649.[28] Toby
Matthew, one of the most prominent Catholic exiles, seems to have been
privy to the greatest range of Bacon's texts. In a letter written some time
after 1608, Bacon refers to having sent his friend 'some copies of my
book of the *Advancement*, which you desired; and a little work of my
recreation, which you desired not'.[29] In 1609 Bacon sent him copies of
the *In felicem memoriam Elizabethae* ('In happy memory of Elizabeth')
and a part of the *Instauratio* described as 'a leaf or two of the Preface,
carrying some figure of the whole work'.[30] The latter seems to have
met with Matthew's approval, for, in what seems to be a reply to his
comments, Bacon writes: 'As for the *Instauration*, your so full approbation thereof I read with much comfort, by how much more my heart is
upon it; and by how much less I expected consent and concurrence in
a matter so obscure.'[31] Another copy of this letter suggests further that
Bacon's text had been admired by those to whom Matthew had shown
it, and thus that the preparatory work on the *Instauratio* was serving its
purpose and finding a network of sympathizers: 'you make me very
glad of your approbation; the rather because you add a concurrence of
opinion with others; for else I might have conceived that affection would
perhaps have prevailed with you'.[32] The praise and advice Bacon received
from his correspondent led him to impart another text, which, from the
description of its 'harshness' and similarity to the Preface, seems likely
to have been the *Redargutio philosophiarum*:

> I send you at this time the only part which hath any harshness; and
> yet I framed to myself an opinion, that whosoever allowed well of that
> preface which you so much commend, will not dislike, or at least
> ought not to dislike, this other speech of preparation; for it is written
> out of the same spirit, and out of the same necessity.[33]

Matthew was thus put into the same position as the 'writer' of the *Redargutio* and entrusted with its continuing circulation. Bacon also hoped that Matthew would control the circulation of his texts, warning him 'you will take care not to leave the writing, which I left with you last, with any man, so long that he may be able to take a copy of it; because first it must be censured by you, and then considered again by me'.[34] Writing to him in October 1609, Bacon responded to warnings that his work might find opposition from clerics by asserting that his only real quarrel with them would be on the matter of his *bête noire*, Aristotle – though this was far from being an entirely secular point of difference:

> I shall have no occasion to meet them in my way, except it be as they will needs confederate themselves with Aristotle, who, you know, is intemperately magnified by the schoolmen; and is also allied (as I take it) to the Jesuits, by Faber, who was a companion of Loyola, and a great Aristotelian.[35]

In the same letter, Bacon stated explicitly his opinion that 'controversies in religion must hinder the advancement of sciences',[36] and while writing to the Catholic Matthew he was also engaged in a correspondence with Lancelot Andrewes.[37] In 1609 Bacon sent Andrewes 'some of this vacation's fruits', perhaps a version of *Cogitata et visa*. He represents the work as a 'recreation' whose purpose is to act as an intellectual purgative, to 'rid my mind of the present cogitation'. Again, it is described as a preparatory piece in the absence of the greater work to come, for 'I purpose to suppress [these miscellanies], if God give me leave to write a just and perfect volume of philosophy, which I go on with though slowly'.[38] Since he is 'forced to respect as well my times as the matter', Bacon asks Andrewes to edit judiciously those parts of the text which may be inappropriate to the times – as it seems he did for *The Advancement of Learning*:

> If your Lordship be so good now, as when you were the good Dean of Westminster, my request to you is, that not by pricks, but by notes, you would mark unto me whatsoever shall seem unto you either not current in the style, or harsh to credit and opinion, or inconvenient for the person of the writer; for no man can be judge and party ... And though for the matter itself my judgement be in some things fixed, and not accessible by any man's judgement that goeth not my way: yet even in those things, the admonition of a friend may make me express myself diversly.[39]

I have shown that in each of the three manuscripts discussed in this essay Bacon is greatly concerned with his texts' effects on their readers;

not simply in relation to the 'currency' or otherwise of his style but more importantly with the experience of reading as part of developing a new form of knowledge. Even in closely argued texts, Bacon implies, any epistemological reconsideration will be experiential rather than logical; just as the dazed state in which the audience emerge from the *Redargutio*'s lecture appears to have little to do with the arguments advanced therein. Similarly, Bacon is convinced that he can refute and supersede the ancients because he is possessed of a particularly privileged way of reading that enables him to distil from their texts all that is valuable and latent in them while dispensing with their faulty methodology (rather as he adapts the allegorical tradition to his own ends in *De sapientia veterum* while mocking previous allegorical interpreters). He is then able in his turn, he suggests, to provide a thread through the labyrinth of the natural philosophical archive for his readers.

The evidence available for the circulation of these texts in anything but the most restricted contexts is, as I have indicated above, virtually non-existent. As essays in particular textual and rhetorical forms they could well have been intended as more or less 'private' works, their primary intended reader Bacon himself. They could, on the other hand, have been designed to find a wider readership at an undefined period in the future: Gruter's placing of *Temporis partus masculus* and *Redargutio philosophiarum* in the collection 'Impetus philosophici' (a difficult title to translate, perhaps best read as 'The onrush of philosophy') argues for a continuing uncertainty about their purpose and leaves their interpretation firmly in the hands of the reader. What is clear, though, is that they all attempt, in their exploration of the potential of different textual forms, to reconceive of the way knowledge is contained in, and transmitted by, texts.

In conclusion I would like briefly to return to a wider consideration of Bacon's model of knowledge. For Foucault, convinced of Bacon's modernity, the novelty of his thought inhered in his foreshadowing of the Cartesian attack on resemblance as the basis of knowledge about the world.[40] Citing the *Novum organum*, Foucault suggests that Bacon's aim was to rid the human mind of its tendency to see similitudes where there are none and enable it to 'become "penetrating" and ultimately perceive the differences inherent in nature'.[41] Looking at *Temporis partus masculus*, *Cogitata et visa* and *Redargutio philosophiarum*, however, one might more profitably locate Bacon's sense of his own modernity as expressed in these preparatory works precisely in his desire to identify similitudes. All three texts articulate a desire to escape from the thrall of the ancients while at the same time locating in their books important lessons for and foreshadowings of Bacon's own philosophy. Foucault admitted the difficulty of attempting to locate discontinuities in the history of thought, but then went on to do so in analyses that cross cultural and linguistic, not to mention considerable temporal, boundaries.[42] If one starts instead by considering in detail the strategies of individual texts such as the ones I have explored in this essay it becomes clear that in the case of Bacon novelty and discontinuity (the new or 'second' philosophy) are conceived of as being of a piece with antiquity and continuity. It is through his ability to discover the nuggets of wisdom concealed in the texts of the ancients and then to transmit them to the minds of his putative readers, present or future, that Bacon hopes to reconceive the acquisition of knowledge in preparation for the philosophy to come. He may be unable to complete that work himself, he admits, but those who manage to read his preparatory texts 'correctly' will have their minds 'chalked up' for its arrival, and will participate in its generation through the new ways of thinking and reading which he has provided.

Notes

1 On Bacon as modern see W. Whewell, *The Philosophy of the Inductive Sciences, Founded upon their History* (London: 1854); Benjamin Farrington, *Francis Bacon: Philosopher of Industrial Science* (London: Lawrence and Wishart, 1951); Max Horkheimer and Theodor W. Adorno, *Dialectic of Enlightenment*, trans. John Cumming (London: Allen Lane, 1973), chapter 1, 'The Concept of Enlightenment', pp. 3–42; at pp. 3–7; Michel Foucault, *The Order of Things*, trans. unknown (London: Routledge, 1970), pp. 51–52. For an elaboration of Foucault's arguments see Timothy J. Reiss, *The Discourse of Modernism* (Ithaca: Cornell University Press, 1982). On Bacon's traditionalism see, for example, Lisa Jardine, *Francis Bacon: Discovery and the Art of Discourse* (Cambridge: Cambridge University Press, 1974); R. E. Larsen, 'The Aristotelism of Bacon's *Novum Organum*', *Journal of the History of Ideas* 23 (1962), 435–450; B. H. G. Wormald, *Francis Bacon: History, Politics and Science 1561–1626* (Cambridge: Cambridge University Press, 1993); Charles Whitney, *Francis Bacon and Modernity* (New Haven: Yale University Press, 1986). For a survey of Bacon's reception see Paolo Rossi, 'Ants, Spiders, Epistemologists', in Marta Fattori (ed.), *Francis Bacon, terminologia e fortuna nel XVII secolo* (Rome: Edizione dell'Ateneo, 1984), pp. 245–260. On Bacon in the eighteenth century see R. C. Cochrane, 'Francis Bacon in Early Eighteenth-century Literature', *Philological Quarterly* 37 (1958), 57–89; on Bacon in the nineteenth century see R. Yeo, 'An Idol of the Market Place: Baconianism in Nineteenth-century England', *History of Science* 23 (1985), pp. 251–298.

2 Francis Bacon, *The Advancement of Learning and New Atlantis*, ed. Arthur Johnston (Oxford, Clarendon Press, 1974), p. 60.

3 Francis Bacon, *Cogitata et visa*, in Benjamin Farrington, *The Philosophy of Francis Bacon: An Essay on its Development from 1603 to 1609 with New Translations of Fundamental Texts* (Liverpool: Liverpool University Press, 1964), p. 76. For ease of reference I use Farrington's translations of these texts throughout. Henceforth all references will be incorporated in the text in the form *F*, followed by page number.

4 Francis Bacon, *Works*, 14 vols, ed. James Spedding, Robert Leslie Ellis and Douglas Denon Heath (London: Longman, 1857–74), vol. 11, pp. 146–147, trans. Spedding.

5 For the theoretical background to this kind of approach, see the essays collected in James Tully (ed.), *Meaning and Context: Quentin Skinner and his Critics* (Princeton: Princeton University Press, 1988).

6 Bacon, *Advancement*, ed. Johnston, p. 141; Jardine, *Francis Bacon*, p. 173.

7 For the dating of the texts see Bacon, *Works*, vol. 3, pp. 524–526 (*Temporis partus masculus*), vol. 3, pp. 544–546 (*Redargutio philosophiarum*), vol. 3, pp. 589–590 (*Cogitata et visa*); Didier Deleule introduction, Francis Bacon, *Récusation des doctrines philosophiques et autres opuscules*, trans. Georges Rombi and Didier Deleule, ed. Didier Deleule (Paris: Presses Universitaires de France, 1987), pp. 6–13.

8 The two chapters of *Temporis partus masculus* are found together in the *Scripta* as part of the *Impetus philosophici* (sigs Vv–[V11]v), with the opening prayer at the very beginning of the book (sig. [*2]v). The manuscript of *Valerius terminus* (British Library Harleian MS 6462), containing the title and first chapter of *Temporis partus masculus* indicates that the three were at some point intended to be together, as they appear in Bacon, *Works*, vol. 3, pp. 527–539 (*Temporis partus masculus*), vol. 3, pp. 557–585 (*Redargutio philosophiarum*), vol. 3, pp. 591–620 (*Cogitata et visa*) and Farrington, *The Philosophy of Francis Bacon*, pp. 59–72. Part of the *Redargutio philosophiarum* is found in the *Scripta* (sigs O2–O6v), while the manuscript supplies the remainder of the text and the title (British Library Harleian MS 6855). *Cogitata et visa* is the first text in the *Scripta* (sigs A–[C7]); the manuscript is Queen's College Oxford MS CCLXXX, fol. 205ff. see Bacon, *Works*, pp. 495–590. For the posthumous transmission of manuscripts from Bacon, via William Boswell, to Gruter see Graham Rees, introduction, Francis Bacon, *Philosophical Studies c. 1611–c. 1619*, ed. Graham Rees, trans. Graham Rees and Michael Edwards, *The Oxford Francis Bacon*, vol. 6 (Oxford: Clarendon Press, 1996), pp. lxx–xcv. See also Peter Beal (compiler), *Index of English Literary Manuscripts vol. I, 1450–1625: Part I, Andrewes–Donne* (London: Mansell, 1980), pp. 17–52.

9 We await the volume in the new Oxford Francis Bacon which will clarify some of the vexed textual questions glanced at here.

10 For Bacon's desire to move from a 'magistral' to a 'probative' model of learning see *The Advancement of Learning*, pp. 35 and 134. He stresses that texts should ideally provoke further inquiry, criticism and speculation – as the form of the aphorism tends to (see Bacon, *Works*, vol. 3, p. 405; Bacon, *Advancement*, p. 34). On Bacon's use of the aphorism see further Brian Vickers, *Francis Bacon and Renaissance Prose* (Cambridge: Cambridge University Press, 1968), Chapter 3, pp. 60–95; Mary Horton, 'Bacon and "Knowledge Broken": An Answer to Michael Hattaway', *Journal of the History of Ideas* 43:3 (July–September 1982), 487–504; Francis Bacon, *The Essays*, ed. John Pitcher (Harmondsworth: Penguin, 1985), Introduction. Stephen Clucas, '"A Knowledge Broken": Francis Bacon's Aphoristic Style and the Crisis of Scholastic

and Humanist Knowledge-systems', in Neil Rhodes (ed.), *Renaissance Prose: New Essays in Criticism* (Binghamton: Mediaeval & Renaissance Texts Society, 1995), pp. 147–172, situates Bacon's use of the aphorism in the Hippocratic tradition, in contrast to the more familiar sententious use of the form. Julian Martin, *Francis Bacon, the State, and the Reform of Natural Philosophy* (Cambridge: Cambridge University Press, 1992), pp. 90–120, draws parallels between Bacon's use of the aphorism in his natural philosophy and his plans for the reform of the laws.

11 Bacon, *Works*, vol. 10, pp. 364–365.

12 *Ibid.*, vol. 1, p. 139; vol. 4, p. 27.

13 On the idols of the mind see *ibid.*, pp. 53–68.

14 Cf. *Novum Organum*, aphorism 3: 'Human knowledge and human power meet in one; for where the cause is not known the effect cannot be produced. Nature to be commanded must be obeyed' (Bacon, *Works*, vol. 1, p. 157; (translation) vol. 4, p. 47).

15 Bacon there defends the use of commonplaces, describing them as 'that which assureth copie of invention, and contracteth judgement to a strength' (Bacon, *Advancement*, p. 129).

16 Ann Blair, 'Humanist Methods in Natural Philosophy: The Commonplace Book', *Journal of the History of Ideas* 53:4 (October–December 1992), 546. See further Ann Moss, *Printed Commonplace-books and the Restructuring of Renaissance Thought* (Oxford: Clarendon Press, 1996).

17 Blair, 'Humanist Methods in Natural Philosophy', p. 547.

18 Cf. Bacon, *Advancement*, p. 99; letter to Bodley p. 89 below.

19 However, it is important to note the extended praise of the advantages of printing at the end of the text, which complicates still further the treatment of communication and its proper modes in this manuscript work (*F*, p. 132).

20 Bacon, *Works*, vol. 10, p. 366.

21 Bacon, *Advancement*, p. 99. The Virgilian hexameter appears first in the *Promus*; see Bacon, *Works*, vol. 7, p. 192. Virgil has a special place in the *Advancement*, accounting for forty-five allusions in the two versions. On Bacon's reading of Virgil see William A. Sessions, 'Francis Bacon and the Classics', in William A. Sessions (ed.), *Francis Bacon's Legacy of Texts: 'The Art of Discovery Grows with Discovery'* (New York: AMS Press, 1990), pp. 237–253; Whitney, *Francis Bacon and Modernity*, pp. 170–171. The reference to the 'lodgings chalked up', of course, also appears in the *Redargutio philosophiarum*; see above, p. 87.

22 Bacon, *Advancement*, p. 99.

23 Francis Bacon, *The Wisedome of the Ancients*, trans. Sir Arthur Gorges (London: 1619), sig. [B7]. See *De sapientia veterum*, sig. C2.

24 Kevin Dunn, *Pretexts of Authority: The Rhetoric of Authorship in the Renaissance Preface* (Stanford: Stanford University Press, 1994), suggests that Bacon 'saw his works as a series of interlocking prefaces' (p. 103). *Temporis partus masculus* promises three books at the outset, but the text consists only of the first two chapters of the first book.

25 Bacon, *Works*, vol. 11, p. 66.

26 *Ibid.*

27 Michèle Le Doeuff argues that Bacon's texts circulated in something approaching such a republic: she adduces the example of Sir Henry Wotton, who read out the

Novum organum to his household when he received his copy from Bacon and undertook the responsibility for its dissemination in Germany. See Francis Bacon, *La Nouvelle Atlantide*, ed. Michèle Le Doeuff, trans. Michèle Le Doeuff and Margaret Llasera (Paris: Flammarion, 1995), p. 39; pp. 39–40.

28 For French translations of Bacon see Michèle Le Doeuff, 'Bacon chez les Grands au siècle de Louis XIII', in Fattori (ed.), *Francis Bacon*, pp. 155–178. Several Bacon manuscripts have been found in the Bibliothèque Nationale; see Graham Rees, 'Bacon's Philosophy: Some New Sources with Special Reference to the *Abecedarium novum naturae*', in Fattori (ed.), *Francis Bacon*, pp. 223–244. Rees, introduction, Bacon, *Philosophical Studies c. 1611–1619*, draws attention to French excitement at news of Bacon's plans to publish in Latin (p. lxxiv, n. 24).

29 Bacon, *Works*, vol. 11, p. 134.

30 *Ibid.*, pp. 132–133.

31 *Ibid.*, pp. 135–136.

32 *Ibid.*, p. 139.

33 *Ibid.*, p. 137.

34 *Ibid.*, p. 9.

35 *Ibid.*, p. 137.

36 *Ibid.*, p. 138.

37 Michèle Le Doeuff stresses the importance of religious toleration to Bacon's thought, citing his letter to Queen Elizabeth advising her not to make martyrs of her Catholic subjects (Bacon, *La Nouvelle Atlantide*, ed. Le Doeuff, pp. 31–33).

38 Bacon, *Works*, vol. 11, p. 141.

39 *Ibid.*

40 Foucault, *The Order of Things*, p. 51.

41 *Ibid.*, p. 52.

42 *Ibid.*, p. 50.

5

Montaigne's *commerce* with women: 'Jusques où va la possibilité?'[1]

ELIZABETH GUILD

T**HE THOUGHTS** of many commentators, including cultural historians and literary theorists, have turned of late to relations with the other or Other. Renewed attention has been paid to sixteenth-century French accounts of encounters with the New World by such writers as Cartier, Thevet and Léry, and to the epistemological, representational and ethical difficulties and blindspots they present to twenty-first-century readers.[2] Among such accounts Montaigne's reflections on the meaning of other, on the space of the other and on the 'new' world in 'Des cannibales' (I, 31) and 'Des coches' (III, 6) stand out in their prevailing openness to what is other and in their refusal of what fuels the drive to colonize, such as commerce.[3] However, as I shall go on to trace here, sites of other commerce in Montaigne's *Essais*, specifically sites of commerce with women, reveal a less open desire to explore the limits to understanding.

In Montaigne's book, *commerce* and commerce are not one and the same, despite the word travelling from a common root in Latin (*merx*, *mercis*, merchandise) into English via the French. Commerce, the exchange of merchandise, is closer in the *Essais* to *trafique*, that is, trade, trading, commerce, barter, business; and, whether *trafique* or traffic, the connotations of the term shade into unscrupulous practice and corruption. In the *Essais* the Conquistadores' exploitation of the natives of the New World is symptomatic of this sort of commerce: in 'Des coches' (III, 6) Montaigne fulminates against these traffickers who have not only *subjuguez* (p. 124) (subjugated (p. 1030)) but also *honteusement abusez* (p. 125) (disgracefully exploited (p. 1030 translation modified)) the natives. Such commerce is presented as not only the means to a shameful end, European despoilment of 'Nature', new territories and peoples; it is *the* contaminant, example of the corrupting greed of the fallen Old World, and more: a betrayal of the Greek and Roman ideals of noble conquest. All for pearls and pepper; these are 'tradesmen's victories' (p. 1031): *'mechaniques victoires'* (p. 125).[4]

We tend to operate a clear distinction these days between traffic (drugs, arms ...) and commerce (legitimate trade, a morally neutral practice and forum). In the *Essais*, too, it is *trafique* that implies corruption and shameful practices and desires, whereas *commerce* has largely morally neutral or positive connotations. It is not, however, without ambiguities. Its most frequent occurrences denote a cluster of unproblematic activities and states (dealings, involvement, contact, human relations and affairs, company, communication, dynamics, knowing about – even societal norms); and at times the connotations are positive, particularly when Montaigne's *commerce* is with books and with friends. *Commerce* might even appropriately describe the somewhat ambivalent relationship between Montaigne's own book and the world of cultural production inhabited by him and his humanist friends, correspondents and readers. As Warren Boutcher has recently argued, although Montaigne himself initially denied (in his *Au Lecteur*) that his *Essais* were intended as 'a commodity on the international cultural market', over time he became aware that 'the book's unmistakable orientation was the field of cultural production ... the international readership of scholars and gentlemen'.[5] After writing comes publication, being bought, lent, read, commented, misread, reread: all are forms of Montaigne's communication (with other men). Such is the circulation and exchange in which his words, once published, are engaged, beyond his own will and desire – a process of both *trafique* and *commerce*.

In recent critical discussions of questions of reading and interpretation in sixteenth-century French writing Montaigne's *Essais* have come to exemplify a new orientation: a shift away from modes of reading subordinate to the authoritative and immobile meaning given in the text, towards a more open process of interpretation actively involving readers in the production of some of the plurality of a text's potential meanings.[6] Witness, it is argued, the endless shifting reflections on texts read and the reading process in the *Essais*, and Montaigne's performances as reader of others and of his own (subjectivity as unfolding in) writing, always under revision, always elusive. Marguerite de Navarre's *Heptaméron* is also cited as a paradigm of this phenomenon: for it folds together the double pleasures of narrative (for narrator and listener) with the ensuing conversations between successive narrators and listeners (five women and five men).[7]

This approach reorients questions of authority, requires a reader more responsible for whatever meanings may emerge and whose thinking and imaginings are drawn towards the horizons of a text's significance; it also allows that there will remain margins and possibilities of meaning beyond both writer's and reader's knowledge and grasp. Therefore it opens up the process of reading beyond the inherited limits (whereby the reader was the faithful transmitter, reading strictly according to prescribed modes and models), and sets new limits, by insisting on what was not yet known and what will remain yet to know in a text.[8] This is more familiar to twenty-first-century readers than the earlier practice; yet it seems important to insist on differences between our reading practices and this approach, and to wonder about remaining limits. If Montaigne's and Marguerite de Navarre's texts gesture towards rich ontological and epistemological shifts and redefinitions of the ethical subject, and are examples of the performance of reading, those examples are double: models and warnings. By coupling Montaigne and Marguerite de Navarre and then by exploring Montaigne's reflections on conversation and *commerce* with women, I shall suggest some gaps and limits to the processes of understanding and interpretation with which Montaigne was so preoccupied, and the ethical impasses and limits of *commerce* between gendered subjects.[9]

There was no flesh-and-blood conversation between Marguerite de Navarre and Montaigne. She died in 1549, when he was just sixteen; the *Heptaméron* had not yet been published, and had remained unfinished; she had already fallen into silence long before Montaigne might have had anything to say. This silence returns within Montaigne's text, but here it is human opinion rather than mortality that dismisses her into silence. His four references to either Marguerite de Navarre or the *Heptaméron*, which he seems to read as if it were a straightforward expression of her ideas, all take their distance from her, even dismissively. This woman, one of the rare women of the time to go into print, seems to figure as an example of a limit within Montaigne's thinking. Here his dismissal resonates with the words of another extraordinary reader nearly four hundred years later, Jacques Lacan: 'they [women] don't know what they are saying, which is all the difference between them and me'.[10] Lacan's apparent dismissal is perhaps open to a corrective interpretation: 'when Lacan says that women do not know, while, at one level, he relegates women outside, and against, the very mastery of his own statement, he was also recognising the binding or restricting, of the parameters of knowledge itself (masculine knowledge irredeemably an erring)'.[11] But however just it may be to allow this ambiguity in Lacan's position, it is difficult not to admit a more generalized ambivalence in his writing: an attachment, a return to mastery even while seeming to upset it. Here we might say that Lacan's writing and Montaigne's, *on women*, converge. And this despite Montaigne being a paradigm for a writing subject acutely attuned to the problems of knowledge as mastery, writing and writing so as to avoid closure, erring in a benign and exploratory sense and admitting difference, on the whole: but not here. She is outside, and mastered, '*en femme*' (III, 5, p. 110) (just like a woman (p. 1014)).

My importation of Lacan is not arbitrary but is the product of three (loose) connections. Firstly, in his writing, after Freud, questions of subjectivity and questions of the feminine are openly intricated and may illuminate the more covert and disavowed relationships and approaches of the earlier text. Secondly, at stake in the *Essais* as in Lacan's writing are, not least, the relations between subjectivity and language: as each demonstrates, language is where meaning circulates and in so doing displaces the subject. Thirdly (and this follows from the second), Lacan's problematizing of the impulse to 'make sense' illuminates this impulse which plays through both the *Essais* and the *Heptaméron*; as Rose comments: 'the stress . . . is on the constant failing within language and sexuality, which meaning attempts to supplement or conceal . . . "making sense" is a supplement, a making good of the lack of subjectivity and language, of the subject in language, against which lack it is set'. A 'making good', that is, that plays along with the illusion of sameness and completion which 'closes off the gap of human desire' – as the concept of 'love', say, 'makes good' the difference, lack, and falling away from meaning in 'sexuality'.[12] This, we might say, returns us to the very issues that drive the conversations of Marguerite de Navarre's *devisants* and fuel Montaigne's love of difference (and inability not to close on feminine sexuality, and with it, speech).[13]

But Lacan's first entrance here is due to a doubling that has become rather a commentator's cliché: his two Marguerites and a question of desire. De Navarre and Duras.[14] Montaigne also has two Marguerites, both de Navarre by marriage. One is figure of difference as negative, inferior and limit, a woman whose judgement in theological, erotic and emotional questions is to be dismissed. The other is thought to be the patroness, 'mother' of his *Apologie*, and is invoked twice, with a show of respect which, while ambiguous, is not dismissive. She is invoked as having given permission to Montaigne's 'Latin': 'J'en use en liberté de conscience de mon Latin, avecq le congé que vous m'en avez donné' (p. 141) (I quote my Latin with freedom of conscience! You, my Patroness, have given me leave (p. 529)).[15] 'Mon Latin', that is, his quoting of verses attributed to Augustus in Martial, *Epigrams*, XI, 21, 3, which turn around the old 'war between the sexes', the belligerent and vengeful economy of fucking, and Augustus's primary relation, to his *mentula* (prick): 'Quid, si mihi vita / Charior est ipsa mentula?' (p. 141) (What if my cock is dearer than life to me? (p. 529)). Montaigne's women readers may well not have understood his Latin, but the force of his 'Latin' is clear enough, with or without his patroness's leave. This is an edgy moment in the essay; it reminds us that reflections on women in the *Essais* are rarely not eroticized, rarely fall out outside a 'phallic' economy. The second invocation of Marguerite is, again, edgy and strategic, but has less to do with sexual difference (although this dimension remains) than with conceptual and theological difference. Montaigne feints, and seems to allow her her defence of Sebond – while using metaphors of sword-play to comment on how he is tactically luring her towards defeat:

> Vous . . . ne refuyrez poinct de maintenir vostre Sebond par la forme ordinaire d'argumenter dequoy vous estes tous les jours instruite, et exercerez en cela vostre esprit et vostre estude: car ce dernier tour d'escrime icy, il ne le faut employer que comme un extreme remede. C'est un coup desesperé, auquel il faut abandonner vos armes pour faire perdre à vostre adversaire les siennes, et un tour secret, duquel il se faut servir rarement et reservéement. (p. 223)

> (Sebond is your author: you will, of course, continue to defend him with the usual forms of argument in which you are instructed every day; that will exercise your mind and your scholarship. The ultimate rapier-stroke which I am using here must only be employed as a remedy of last resort. It is a desperate act of dexterity, in which you must surrender your own arms to force your opponent to lose his. It is a cover blow which you should only use rarely and with discretion. (p. 628))

The metaphors require no comment; and the strategy – alluringly revealed – belongs to one who remains confident he runs no risk of loss.

Marguerite de Navarre, on the other hand, is accorded neither respect nor possibility of dialogue or exchange in all Montaigne's (failed) encounters with her, in I, 13, I, 56, II, 11 and III, 5. In I, 13 her views on a matter of etiquette are cited so as to be rejected as 'vains offices' (p. 89) (vain obligations (p. 50)): her empty formalities figure as the antithesis to the authentic manners of 'ma maison' (p. 89) (in my home (p. 50)). The mechanism is similar in the second and third encounters: she serves a source of example of women's lack of judgement and Montaigne's superiority. In I, 56 the matter is theology:

La Royne de Navarre, Marguerite, recite d'un jeune prince . . . qu'allant
à une assignation amoureuse, et coucher avec la femme d'un Advocat
de Paris, son chemin s'adonnant au travers d'une Eglise, il ne passoit
jamais en ce lieu saint, alant ou retournant de son entreprinse, qu'il
ne fit ses prieres et oraisons. Je vous laisse à juger, l'ame pleine de ce
beau pensement, à quoy il employoit la faveur divine! Toutesfois
elle allegue cela pour un tesmoignage de singuliere devotion. Mais
ce n'est pas par cette preuve seulement qu'on pourroit verifier que les
femmes ne sont guieres propres à traiter les matieres de la Theologie.
(p. 384)

(Queen Margaret of Navarre relates the tale of a young 'prince' . . . ;
whenever he was out on an assignation (lying with the wife of a Parisian
barrister) he would take a short-cut through a church and never failed
to make his prayers and supplications in that holy place on the way
there and on the way back. I will leave you to judge what he was
asking God's favour for when his soul was full of such fair cogitations!
Yet she cites that as evidence of outstanding devotion. But that is not
the only proof we have of the truth that it hardly befits women to
treat Theological matters. (p. 363))

Montaigne is alert to the characteristic confusions and convergences of
the erotic and the spiritual in the *Heptaméron,* but does not allow that
within this woman's writing the ambiguities and slippages are already
knowingly in play. Then in II, 11, Montaigne asserts his understanding
of masculine sexuality and honour over hers:

Je ne prens pour miracle, comme faict la Royne de Navarre en l'un
des contes de son *Heptameron* . . . ny pour chose d'extreme difficulté,
de passer des nuicts entieres, en toute commodité et liberté, avec une
maistresse de long temps desirée, maintenant la foy qu'on luy aura
engagée de se contenter des baisers et simples attouchemens. (p. 99)

(I do not regard it as a miracle, as the Queen of Navarre does in one
of the tales in her *Heptameron* . . . nor even as a matter of extreme
difficulty, to spend nights at a time with a mistress long yearned for,
in complete freedom and with every opportunity, while keeping
my promised word to her to content myself with simple kisses and
caresses. (p. 481))

Montaigne has disregarded the plurality of views articulated in her text
and chosen to extract just one, which he has identified with the author.
This gesture – appropriate/dismiss – belongs to a habit of mastery and
denial of difference he would usually question or resist. In each instance
she is accused of excess or lack (in relation to his position) – that is, we

might say without more ado, accused of being a woman, 'en femme', the phrase which disposes of what she has to say even about women, in III, 5: 'Et Marguerite, Royne de Navarre, alonge, en femme, bien loing l'avantage des femmes, ordonant qu'il est saison, à trente ans, qu'elles changent le titre de belles en bonnes' (p. 110) (Queen Margaret of Navarre (just like a woman) greatly extends the privileges of women when she ordains that it is time for them to change the title *beautiful* for *good* after they have reached thirty (p. 1014)).

Most critical discussions of Montaigne's reflections on women focus on this essay, which returns readers most squarely to issues of sexuality. I shall discuss it only briefly, for it has already had much attention;[16] I want to concentrate instead on two other essays, 'De trois commerces' (On three kinds of social intercourse) (III, 3), and 'De l'art de conferer' (On the art of conversation) (III, 8). I shall use *commerce* to amplify *conference* and trace out in both essays the limits to Montaigne's knowledge and to his enjoyment of difference and otherness when it comes to *commerce* with women.

'Sur des vers de Virgile' is an extravagant exploration containing reflections on sexuality which span the compass of its day: from misogynist conservatism to recognition of some of the ideological constraints on women and the fears and fantasies that maintain the 'brigue et riotte entre elles et nous' (p. 69) (quarrelling and brawling between women and men (p. 964)). It is quite a performance, perhaps its most seductive ploy in all its canny repertoire of strategies of seduction ('ce chapitre me fera du cabinet' (p. 62) (this chapter will get me into their boudoirs (p. 956, translation modified)) being that, whilst its desire seems to be to penetrate, in fact its strategies include those of flirtation. The essay, which is one of the earliest reflections on or articulations of the 'alliteration perpetuelle' of textual and erotic pleasure, remains seductive so long as possibilities remain open, and it allows 'faveur et saveur' (p. 62) (intimacy and savour (p. 956)), explores ambiguities, refuses to legislate sexuality, makes it a matter finally of 'nous' and 'les femmes'. Yet despite its gestures of openness and mobility it frequently arrests its inquiry with a generalization, such as an appeal to 'nature'; and even if the gesture is subsequently modified or even contradicted, it will be followed by another generalization. Whilst the effect may be to question this conceptual habit, it is not a full erasure or questioning so acute as to cancel the weight of the earlier assertion(s), and all still turn on an irrefutable distinction between 'elles et nous'. However, that distinction does collapse in the middle of the following passage about the languages of sexuality and sources of sexual knowledge.

Nous les [i.e. les femmes] dressons dès l'enfance aus entremises de l'amour ... la police féminine a un trein mysterieux, il faut le leur quitter ... Qu'elles se dispensent un peu de la ceremonie, qu'elles entrent en liberté de discours, nous ne sommes qu'enfans au pris d'elles en cette science. Oyez leur representer nos poursuittes et nos entretiens, elles vous font bien cognoistre que nous ne leur apportons rien qu'elles n'ayent sçeu et digeré sans nous. Seroit-ce ce que dict Platon, qu'elles ayent esté garçons desbauchez autresfois ... Il n'est ny parole, ny exemple, ny démarche qu'elles ne sçachent mieux que nos livres: c'est une discipline qui naist dans leurs veines ... que ces bons maistres d'escole, nature, jeunesse et santé leur soufflent continuellement dans l'ame; elles n'ont que faire de l'apprendre, elles l'engendrent ... Qui n'eut tenu un peu en bride cette naturelle violence de leur desir par la crainte et honneur dequoy on les a pourveues, nous estions diffamez. Tout le mouvement du monde se resoult et rend à cet accouplage; c'est une matiere infuse par tout, c'est un centre où toutes choses regardent. (pp. 71–72)

(We train women from childhood for the practices of love ... feminine polity goes its own mysterious way: we must leave it entirely to them ... Just let them dispense with a little ceremony and become free to develop their thoughts: in knowledge of such things we are babes compared with them. Just listen to them describing our pursuit of them and our rendezvous with them. They will soon show you that we contribute nothing but what they have known and already assimilated independently of us. Could Plato be right when he said that in a former existence girls had been lascivious boys! ... There is no word, no exemplary tale and no stratagem which women do not know better than our books. The doctrines which nature, youth and good health (those excellent schoolmasters) ceaselessly inspire in their souls are born in their veins ... They do not need to learn them: they give birth to them ... If the ferocity of their desires were not somewhat reined in by that fear for their honour with which all women are endowed, we would all be laughing-stocks. The whole movement of the world tends and leads towards copulation. It is a substance infused through everything; it is the centre towards which all things turn. (pp. 966–968))

'Amour' slides towards 'accouplage', as Montaigne's thoughts on feminine sexual knowledge unfold. Sexual desire and the desire to know are folded together in this passage, both Montaigne's and that of the women whose desire and knowledge so fascinate him. What lures him is what women know beyond what they learn from men or with men's permission, and whilst at one moment he seems content that this remain '*mysterieux*', by the end of the passage cited he is falling back into the conventional discourse of honour as safeguard of women and of men from women, setting this against the all-pervasiveness of female sexuality. Given the theme of sexuality, and given that Montaigne's reflections take in the paradoxes of censorship (revealing what would be concealed), it seems appropriate enough to wonder what this passage reveals of Montaigne's desire, beyond his grasp.

Later in the essay Montaigne reflects on love as incommensurate with any other economy or relation: it is 'un commerce qui a besoin de relation et de correspondance: [et qui] ne se paye que de mesme espece de monnoye' (p. 109). (Love is a commerce which requires interrelationship and reciprocity ... This one can only be repaid in the same coin (p. 1012)). Love is like only itself; furthermore, love is, perhaps, of what is like oneself, or of what one would like to be like. Here and throughout this essay Montaigne's thoughts are drawn away from love and towards sexuality and the difference between 'elles et nous'; constantly drawn, but still eluded: this remains the horizon of meaning. Montaigne wants this essay to penetrate his women readers; his writing is penetrated, saturated by his desire to know the impossible more, if not all, about women's knowledge and desire. Montaigne is not Tiresias but might long to be.

Tiresias had appeared some pages earlier, in his usual guise, as the example of the one supposed to know (about) both men's and women's desire and pleasure, having been 'tantost homme, tantost femme' (p. 69) (first a man and then a woman (p. 964)). Only Tiresias has the knowledge Montaigne desires. But here he jokes: perhaps girls were boys in a former existence; how else to explain how much more they seem to know than men do of men's own desires? So much so that they make children of men. Infantilize or tantalize? Women's 'liberté de discours' (freedom of speech) is very seductive; how much might men not want to know what women know of them that they do not? Besides, although it may be only a joke, what does Montaigne's fantasy of girls who were boys imply for his usually clearly distinct 'elles et nous'? What does it suggest of forbidden or disavowed desires? Here sameness and difference begin to slide, and Montaigne can recover his sense of distinction and stable meaning by only reiterating masculine commonplaces about women's desire, and by putting women in their place with his reference to 'la crainte et honneur dequoy on les a pourveues'; that is, a dishonourable honour for it is not proper to women but acquired from men, and is an effect of fear rather than an ethical impulse.

However, the topic is too seductive for Montaigne to abandon it to this semblance of conclusion and regulation. 'Accouplage' is 'infuse par tout'; it is the 'centre où toutes choses regardent'. All is intercourse; Montaigne's thoughts soon turn to that part of his body that 'me faict plus proprement homme ... que toute autre' (p. 102) (none [of my members] makes me more properly a man than that one (p. 1004)), as being a god in many cultures. In so doing he pins the meaning of 'accouplage' to sexuality, and continues to bear women in mind. But when it comes to the intercourse for which he has a passion, social rather than sexual, he excludes women from what is richest in his experience of it, coupling women almost exclusively with sexual relations rather than conversation.

What is most marked about the place of women in 'De l'art de conferer' is their absence.[17] When women do figure, they are assimilated to children and the insane, or they have an ambiguous and marginal value, when, for instance, the 'caquet des harengeres' (p. 141) (the cackle of fishwives (p. 1049)) is preferred to schoolmen's logic, or when their words are considered for lack of anything else: 'où l'un plat est vuide du tout en la balance, je laisse vaciller l'autre, sous les songes d'une vieille' (p. 138) (when one scale in the balance is quite empty I will let the other be swayed by an old woman's dreams (p. 1046)). Here 'les songes d'une vieille' connotes both superstition and what has only fractionally more significance than empty air – and what value and fascination dreams may hold is evaporated by their being an old woman's, figure of infertility and cultural marginality. Nor is the preference for the talk of 'harengeres' to the women's credit. If anything, the comparison serves to heighten the contempt for logic-chopping; it is a deliberate flash of vulgarity to show up the enervation of these (less than) men's uses of language; women's talk figures in so far as, through the aural proximity of *harengere* and *harangue(r)*, Montaigne can persuade of his point through his own more colourful and creative rhetoric. It enters the text, that is, to be trafficked in this vying between men.

Women may only appear in 'De l'art de conferer' either in the already overused and hollowed-out assimilation to children and the insane (as unfit for public office), or as examples of Montaigne's own artful language, and of their belonging less on the side of art qua culture and rational thinking than on the side of nature, the primitive or superstitious, the *inculte*. Their difference or otherness, here, has little resonance: dreams may be the site of knowledge both desired and feared in its otherness to conscious thought, but that potential significance is muted by the dreamer being only an old woman; and if the *harengeres* speak, it is only *caquet*, which at the close of 'Sur des vers de Virgile' is seamlessly assimilated to *flux* (diarrhoea), and connotes an excess or lack in relation to proper speech. However in 'De trois commerces', in which Montaigne reflects on the pleasures and consequences of engaging with women, women represent a more potent otherness or difference, or conversely suggest a lack of difference that Montaigne disavows. 'De l'oisiveté' (Of idleness) (I, 8) sheds light on this.[18]

This short essay turns around an elaborate comparison between an idle mind and, firstly, fallow land which, being left, will 'foisonne[r] en cent mille sortes d'herbes sauvages et inutiles' (p. 69) (abound in hundreds and thousands of different kinds of useless weeds (p. 30)) and, then, through a very conventional analogical turn, an idle womb (womb as earth in which man sows seed). Far from remaining in a state of rest or neutral 'health' this will risk producing not 'une generation bonne et naturelle' (p. 69) (good natural offspring (p. 30)) (which requires semen) but 'des amas et pieces de chair informes' (p. 69) (shapeless lumps of flesh (p. 30)). Montaigne's melancholy mind, likewise, is in danger of producing offspring which are far from 'bonne et naturelle': 'm'enfante tant de chimeres et monstres fantasques ... sans ordre et sans propos' (p. 70) (it gives birth to so many chimeras and fantastic monstrosities ... without order or fitness (p. 31)). This is not the place to explore the physiology and ideology behind Montaigne's ideas on fertility and conception;[19] but this analogy is germane to an understanding of Montaigne's *commerce* with women. Women on their own without men are in a state of lack; they represent nature and lack together, lack which is natural (within nature) but also unnatural, identified with what is monstrous, inchoate, and even outside language. It is to cure this 'estrangeté' (p. 70) (strangeness (p. 31)) that Montaigne starts to write; women, on the other hand, cannot cure themselves of the *estrangeté* they bear within. Here, then, women remain doubly subject to men as ejaculators and as writers. Women figure as excess and lack, here, within Montaigne's curative reflections on himself, and remain in a state of excess and lack, unlike Montaigne who can overcome his *estrangeté*, all the more so by writing it out on to women who cannot. However, I want to suggest that in III, 3 what women are left to embody for Montaigne of *estrangeté*, that is, strangeness, and otherness within, a margin of unknowableness beyond the acknowledgement of lack on which he insists throughout the *Essais*, ghosts him, and returns as a symptom of what he fears in relation to himself.

What Montaigne wants in his 'commerce' (social intercourse) is 'accointances qui reviennent à mon goust' (p. 36) (any acquaintanceship which corresponds to my tastes (p. 924)); although no one else can come close to his ideal, La Boëtie, with whom friendship allowed a merging of subjectivities, likeness is what appeals and sets the frame within which specific differences can flourish. His reflections in this essay begin with friendships with men, move on to *commerce* with women, shift back to ideals of masculine 'privauté' (intimacy) (p. 39), on to another sort of *commerce* with women which had already emerged as the grounds of the earlier dealings, and come to rest on his reading – the pleasure most his own, and which in a sense most distinguishes him from women in terms of what sort of commerce he believes to be to their 'goust'.

In a 1992 article Neil Kenny traced out with great finesse the complexities and ambiguities of Montaigne's reflections on *commerce* with women in this essay.[20] He demonstrates that what troubles Montaigne and contributes to the marginalization of women is that they disturb an economy he would rather remain reliably in place, namely the distinction between appearances and 'reality', surface and substance, natural and artificial, own and borrowed. Women who are seduced by 'sçavans' into adopting an appearance of learning, merely parroting an already deceptive rhetoric, demonstrate that they cannot tell the difference between the 'real thing' and an abusive imitation. '[Les sçavans] ont en ce temps entonné [de leur magistère] si fort les cabinets et oreilles des dames que, si elles n'en ont retenu la substance, elles en ont la mine . . . La doctrine qui ne leur a peu arriver en l'ame, leur est demeurée en la langue' (pp. 37–38) ([The scholars] have funnelled so much of [their mastery of their subject] into the ears of the ladies in their drawing-rooms that, even if those ladies of ours have retained none of the substance, they look as though they have. . . . The doctrine which they have learned could not reach their minds so it has stayed on their tongues (pp. 926– 927)). Montaigne considers this symptomatic of a wider failing among even the best of women: 'elles cachent et couvrent leurs beautez soubs des beautez estrangeres' (p. 38) (they hide and drape their own beauties under borrowed ones (p. 927)). Thus far Montaigne's attack on women only reproduces familiar topoi, and the old oppositions between the positive values epitomized by men and their negatives embodied by women remain straightforwardly in place (except for an emasculating touch in his criticism of 'sçavans': if they 'font parade' then there is implicitly something too close to the 'feminine' in their behaviour). It is in what Montaigne describes as women's proper place that the oppositions such as nature/art(ifice), substance/surface, appearance/reality collapse; for their role is 'farder le fard' (p. 38) (add yet more make-up to their make-up (translation mine)). This phrase resonates with a more abyssal moment at the end of II, 12; there in the thick of a very long quotation from Plutarch (originally neither indicated nor recognized), being is described as 'devenant tousjours autre d'un autre' (p. 267) (becoming ever an other of an already other being (translation mine)): here in III, 3 it is women who are the figures of difference, in whom the relation between essence and inessential seems to be undecidable. Women's difference and ambiguity are a vanishing point which will return in the second passage in this essay, and I shall come to this shortly. Before, though, it is important to attend to what Montaigne equivocally suggests about women's desire for knowledge. Montaigne does not disguise how women are subject to men: subject if they keep their proper place, which is 'vivre aymées et honnorées' (p. 38) (to live loved and honoured (p. 927)); subject, too, if they learn rhetoric, logic and so on, for these are not routes to learning and understanding (which should unbind the individual) but rather, according to Montaigne, rooted in men's desire to maintain their power over women: 'j'entre en crainte que les hommes qui le leur conseillent, le facent pour avoir loy de les regenter soubs ce tiltre' (p. 38) (I begin to fear that the men who counsel them to do so see it as a way of having a pretext for manipulating them (p. 927)). A canny observation, doubly so: for, in drawing attention to this ploy, Montaigne keeps women subject: he defends them while reminding that they are blind to their situation, and they, as an example in his text, remain subject to the needs of his developing reflections – which will always return to and derive from his own pleasures and desire for knowledge.

This habit of subjection is confirmed four sentences later, when he prescribes appropriate reading for women: 'Si toutesfois il leur fache de nous ceder en quoy que ce soit, et veulent par curiosité avoir part aux livres' (p. 38) (Should it nevertheless irk them to lag behind us in anything whatsoever; should they want to share in our books out of curiosity (p. 927)). That is, women's desire for knowledge is saturated with *mauvaise foi*: it is conditional on their relationship to men, a refusal to stay in their proper place ('il leur fache de nous ceder en quoy que ce soit'), and derives from 'curiosité', which reminds us that as readers we are all daughters of Eve and Pandora.

When Montaigne returns to the theme of *commerce* with women some paragraphs later, he is less than interested in their minds: in this 'doux' commerce, it is 'les graces corporelles' rather than 'les graces de l'esprit' (p. 42) (graces of the body . . . graces of the mind (translation mine)) that matter. What women might learn with profit, he has already touched on, summarily, and moved on with a punctual distinction between them and himself. Women are creatures of disguise, 'tout en montre' (all show (p. 38)) and yet opaque; Montaigne, on the other hand, proclaims himself to be all on show, undisguised: 'tout au dehors et en evidence' (p. 38) (I am all in evidence; all of me is exposed (p. 928)). Belief in this claim dissolves in the light of the coyness and disavowals of the next passage on *commerce*, when he returns to the desired relationship with women that his first passage wove around: flirtation, seduction; he insists that men's relations with women are erotic: 'que leur faut-il, que vivre aymées?'

He has in mind 'belles et honnestes femmes' (p. 40) (beautiful and honourable women (p. 929)); 'belles' is added in the 1595 edition, which acts as a hinge between this passage, the earlier one, and the themes of beauty, the erotic and difference that will be folded together over the following pages. Where friendship between men is an 'exercice des ames' (p. 39) (exercising our souls (p. 928)) and is equated with art, commerce with women, however sweet, is dangerous; both, he is quick to say, as a source of disease, and because a man runs the risk of losing those qualities that help maintain him on the side of the masculine: order, judgement, measure. Passion might make him just like a woman.

Montaigne insists in this essay on his candour: he is 'tout au dehors et en evidence' (p. 38), he will show his flaws, his 'erreurs de . . . jeunesse' (p. 42) (errors of my youth (p. 931)), for he does not want to be thought better than he is ('qu'on [ne] me tienne pour meilleur que je suis' (pp. 41–42) (being a man who does not ask to be thought better than I am (p. 931)). But what if this transparency is a cover story, within the unfolding narrative of sexual difference, likeness and improper desire? Montaigne differentiates between himself and women by claiming to be all on show, nothing to hide, whereas women are all show and all hidden ('farder le fard'); the difference between their own beauty and 'beautez estrangeres' (p. 38) (borrowed beauties (p. 927)) is not clear; and, when women make a show of what makes them women, they reveal that there is nothing to see. In a critical moment, veiled as an exotic example which seems safely to locate difference as alien, as 'not here', but may be read as a gesture of disavowed curiosity, very close to home, Montaigne's thoughts turn to sexual difference, and to how that difference is known. 'Les filles Brachmanes qui ont faute d'autre recommandation, le peuple assemblé à cri publiq pour cet effect, vont en la place, faisant montre de leurs parties matrimoniales, veoir si par là aumoins elles ne valent pas d'acquerir un mary' (p. 41) (when the daughters of the Brahmans have nothing else to recommend them, the town-crier calls the people together in the market-place expressly for them to show off their organs of matrimony to see whether they at least can be worth a husband to them (p. 930)). This is difference seen as absence of likeness, and this public revelation of lack uses an alien culture to expose what is otherwise so shameful that it must be hidden (though already hidden). But all the showing and looking in the world cannot give Montaigne the knowledge that he seeks, of women's desire: he knows that this will remain hidden, among women, in women's commerce with each other, so long as men are 'all show': 'elles se r'alient et rejettent à elles mesmes, ou entre elles' (p. 41) (women turn in on themselves and have recourse to themselves or to other women (p. 930); and the commerce he describes with women remains one of lack of relation, retreat into difference.

Is this because women are required to represent a difference *within* subjectivity that Montaigne cannot quite acknowledge? Or is it because desire is no respecter of difference? Let us take this question first. Beauty is represented as women's 'vray avantage' (p. 42) (true privilege (p. 931)). Or, we might say, what men want in women is beauty. It is proper to women: 'si leur' (p. 42) (so much more proper to them (p. 931)). And yet Montaigne's plain assertions about the specificity of women and their beauty fail to hold; what is proper, natural, their own, slides into borrowed beauty, in the end the difference cannot be established between own and not own ('farder le fard'). This is less troubling, textually, than the capacity of beauty to disrupt the difference between men and women, and to arouse improper desires: '[La beauté] est si leur que la nostre, quoy qu'elle desire des traicts un peu autres, n'est en son point que confuse avec la leur, puerile et imberbe. On dict que chez le grand Seigneur ceux qui le servent sous titre de beauté, qui sont en nombre infini, ont leur congé, au plus loin, à vingt et deux ans' (p. 42) (Beauty is the true privilege of noblewomen. It is so much more proper to them than ours is to us men, that even though ours requires slightly different traits, at its highest it is boyish and beardless, and therefore confounded with theirs. They say that in the place of the Grand Seigneur males chosen to serve him for their beauty – and they are countless in number – are sent away at twenty-two at the latest (p. 931)). Not only does masculine beauty turn out to be confusible with feminine beauty; but – and once again, too close to home – the story has to be told as having to do with foreigners, here the infidel (and therefore no stranger to improper desires) it triggers a fantasy of countless beautiful young men just waiting to meet the master's desire. This slippage reminds of the fantasy of girls-who-were-boys in III, 8: another vanishing point in Montaigne's writing on knowledge and desire, which leaves the reader not knowing, but wondering, whether this speaks of a desire not 'known' by the writer, desire for what is same but also different (for beauty does not cease in Montaigne's text to be primarily feminine) – and lack of desire for what is different as represented *in extremis* by the Brahman women.

This is to suggest that there is something that Montaigne does not let himself see, does not know – beyond/other to his insistence on his knowledge being conditional on recognising that he does not know. But this not knowing tends to be the gesture of a radical thinker rather than that of a man describing the pleasures of different kinds of intimacy. This introduces a distinction (thinker/man) that seems to go against the grain of Montaigne's writing about himself; it seems analogous to the *spirituel/corporel* distinction that he attributes to women and so to his relations with them. But we might put it otherwise: women bear the burden of representation of the difficulties and dislocations of the relations between the *spirituel* and the *corporel*, which are neither distinct nor coincident; nor are they fully known. In focusing on beauty, girls/boys and knowledge, I have sought to suggest that the tensions between sameness and difference cannot admit the otherness of women – least of all when they have to figure Montaigne's own otherness. Sexuality is here the vanishing point of meaning and that there is no relation between men and women so long as women and men's difference, sameness and otherness remain imaginary and constantly move around each other, while women's desire remains imaginary, and while the otherness of men's desire remains disavowed. Not surprising that according to Montaigne the problem with women is that 'elles ne se cognoissent point assez' (p. 38) (they do not know enough about themselves (p. 927)). They have to represent the lack of (enough) self-knowledge; this is the place of the other: to bear the burden of his fear that this might be his lack, and of their own (other) self-knowledge and desire not being recognized – or strictly delimited as existing in relation to, and conditional on, men, in, for instance, the 'commerce' women enjoy among themselves because of men's 'trahison' (p. 41) (treachery (p. 931)).

Montaigne's instance of the Brahman women is an example of shame and exposure; but it is double exposure, and, as with the photographic image, the resulting representation may have more potential for significance than was imagined. These women reveal what is usually most private in the hope of satisfying their desire (a husband); but in Montaigne's cultural dislocation it is an example of women's folly, vanity, self-delusion: 'c'est qu'elles ne se cognoissent point assez', as it were, and it is to their shame. But is it not equally a shameful example, covertly inviting and licensing the pleasures of masculine voyeuristic fantasy while seeming to take its distance? Is it not possible to read this as a symptom of an anxiety disguised precisely at such moments of apparent clarity and exposure as to women's desire?

'All the difference between them and me' is pinned to anatomy, as if difference were representable. The move is one of triple closure: on understanding (women) in all their differences, on the ethics which seem otherwise to govern his thinking, and on self-understanding. Here Montaigne veers away from the dangers of unmasterable ambiguities and from a potentially intolerable not knowing; he fails to recognize the other as other, and makes a sacrifice of otherness and openness to the representation of difference.

Notes

1 Michel de Montaigne, *Essais*, I, 27, ed. A. Micha (Paris: Garnier-Flammarion, 1969), p. 228. All references hereafter are to this edition. All English translations, unless otherwise stated, are from M. A. Screech, *Michel de Montaigne, The Complete Essays* (London: Penguin Classics, 1993).

2 See in particular among the many studies: M. de Certeau, *Heterologies: Discourse on the Other*, trans B. Massumi (Minneapolis: University of Minnesota Press, 1985); see also S. Greenblatt, *Marvellous Possessions: The Wonder of the New World* (Oxford: Clarendon Press, 1991); F. Lestringant's several studies including *Le Cannibale: grandeur et decadence* (Paris: Librairie Académique Perrin, 1994); A. Pagden, *European Encounters with the New World: From Renaissance to Romanticism* (New Haven and London: Yale University Press, 1993); and T. Todorov, *The Conquest of America: The Question of the Other* (New York: Harper and Row, 1984).

3 Specific studies of this aspect of the *Essais* include M. Blanchard, *Trois portraits de Montaigne: essai sur la représentation à la Renaissance* (Paris, Nizet: 1990), ch. II, and G. Defaux, 'Un cannibale en haut de chausses: Montaigne, la différence et la logique de l'identité', *Modern Language Notes* 97 (1982), 919–957, and C. Blum, M.-L. Demonet and A. Tournon (eds), *Montaigne et le nouveau monde: actes du colloque de Paris, 18–20 mai 1992* (Mont-de-Marsan: Editions interuniversitaires, 1994). On Montaigne and commerce in the economic sense see P. Desan, *Les Commerces de Montaigne: le discours économique des Essais* (Paris: Nizet, 1992).

4 On pepper as commodity and currency, and on the intrication of Renaissance trade, consumerism, politics and culture see Lisa Jardine, *Wordly Goods* (London: Macmillan, 1996). With reference to scruples such as Montaigne's see in particular chapter 6.

5 Warren Boutcher, '"Le Moyen de voir ce Seneque escrit à la main": Montaigne's *Journal de Voyage* and the politics of *science* and *faveur* in the Vatican Library', in J. O'Brien (ed.), *(Ré)Interprétations: études sur le seizième siècle, Michigan Romance Studies*, XV (Ann Arbor: University of Michigan Press, 1995), pp. 177–214 (pp. 188–189).

6 See for example T. C. Cave, 'The Mimesis of Reading in the Renaissance', in J. D. Lyons and S. G. Nichols (eds), *Mimesis: From Mirror to Method, Augustine to Descartes* (Hanover and London: University Press of New England, 1982), pp. 148–165.

7 See Cave's essay and also, for example, M. Jeanneret, 'Modular Narrative and the Crisis of Interpretation', in J. D. Lyons and M. B. McKinley (eds), *Critical Tales: New Studies of the Heptaméron and Early Modern Culture* (Philadelphia: University of Pennsylvania Press, 1993), pp. 85–103.

8 For further discussion see T. C. Cave, *The Cornucopian Text: Problems of Writing in the French Renaissance* (Oxford: Oxford University Press, 1979) and S. Rendall, *Distinguo: Reading Montaigne Differently* (Oxford: Clarendon, 1992).

9 For discussion of related aspects of Montaigne's writing beyond the scope of this discussion see R. D. Cottrell, *Sexuality/Textuality: A Study of the Fabric of Montaigne's 'Essais'* (Columbus: Ohio State University Press, 1981); and L. Kritzman, *The Rhetoric of Sexuality and the Literature of the French Renaissance* (Cambridge: Cambridge University Press, 1991).

10 Jacques Lacan, 'God and the *Jouissance* of The Woman', trans J. Rose, in J. Mitchell and J. Rose (eds), *Feminine Sexuality: Jacques Lacan and the École Freudienne* (London: Macmillan, 1982), pp. 137–148 (p. 144).

11 Rose, *Feminine Sexuality*, p. 51.

12 See Rose, *Feminine Sexuality*, pp. 46–47.

13 Marie de Gournay, editor and champion of Montaigne, is none the less an early implicit critic, for in her *Grief des Dames* (1626) she attacks all men's dismissal of women's speech and the possibility of conversation between men and women; for instance: 'il n'y a si chétif, qui ne les rembarre avec approbation de la pluspart des assistans, quand avec un sousris seulement, ou quelque petit branslement de teste, son éloquence muette aura dit: "C'est une femme qui parle"' (see M. Schiff, *La Fille d'alliance de Montaigne: Marie de Gournay* (Paris: Champion, 1910), pp. 89–97 (pp. 90–91)). (There is not even the puniest of men who does not rebuke them with the assent of most of those present, when with just a smile or a nod of the head, his silent eloquence proclaims: It is only a woman speaking (trans M. Bijvoet, in K. M. Wilson and F. J. Warnke (eds), *Women Writers of the Seventeenth Century* (Athens and London: University of Georgia Press, 1989) (p. 19))).

14 J. Lacan, 'Hommage fait à Marguerite Duras, du ravissement de Lol V. Stein', *Cahiers Renaud-Barrault* 52 (December 1965), 7–15.

15 Montaigne, *Essais*, II, 12, p. 141.

16 See for instance B. Bowen, 'Montaigne's Anti-Phaedrus: "Sur des vers de Virgile" (*Essais* III,v)', *Journal of Medieval and Renaissance Studies* 5 (1975), 107–121; D. Coleman, 'Montaigne's "Sur des vers de Virgile": Taboo Subject, Taboo Author', in R. R. Bolgar (ed.), *Classical Influences on European Culture A.D. 1500–1700* (Cambridge: Cambridge University Press, 1976), pp. 135–140; R. D. Cottrell, *Sexuality/Textuality*; L. Kritzman, 'My Body, My Text: Montaigne and the Rhetoric of Sexuality', *The Journal of Medieval and Renaissance Studies* 13:1 (1983), 75–89; M. McKinley, '"Salle/Cabinet": Literature and Self-disclosure in "Sur des vers de Virgile"', in D. Frame and M. McKinley (eds), *Columbia Montaigne Conference Papers* (Lexington: French Forum, 1981), pp. 84–104; and J. Starobinski, *Montaigne en mouvement* (Paris: Gallimard, 1982).

17 For further discussion of this essay in terms of questions of reading see Rendall, *Distinguo*, ch. 4.

18 For further discussion of this essay see M. Screech, *Montaigne and Melancholy* (London: Duckworth, 1983).

19 See T. Laqueur, *Making Sex*, especially chs 2–4, and I. MacLean, *The Renaissance Notion of Woman* (Cambridge: Cambridge University Press, 1980).

20 N. Kenny, 'Montaigne et "les bien-nées . . . attachées à la rhétorique": autour d'un passage de l'essai "De trois commerces"', in J. O'Brien, M. Quainton and J. J. Supple (eds), *Montaigne et la rhétorique: actes du colloque de St Andrews (28–31 mars 1992)* (Paris: Honoré Champion, 1995), pp. 203–219.

—6—

'This ripping of auncestors': the ethnographic present in Spenser's *A View of the State of Ireland*

WILLY MALEY

I N THIS ESSAY, I want to suggest that Edmund Spenser's *A View of the State of Ireland*, written in 1596 and published in 1633, is a far more sophisticated treatise than much of the criticism that it has engendered would imply. Specifically, I shall argue that Spenser's strategy in the *View* is not one of straightforward denigration of the Irish, but is rather one of displacement and subterfuge, no less racially motivated, in which the discussion of Irish identity is a side-show, and the main event is an interrogation of English, Scottish, British and European identity formation. It is precisely by means of a determined process of oversight, that is, by ignoring the Irish as such, that Spenser is able to effect the desired goal – the elimination of the native.

In an incisive essay on the representation of race in English Renaissance culture, Lynda Boose sees Spenser's *View* as a founding document of racism:

> If 'race' originates as a category that hierarchically privileges a ruling status and makes the Other(s) inferior, then for the English the group that was first to be shunted into this discursive derogation and thereafter invoked as almost a paradigm of inferiority was not the black 'race' – but the Irish 'race'.

Boose places the *View* within a discourse in which 'the derogation of the Irish as "a race apart" situates racial difference within cultural and religious categories rather than biologically empirical ones'.[1] My argument centres on the premise that the Irish are for Spenser less 'a race apart' than 'a race aside', and that they afford him a unique opportunity, through a series of subtle displacements, to explore questions of identity and difference that go beyond the immediate Irish context.

Despite the fact that Spenser's *View* is arguably one of the most difficult colonial discourses any reader may expect to encounter, standard criticism tends to portray it as an uncomplicated exercise in anti-Irish sentiment. The upshot of a peculiar conjunction of embarrassment and anger is that the text attracts commentary of the most simplistic sort. While inevitable as the necessary first stage in a critical process, the mere cataloguing of negative images obviously has its limitations, yet criticism of Spenser and Ireland continues to dwell on a perceived anti-Irishness. Spenser has been singled out for attention as being obsessed with 'race' in a way that his contemporaries were not. Brendan Bradshaw alleges that Richard Beacon and William Herbert, two of Spenser's fellow undertakers on the Munster Plantation, do not resort to the kind of ethnology employed by Spenser.[2] For Margaret MacCurtain, 'Spenser's delineation of the origins and history of the Irish could almost be termed an essay in anthropology'.[3] An earlier generation of Spenser scholars attached less weight to the time Spenser spends on issues of racial composition, colonial legacy, national identity and cultural inheritance. Rudolf Gottfried's assertion 'that the antiquities are a completely separable element, a kind of historical decoration on the facade of the *View*; if they are also flimsy in character, they cause no weakening of its broad and solid structure' is no longer accepted wisdom.[4] Where Gottfried sees a façade, Ciarán Brady sees patience, purpose and planning in Spenser's ethnographic orientation. Yet having insisted on the centrality of Spenser's treatment of racial origins, Brady concludes that the sophisticated ethnology he constructs is merely a humanist pretext for homicidal policies:

> Thus the elaborate discussions of classical and modern authorities and the ingenious analysis of etymologies were intended to show that Spenser's credit as a scrupulous and sincere scholar remained good. The killing would be justified not simply on grounds of crude expediency but in terms of the highest humanist discourse as well.[5]

Tracey Hill likewise draws a direct link between the cultural denigration of the Irish and the need for colonial violence: 'In *A View*, the indigenous Irish are constructed as ethnically debased and intrinsically unruly; it therefore follows that a policy of extreme military repression is required to control them.'[6]

My contention will be that Spenser's chief strategy in the *View* is to efface rather than deface the Irish. From a theoretical perspective, I am concerned with what postcolonialism can learn from Renaissance texts such as Spenser's and what readers of the *View* can gain from an awareness of postcolonial criticism. Spenser's text, published posthumously, remains timely. Sir James Ware's edition of 1633 was entitled *A View of the State of Ireland.* Ware dropped the 'present' from the title in an effort to forget the past. But the past, like the post, keeps coming back to haunt us. The *View* remains caught up in the present. Ware, in his preface, praises Spenser thus: 'His proofes (although most of them conjecturall) concerning the originall of the language, customes of the Nations, and the first peopling of the severall parts of the Iland, are full of good reading; and doe shew a sound judgment.'[7] Note that Ware pluralizes national identity, in keeping with Spenser's preoccupation with multiple origins and affiliations.

The *View* is to a large extent an extended essay in multiculturalism. Its rehearsal of origins and identity, antiquity and early modernity, dialogism and development, makes it an ideal starting-point for a meditation on the applicability of postcolonial theory to the period. The key terms of postcoloniality – ambivalence and hybridity – are seldom invoked in discussions of Spenser's Irish experiences. A theory most intimately and obviously associated with late modern, or even postmodern, culture, postcolonial criticism can arguably both inform, and be informed by, early modern texts and contexts. In this regard, Spenser's treatise is an ideal test-case for the applicability of postcolonial theory to Renaissance texts.

Postcolonialism offers a valuable critical register for dealing with a text such as the *View*. Yet one recent response suggests that the simplified version of the poet's colonial ideology that obtains in Renaissance studies is being reproduced without significant alteration in a form of criticism which one would have expected to be more attentive to historical differences. Edward Said places Spenser unproblematically at the core of a particular Western colonial tradition: 'Since Spenser's 1596 tract on Ireland, a whole tradition of British and European thought has considered the Irish to be a separate and inferior race, usually unregenerately barbarian, often delinquent and primitive.'[8] In what follows, I aim to suggest that the perspective that sees Spenser's tract as part of nothing but the same old story of unadulterated anti-Irish racism from Giraldus Cambrensis to the present is fundamentally flawed, exactly because Spenser's overriding concern is not with the margins but with the mainstream, that is, he is preoccupied with using the complexities of the Irish colonial milieu as a means of refiguring metropolitan identities.

One reason why it does not make sense to read the *View* in terms of a recognizable Anglo-Irish conflict that retrospectively superimposes a modern standpoint onto the sixteenth and seventeenth centuries is that Spenser's attitude to Englishness is as important as his opinion of the Irish. This fact has not generally been acknowledged by previous scholars, and as a result the traditional simplistic division between English and Irish cultures has been allowed to inhibit a properly historical reading of Spenser's work.

My starting-point is the treatment of national formation, for it is here, with Spenser's inventive ethnography, that the key to the author's attitude to his immediate political context is to be found. Spenser's genealogy of Ireland is compelling. He does not fix the Irish in an ethnographic present and a seamless past. Both speakers in the dialogue, Irenius the informed innovator and Eudoxus the searching sceptic, work together to undermine established prejudices. In fact, Irenius begins by insisting on the mixed and multiple origins of the country:

> Before we enter into the treatie of their customes, it is first needfull to consider from whence they first sprung; for from the sundry manners of the nations, from whence that people which now is called Irish, were derived, some of the customes which now remain amongst them, have been first fetcht, and sithence there continued amongst them; for not of one nation was it peopled, as it is, but of sundry people of different conditions and manners. But the chiefest which have first possessed and inhabited it, I suppose to bee Scythians. (p. 44)

Note that Spenser cannot resist the pun, 'sithence' – 'since then' – foreshadowing 'Scythians'. Eudoxus interrupts at this point to ask: 'How commeth it then to passe, that the Irishe doe derive themselves from Gathelus the Spaniard?' Irenius explains:

> They doe indeed, but (I conceive) without any good ground. For if there were any such notable transmission of a colony hether out of Spaine, or any such famous conquest of this kingdome by Gathelus a Spaniard, as they would faine believe, it is not unlikely, but that the very Chronicles of Spaine, (had Spaine then beene in so high regard, as they now have it) would not have omitted so memorable a thing, as the subduing of so noble a Realme to the Spaniard, no more then they doe now neglect to memorize their conquest of the Indians, especially in those times, in which the same was supposed, being nearer unto the flourishing age of learning and Writers under the Romanes. (p. 44)

Irenius, having dispensed with the Irish claim to Spanish provenance, comments:

> But the Irish doe heerein no otherwise, then our vaine English-men doe in the Tale of Brutus, whom they devise to have first conquered and inhabited this land, it being as impossible to proove, that there was ever any such Brutus of Albion or England, as it is, that there was any such Gathelus of Spaine. (p. 44)

Several critics have commented on this provocative passage, undermining a prominent British origin-myth, which appears to be at odds with Spenser's attitude in *The Faerie Queene*, although Andrew Hadfield has argued eloquently for a consistent scepticism in both instances.[9] Judith Anderson says of the apparently anomalous undermining of the Brutus myth:

> Nowhere in Spenser's writings is the split between two different versions of truth more obvious than in his treatment of the Brutus legend, first in poetry and then in history. Nowhere else does he so thoroughly debunk popular myths of origin – indeed, popular antiquities – as in the *View*.[10]

Perhaps the most balanced perspective is offered by John Breen, who astutely observes: 'In the *View* Irenius appears to cast doubt upon the authenticity of the story concerning Britain's mythic origins [. . .] However, it would be rash to suggest that, based on Irenius' comment, Spenser did not believe in the Brutus myth's romantic and nationalistic import'.[11] Again it is a matter of effect rather than essence. The Brutus Myth may be ridiculed in the *View*, but only in order to insinuate the Myth of Arthur, trading one origin-myth for another in a covert operation to assert a more pertinent prior British claim that will countermine the idea of England's Irish colony being a gift of the Pope to Henry II.

Spenser's Irish genealogy is interlaced with conflicting perspectives on British origin myths. Kim Hall speaks of an 'ethos of language and national/ethnic competition . . . which is concerned in many ways with the legal, cultural, and economic ramifications of the union of cultures under imperialism'.[12] Hall points out that in Spenser's text: 'Cultural and political differences between the English, the Scottish, and the Irish are distilled to problematic linguistic differences, the overcoming and assimilation of which is the first step in an imperialist project'.[13] Though written before the accession of James I, the *View* is a text of Union as well as of Empire.

Tom Healy suggests that 'Spenser proposes that Irish savagery excels anything that could be associated with England's most apparent enemy, Spain', but Spenser's refutation of the claim to Spanish descent is, as we have seen, qualified and strategic.[14] Moreover, Healy overlooks, as do many readers, a vital Scottish component.[15] Having despatched the myth of Brutus, Irenius applies himself to the ethnic make-up of Ireland, arguing that the Scythians are Scots, and going so far as to declare that 'Scotland and Ireland are all one and the same'. When Eudoxus expresses astonishment at the existence of two Scotlands, Irenius explains that there are not two countries called Scotland but two kinds of Scots, with one variety situated in the north of Ireland (p. 45). During this genealogical journey, Irenius claims to be drawing on bardic sources. Eudoxus warns him not to take the Irish chronicles too seriously, but Irenius responds by declaring that all chronicles are doubtful, before going on to claim that the Irish had letters before the English:

> neither is there any certaine hold to be taken of any antiquity which is received by tradition, since all men be lyars, and many lye when they wil; yet for the antiquities of the written Chronicles of Ireland, give me leave to say something, not to justifie them, but to shew that some of them might say truth. For where you say the Irish have alwayes bin without letters, you are therein much deceived; for it is certaine, that Ireland hath had the use of letters very anciently, and long before England. (p. 47)

Citing this passage, Ciarán Brady notes that Spenser 'did not suggest that the Scythians or the Gaelic Irish were generally and totally inferior to more advanced civilizations; and in a number of cases, most interestingly in regard to the acquisition of literacy, he conceded that the Celts were far more advanced than the Anglo-Saxons'.[16] Having insisted on the validity, however qualified, of the Irish sources, Irenius then argues that the Gaules first inhabited Spain, then settled in Ireland. This comes as a great surprise to Eudoxus, since it flies in the face of the sources as he knows them:

> Surely you have shewed a great probability of that which I had thought impossible to have bin proved; but that which you now say, that Ireland should have bin peopled with the Gaules, seemeth much more strange, for all the Chronicles doe say, that the west and south was possessed and inhabited of Spaniards: and Cornelius Tacitus doth also strongly affirme the same, all which you must overthrow and falsifie, or else renounce your opinion. (p. 48)

But far from renouncing his opinion, Irenius presses his case, and continues with his iconoclastic ethnography. All are not Spaniards, he says, who come out of Spain:

> Neither so, nor so; for the Irish Chronicles (as I shewed you) being made by unlearned men, and writing things according to the appearance of the truth which they conceived, doe erre in the circumstances, not in the matter. For all that came out of Spaine (they being no diligent searchers into the differences of the nations) supposed to be Spaniards, and so called them; but the ground-work thereof is neverthelesse true and certain, however they through ignorance disguise

the same, or through vanity, whilst they would not seem to be ignorant, doe thereupon build and enlarge many forged histories of their
owne antiquity, which they deliver to fooles, and make them believe
for true. (pp. 48–49)

Eudoxus wonders why it is 'that the Irish doe so greatly covet to fetch
themselves from the Spaniards, since the old Gaules are a more auncient
and much more honourable nation?' Irenius, in keeping with Spenser's
opportunistic approach to origin-myths, as idiomatic strategies rather
than stable identities, responds thus:

Even of a very desire of new fanglenes and vanity, for they derive
themselves from the Spaniards, as seeing them to be a very honourable people, and neere bordering unto them: but all that is most
vaine; for from the Spaniards that now are, or that people that now
inhabite Spaine, they no wayes can prove themselves to descend;
neither should it be greatly glorious unto them; for the Spaniard that
now is, is come from as rude and savage nations as they, there being,
as there may be gathered by course of ages, and view of their owne
history, (though they therein labour much to enoble themselves) scarce
any drop of the old Spanish blood left in them; for all Spaine was first
conquered by the Romans, and filled with colonies from them, which
were still increased, and the native Spaniard still cut off. (pp. 49–50)

When Irenius denies Spanish origins for tactical reasons – in order to
ward off Spanish claims – he does so by pointing to the mixed origins of
the Spanish. Irenius lists the nations that overran Spain, including the
Carthaginians, Goths, Huns, and Vandals, 'And lastly all the nations of
Scythia, which, like a mountaine flood, did over-flow all Spaine, and
quite drowned and washt away whatsoever reliques there was left of
the land-bred people, yea, and of all the Romans too'. Irenius details the
conquests and colonizations of Spain, and effectively does for Spain, in
his radical ethnology, what he is doing for Ireland – tears up the roots
of its ancestry, leaving 'no pure drop of Spanish blood, no more then of
Roman or Scythian':

So that of all nations under heaven (I suppose) the Spaniard is the
most mingled, and most uncertaine; wherefore most follishly doe the
Irish thinke to enoble themselves by wresting their auncientry from
the Spaniard, who is unable to derive himself from any in certaine.
(p. 50)

Eudoxus cautions Irenius against speaking so sharply 'In dispraise of
the Spaniard, whom some others boast to be the onely brave nation
under the skie'. Irenius denies the charge:

> So surely he is a very brave man, neither is that any thing which I
> speake to his derogation; for in that I said he is a mingled people, it is
> no dispraise, for I think there is no nation now in Christendome, nor
> much further, but is mingled, and compounded with others: for it
> was a singular providence of God, and a most admirable purpose of
> his wisedome, to draw those Northerne Heathen Nations downe into
> those Christian parts, where they might receive Christianity, and to
> mingle nations so remote miraculously, to make as it were one blood
> and kindred of all people, and each to have knowledge of him.
> (pp. 50–51)

Thus the apparent 'denigration' of the Spanish leads into an acknowledgement of the mixed origins of all nations.

Irenius notes in passing the tendency of the Irish 'to call any stranger
inhabitant there amongst them, Gald, that is, descended from the Gaules',
and having described Ireland as Scotia Major, and Scotland as Scotia
Minor, he claims that 'Ireland is by Diodorus Siculus, and by Strabo,
called Britannia' (p. 52). Eudoxus, recovering from the series of jolts his
knowledge of history has suffered, summarizes the story so far:

> Now thus farre then, I understand your opinion, that the Scythians
> planted in the North part of Ireland: the Spaniards (for so we call
> them, what ever they were that came from Spaine) in the West;
> the Gaules in the South: so that there now remaineth the East parts
> towards England, which I would be glad to understand from whence
> you doe think them to be peopled.
>   *Iren.* Mary I thinke of the Brittaines themselves, of which though
> there be little footing now remaining, by reason that the Saxons
> afterwards, and lastly the English, driving out the inhabitants thereof,
> did possesse and people it themselves. (p. 52)

On this point, Roland Smith noted that 'Spenser's theory that south-
eastern Ireland was "peopled from the Brittons" has been abandoned
only recently by modern scholars'.[17] Smith maintains that 'Spenser's
theory that "Irelande received muche people afterwarde from the
Saxons" has more to recommend it than has his theory of British
migration'.[18]

Irenius concludes that the English displaced the British in Ireland,
and that the Irish are more closely linked to the Scots than the Spanish.
Reeling from these culture shocks, Eudoxus praises Irenius for 'This
ripping of auncestors' (p. 53). No sooner has he sat back than Irenius
has him out of his chair again. The English, it emerges, are the real villains
of the piece. The Old English, the descendants of the original medieval

colony, come in for more severe criticism than the Gaelic Irish. Irenius unsettles Eudoxus again by declaring that the chief abuses of the Irish are grown from the English, and indeed that the Old English are more reprehensible than the native Irish. Eudoxus is astonished to learn that of the remnants of the English pale not all remain English:

> What is this that you say, of so many as remaine English of them? Why? are not they that were once English, English still?
>
> *Iren.* No, for some of them are degenerated and growne almost mere Irish, yea, and more malitious to the English then the Irish themselves.
>
> *Eudox.* What heare I? And is it possible that an Englishman, brought up in such sweet civility as England affords, should find such likeing in that barbarous rudenes, that he should forget his owne nature, and forgoe his owne nation! how may this bee, or what (I pray you) may be the cause thereof? (p. 54)

Irenius postpones his answer, and confesses to digressing from his original purpose – to set out the customs of Ireland – but the digression proves necessary, as a way of reinforcing the point that the present state of Ireland can be understood only with reference to its past, thus the detour that reconstitutes its various inhabitants. While the meditation on the Scottish/Scythian origins of the Irish yields to an examination of Old English corruption, Irishness remains throughout a mobile marker of wildness rather than an essential property. Irenius regrets that some of the Old English 'are almost now growne like the Irish', and 'have quite shaken off their English names, and put on Irish that they might bee altogether Irish'. Eudoxus is vexed at the notion 'that any should so farre growe out of frame that they should in so short space, quite forget their countrey and their owne names!', a cultural amnesia that he considers to be 'a most dangerous lethargie' (p. 68). But it transpires that the Old English have not so much forgotten their origins as remembered them all too faithfully. Thus it unfolds that the garments of the Irish, including the mantle, of which so much has been written in Spenser criticism, are English after all. Irenius, incurable iconoclast that he is, gives another turn of the screw when he boldly states, in response to the query from Eudoxus as to whether the mantle and other items of clothing are 'Irish weedes':

> No: all these which I have rehearsed to you, be not Irish garments, but English; for the quilted leather jack is old English: for it was the proper weed of the horseman, as you may read in Chaucer, when he describeth Sir Thopas apparell and armour, as hee went to fight gainst the gyant,

> in his robe of shecklaton, which is that kind of guilded leather with
> which they use to imbroyder their Irish jackets. And there likewise by
> all that description, you may see the very fashion and manner of the
> Irish horseman most truely set forth, in his long hose, his ryding
> shooes of costly cordwaine, his hacqueton, and his haberjeon, with all
> the rest thereunto belonging. (p. 73)

Eudoxus finds it hard to believe that aspects of costume universally held
to be Irish are actually English, but Irenius insists: 'No sure; they be
native English, and brought in by the Englishmen first into Ireland'.
Now we can begin to see the subtlety of Spenser's strategy. Not only are
the Irish not Irish, and the Spanish not Spanish, but the English are not
English.[19] Moreover, the Irish are really Scots, but they are Scots in
English clothing. Irenius even claims the infamous Irish 'Galloglasses'
as English: 'the which name doth discover them also to be auncient
English: for *Gall-ogla* signifies an English servitour or yeoman' (p. 74).
There is no point in doing as others have done and pointing out that
this is a mistake on Spenser's part, and one of many. That would be to
read as an historian the text of a poet. Like all such myth-takes, it is less
an error than an angle.

Later, Irenius compares the Old English with the Irish 'which,
being very wilde at the first, are now become more civill; when as these,
from civillity, are growne to be wilde and meere Irish' (p. 143). Here,
'Irish' is not simply another word for 'barbarous' but a term of opposition, in this case opposition to another wave of colonizers. It is as if
Spenser wishes to unravel Irish identity to the point of erasure. For the
Old English, the loss of cultural memory – 'that he should forget his
owne nature' – is catastrophic, but for the Irish to lose themselves is
salutary.

Spenser presses home the idea of a time lag, arguing that the feudal
nature of the Old English, their unwillingness to embrace modern English
values, is the real problem. Irenius expounds a theory of culture that
shows the first English colonial establishment to have been left behind
by history. The Old English rebellions of the post-Reformation years –
Kildare, Butler, Desmond – are put down to a regressive baronial state.
Spenser is in many ways attacking his elders and betters. If one consequence of colonization was the displacement of class, then another was
the intensification of class struggle within the theatre of colonialism.
Paradoxically, Spenser's perspective is on one level socially progressive,
laying the blame for the present state of Ireland at the door of the first
colonists, a 'caste' who are cast off, throwbacks to an earlier English
culture:

Now this you are to understand, that all the rebellions which you see from time to time happen in Ireland, are not begun by the common people, but by the lords and captaines of countries, upon pride or wilfull obstinacy against the government, which whensoever they will enter into, they drawe with them all their people and followers, which thinke themselves bound to goe with them, because they have booked them and undertaken for them. And this is the reason that in England you have such few bad occasions, by reason that the noble men, however they should happen to be evill disposed, have no commaund at all over the communalty, though dwelling under them, because that every man standeth upon himselfe, and buildeth his fortunes upon his owne faith and firme assurance: The which [. . .] will worke also in Ireland. For by this the people are broken into small parts like little streames, that they cannot easily come together into one head, which is the principall regard that is to be had in Ireland, to keepe them from growing unto such a head, and adhering unto great men. (p. 140)

Irenius is at pains to establish that the English ruling class in Ireland are more blameworthy than the general population: 'for sure in mine opinion they are more sharpely to be chastised and reformed then the rude Irish, which, being very wilde at the first, are now become more civill; when as these, from civillity, are growne to be wilde and meere Irish' (p. 143). This fugitive Irishness into which the Old English are in danger of falling repeatedly assumes the form of an underdeveloped Englishness. It is a question of the arrested development of a colonial community, caught in limbo, and refusing to make way for a new generation of reforming native English.

In an authoritative intervention, Deborah Shuger interrogates Spenser's use of classical republican sources in the *View*, which emerges in her reading as primarily an anti-aristocratic tract.[20] Shuger sees the central conflict in Spenser's work as one between a warrior aristocracy and a rural gentry, with Spenser on the side of the latter. Her key point is that the 'georgic vision' of peace and civility through cultivation – in all its senses – 'ranges itself against a still-powerful attraction, even among scholarly humanists, to heroic barbarism'.[21] Spenser the aspiring gentleman is seduced by the glamour surrounding the overmighty subjects who block his progress. This opposition of English identities, Old and New, creates productive tensions, in prose and poetry alike. In mapping out his distance from the court, and in representing in aesthetic terms a feudal culture to which he was outwardly opposed, Spenser sourced reserves of social energy that radiate in his work.

As for the Irish themselves, those who are not written out of the story, they are gullible rather than malignant. They follow the Old

English, but, again ironically, unlike the latter, they are not beyond the pale. Naming is crucial as a means of taming. Thus Irenius observes:

> that whereas all men used to be called by the name of their septs [or clans], according to the severall nations, and had no surnames at all, that from henceforth each one should take upon himselfe a severall surname, either of his trade and facultie, or of some quality of his body or minde, or of the place where he dwelt, so as every one should be distinguished from the other, or from the most part, wherby they shall not onely not depend upon the head of their sept, as now they do, but also in time learne quite to forget his Irish nation. And herewithall would I also wish all the O's and Mac's, which the heads of septs have taken to their names, to bee utterly forbidden and extinguished. For that the same being an ordinance (as some say) first made by O'Brien for the strengthning of the Irish, the abrogating thereof will asmuch infeeble them. (pp. 147–148)

This is a further example of a rhetorical strategy that seeks to abolish Irish identity at a stroke. If demonizing is one colonialist approach to the Other, then dematerializing is another. Invisible natives are easier to handle than negative stereotypes.

Closing the earlier genealogical phase of his discourse, Irenius remarked: 'And thus you have my opinion, how all that Realme of Ireland was first peopled, and by what nations.' The Old English put out the British and are themselves now 'degenerate'. The Scots, or Scythians, are the other culprits. The Irish customs that Irenius abhors, and which critics often read as evidence of anti-Irish sentiment, are Scythian, which for Spenser's purposes means Scottish.

In the *View*, Spenser attacks the Spanish and the Scottish (Scythians), and dismisses the myth of Brutus, while retaining the claim that Arthur conquered Ireland (p. 52). Moreover, he reserves his strongest criticisms of native Irish society not for the Gaelic Irish – whose aboriginality he throws into question – but for the 'Old English', the descendants of an earlier phase of English settlement:

> for the chiefest abuses which are now in that realme, are growne from the English, and some of them are now much more lawlesse and licentious then the very wilde Irish: so that as much care as was by them had to reforme the Irish, so and much more must now bee used to reforme them; so much time doth alter the manners of men. (p. 67)

In another shift of emphasis, Irenius repeats his claim that the Old English have become Irish – 'and are now growne as Irish, as O-hanlans breech, as the proverbe there is' – only to then cancel this out by attributing the most harmful Irish customs to the (Old) English themselves:

> You cannot but hold them sure to be very uncivill; for were they at the best that they were of old, when they were brought in, they should in so long an alteration of time seeme very uncouth and strange. For it is to be thought, that the use of all England was in the raigne of Henry the Second, when Ireland was planted with English, very rude and barbarous, so as if the same should be now used in England by any, it would seeme worthy of sharpe correction, and of new lawes for reformation, for it is but even the other day since England grew civill.
> (p. 70)

Implicit in this last point is the prospective alienation of the New English themselves. As Patricia Coughlan remarks: 'As Scythians are to Greeks and wild men are to the civil, so the Irish are to the English: but so too, in a sense, are the colonists and officials in the field to the distant metropolitan policy-makers'.[22] Irenius goes further, and maintains that it matters little when addressing the 'evill customes' of the Old English whether these originate among the Irish or the English. What matters is that it is the 'degenerate' English who are the problem. The twin pitfalls facing English colonists are fosterage and intermarriage (p. 71). Patricia Fumerton contends that for Spenser 'fears of interracial alliance are very explicitly linked to fears of assimilation of the ruler by the ruled'.[23]

It is not simply a question of what has befallen the Old English since their arrival in Ireland, but of how things have moved on in England during their lengthy absence in the land that time forgot. Indeed, it emerges that it is not so much that the Old English have gone native as that they have retained earlier English manners that are obsolete in the metropolis. It is the medieval English culture of the first wave of planters that is now erroneously regarded as Irish. Thus many habits regarded as Irish are in fact English, and if they seem uncivil this is because the original English colonists were far less cultured than their sixteenth-century counterparts. Irenius excludes the English in Ireland from England's newly established civility, thus justifying the fresh influx of (New) English colonists. Spenser's antiquarian digressions on Irish origins are actually cleverly masked allusions to contemporary affairs. Far from being an inveterate opponent of all things Irish, Spenser is at odds with a particular form of Englishness which sits uncomfortably with his own vision of English national identity, and consequently his meditation on English and Irish origins is more subtle than critics have allowed. Moreover, the representation of the Irish as barbarous, through the trope of Scythian origins, is complicated by the fact that Spenser sees the Spanish and the Scots as the conduits of Scythian barbarity.

Few critics have grasped the extent to which Spenser's principal targets in his prose dialogue are the Scots and the Old English. Commentators quick to point out the anxiety about Spanish and Scythian influence fail to see that the twin threats of primitivism and invasion cohere in the spectre of the Ulster Scots, while the Old English themselves constitute an internal enemy that is backward precisely because it represents an ancient and untenable form of 'English' identity. The Irish are not too barbarous to be Scottish, and the Spanish themselves are, according to Irenius, mixed like all races. In the case of the Spanish there has been a cultural traffic with North Africa that blurs the boundaries of what is European and what is 'outside' or 'other'. But lest we take this as a slur on the Spanish we recall that for Irenius 'there is no nation now in Christendome, nor much further, but is mingled, and compounded with others' (p. 51). Spenser's scepticism regarding purity of origins is clearly an attempt to side-step the claims of the Old English to be more English than the New English, for not only is there no such originary Englishness but in its earliest manifestation Englishness is so rudimentary as to be compatible with rude Irishness.

Spenserians have hitherto maintained that the elaborate ethnology that Spenser constructs in the *View* is either a façade or a front for colonial violence against the Irish. I would argue that the poet's strategy is very deliberate and intended to be highly persuasive in terms of reasserting the English claim to Ireland in the face of Spanish and Scottish counter-claims, and arguing for the overthrow of the original English colony, now hopelessly corrupt. Spenser's insistence upon Scythian origins was structured by an underlying fear of Spanish and Scottish intervention in Ireland. Clare Carroll makes the link between the forms of otherness utilised by Spenser when she states that: 'In *A View* . . . by social level, religion, and what for Spenser is a non-European ethnic identity (alternately Scythian, African, or Moorish) the Irish are constituted as one inferior category'.[24] But Spenser wants at one and the same time to distinguish between the ruling Old English elite and their more subservient and malleable Irish subordinates, and to merge the 'non-European' with the 'European', since he uses Scythian to imply both Spanish and Scottish.

Spenser's subtle and varied use of past antiquities to inform and offset the ethnographic present has not always been appreciated. Critics have looked to the *View* not for ambivalence and hybridity but for an anti-Irish polemic that they can comfortably and self-righteously denounce. The case I am trying to make is one that illustrates the ways in which Spenser actually deflects the gaze from the Irish to a Scythianism he imputes to Spanish and Scottish immigrants, and a barbarity that he attributes to earlier English settlers. It is therefore a question, literally, of ignorance rather than knowledge, of *not knowing* the Irish, that is, of displacing them. The disappearing act, or sleight of hand, that Spenser effects, the way in which he effectively erases the local inhabitants from the canvas he is painting, is much more interesting, to me at least, than the conventional view that sees him as an unashamed calumniator of the Irish. Of course, it could be argued that the text says what it does not say, and that the exclusion of the Irish is still a racist move, but the fact remains that Spenser's strategy is one of displacement and deferral rather than an unexamined essentializing animosity.

A grounded and immediate attitude to cultural and national differ-ence informs the *View*'s antiquarian ethnography. In its rehearsal of identity and difference, this important document draws an altogether more complex figure than is suggested by received opinion. The focus on Irishness and anti-Irish racism has concealed other ethnicities, and glossed over the tensions in Spenser's text, specifically the slippage between Old English and Irish, and Scythian and Scottish. By obsessing about Ireland critics have let England – and others – escape examina-tion.[25] The discourse on racial origins is intimately bound up with the excavation of British and European origin-myths. Spenser's versatile and varied use of past antiquities to inform and offset contemporary matters – including the matter of Britain – has not always been appreci-ated, except as a thin veil for his infamous anti-Irish views, so infamous as to require little elucidation. Spenser constructs knowledge of the Irish only as an absent Other, disoriented by barbarous foreign implants variously construed as Spanish, Scottish, and even English. Colonial identity is not a unified ideology whose goal is to alienate an integral native culture. In a problematic 'British' context, the meshing of Anglo-Irish and Scottish differences implies a delicate matrix of con-tested positions erected over an abyss. Any discussion of the *View* has to take its delving into mythological origins seriously, since there is a question of policy at issue.

My own feeling is that Spenser's deft interweaving of different elements of cultural and national identity in Ireland points to an aware-ness of the vicissitudes of what historians have come to refer to as the 'British Problem', that is, the painstaking process by which the British state was formed.[26] Ireland was, and arguably remains, a seed-bed of

British identity as well as a fraught locus of colonial otherness, and standard criticism of the *View* that concentrates exclusively on its putative anti-Irish sentiments does not begin to do justice to the various twists and turns of this disturbing and challenging text. Spenser's English-oriented ethnogenesis, his concern with the Scythian connection as a way of asserting New English supremacy, reveals a preoccupation with the present, and with discrediting Spanish and Scottish claims to Ireland rather than debasing the Irish 'themselves'. There are elements of in-betweenness and anachronism here that demand attention. In his 'ripping of auncestors', Spenser showed himself to be attuned to the ethnographic present. The critical tradition that sees the Irish as all too visible in the *View*, victimized and vilified, may find it difficult to accept that they are part of a mesmerizing vanishing act. As a proponent of *recolonization* at the expense of English and Scottish incumbents, Spenser's creative energies were devoted not to berating the native Irish, or even accounting for them, but to taking them out of the equation.

Notes

1 Lynda E. Boose, '"The getting of a lawful race": Racial Discourse in Early Modern England and the Unrepresentable Black Woman?', in Margo Hendricks and Patricia Parker (eds), *Race, Women and Writing in Early Modern Europe* (London: Routledge, 1994), p. 36. *A View of the State of Ireland* is not simply a controversial text on account of its contents, but a disputed document as a result of its publishing history. The gap between the brief entry in the Stationers' Register of 14 April 1598 announcing its arrival, but with authorship unattributed, and its eventual publication in 1633 has prompted heated debate around issues of authorship and censorship. Most critics accept the attribution to Spenser made by the text's first editor, Sir James Ware, in 1633, and followed by all subsequent editors, but Jean Brink has asked pressing questions as to why this important item was excluded from Spenser's corpus until Ware's intervention. For a concise overview of the arguments around the tract's alleged suppression see Andrew Hadfield, 'Was Spenser's View of the Present State of Ireland Censored? A Review of the Evidence', *Notes and Queries* 240 (1994), 459–464. The key perspective on the issue of authorship is Jean Brink, 'Appropriating the Author of *The Faerie Queene*: The Attribution of the *View of the Present State of Ireland* and *A Brief Note of Ireland* to Edmund Spenser', in Peter E. Medine and Joseph Wittreich (eds), *Soundings of Things Done: Essays in Early Modern Literature in Honor of S. K. Heninger Jr.* (Newark: University of Delaware Press, 1997), pp. 93–115. Brink's case is challenged most forcibly in Andrew Hadfield, 'Certainties and Uncertainties: By Way of a Response to Jean Brink', *Spenser Studies* 12 (1998), 197–202.

2 Brendan Bradshaw, 'Robe and Sword in the Conquest of Ireland', in C. Cross, D. Loades and J. J. Scarisbrick (eds), *Law and Government under the Tudors: Essays Presented to Sir Geoffrey Elton on his Retirement* (Cambridge: Cambridge University Press, 1988), p. 153.

3 Margaret MacCurtain, 'The Roots of Irish Nationalism', in Robert Driscoll (ed.), *The Celtic Consciousness* (Edinburgh: Canongate, 1982), p. 373.

4 Rudolf B. Gottfried, 'Spenser as an Historian in Prose', *Transactions of the Wisconsin Academy of Sciences, Arts and Letters* 30 (1937), 328.

5 Ciarán Brady, 'Spenser's Irish Crisis: Humanism and Experience in the 1590s', *Past and Present* 111 (1986), 38.

6 Tracey Hill, 'Humanism and Homicide: Spenser's *A View of the Present State of Ireland*', *Irish Studies Review* 4 (1993), 4.

7 Andrew Hadfield and Willy Maley (eds), *Edmund Spenser, A View of the State of Ireland (1633): From the First Printed Edition* (Oxford and Malden, Mass.: Blackwell, 1997), p. 6. All further references to the *View* are by page number in the text.

8 Edward W. Said, *Culture and Imperialism* (London: Vintage, 1994), pp. 284–285.

9 Andrew Hadfield, '"Who knowes not Colin Clout?": The Permanent Exile of Edmund Spenser', in *Literature, Politics and National Identity: Reformation to Renaissance* (Cambridge: Cambridge University Press, 1994), pp. 193–194.

10 Judith H. Anderson, 'The Antiquities of Fairyland and Ireland', *Journal of English and German Philology* 86:2 (1987), 202–203.

11 John Breen, 'Imagining Voices in *A View of the Present State of Ireland*: A Discussion of Recent Studies Concerning Edmund Spenser's Dialogue', *Connotations* 4:1–2 (1994–95), 126.

12 Kim F. Hall, *Things of Darkness: Economies of Race and Gender in Early Modern England* (Ithaca and London: Cornell University Press, 1995), p. 145.

13 Hall, *Things of Darkness*, p. 146.

14 Thomas Healy, 'Civilisation and its Discontents: The Case of Edmund Spenser', in *New Latitudes: Theory and English Renaissance Literature* (London: Edward Arnold, 1992), p. 89.

15 I have mapped out in some detail the neglected Scottish dimension of the *View* in chapter 7 of *Salvaging Spenser: Colonialism, Culture and Identity* (London: Macmillan, 1997), pp. 136–162.

16 Brady, 'Spenser's Irish Crisis', p. 30.

17 Roland M. Smith, 'More Irish Words in Spenser', *Modern Language Notes* 59:7 (1944), 473.

18 *Ibid.*, p. 476.

19 I have expounded at length upon the varieties of Englishness found in early modern Ireland in chapter 3 of *Salvaging Spenser*, pp. 48–77.

20 Deborah Shuger, 'White Barbarians: Irishmen, Indians and Others in Spenser's *View*', *Renaissance Quarterly* 50:2 (1997), 494–525.

21 *Ibid.*, p. 519.

22 Patricia Coughlan, '"Some secret scourge which shall by her come unto England": Ireland and Incivility in Spenser', in Patricia Coughlan (ed.), *Spenser and Ireland* (Cork: Cork University Press, 1989), p. 70.

23 Patricia Fumerton, 'Exchanging Gifts: The Elizabethan Currency of Children and Poetry', *English Literary History* 53 (1986), 256.

24 Clare Carroll, 'The Construction of Gender and the Cultural and Political Other in *The Faerie Queene* 5 and *A View of the Present State of Ireland*: The Critics, the Context, and the Case of Radigund', *Criticism*, 32:2 (1990), 167.

25 I have taken issue elsewhere with the critical tendency that allows Ireland to overrun Spenser's work. See my '"To weet to work *Irenaes* franchisement": Ireland in *The Faerie Queene*', in *Spenser in Ireland: 'The Faerie Queene', 1596–1996, The Irish University Review* 26:2 (Autumn/Winter 1996), special issue, ed. Anne Fogarty, 303–319.

26 Until now the 'British Problem' has been dealt with almost exclusively by historians. See for instance, Brendan Bradshaw and Peter Roberts (eds), *British Consciousness and Identity: The Making of Britain, 1533–1707* (Cambridge: Cambridge University Press, 1998). The literary critics have their say in David Baker and Willy Maley (eds), *British Identities and English Renaissance Literature* (Cambridge: Cambridge University Press, 2002).

—part three—

Knowing otherwise

7

Mobility and the method: from Shakespeare's treatise on Mab to Descartes' *Treatise on Man*

MARIE GARNIER-GIAMARCHI

THIS ESSAY is an attempt to redefine literary history along non-linear, cross-historical lines. A local textual event can be shown to operate not so much as an interpretative key to other works on which it would have some historical resonance but rather as an operative skeleton key that can be displaced and brought to bear on texts belonging to a distant or apparently unrelated discursive network. In an effort to resist linear procedures, the delocalized practice of literary history involves oblique readings and lateral encounters. The literary text, the Queen Mab speech from *Romeo and Juliet*, is here read in the vicinity of an excerpt from Descartes' *Treatise on Man*. Shakespeare and Descartes are confronted, not in order to pull the Shakespearian text on to the path of modernity but to show traces of Shakespearian 'mobility' in the philosophical text – a reflection that could be pressed as far as Shelley's *Queen Mab*,[1] though not within the format of an essay. Mobility, another word for lateral displacement, is here taken as a key term, a substitute for linear models of influence and positivist historicizing. It is encrypted in and diffracted by figures such as Mab, who operates in what follows as a theory substitute, a mobile literary touchstone that signals the madness beneath the method, the lateral beneath the literal, hovering in mid-air between theory and text.

In spite of the vast amount of criticism devoted to Mercutio since the 1980s, few recent readings of *Romeo and Juliet* have granted any attention to the text of the Queen Mab speech, to the paronomastic ploys the piece rests on, the polarities of *dream* and *drum*. Clifford Leech's essay concludes with a critically uncouth paragraph on Queen Mab, apparently no fit conclusion to a study entitled 'The Moral Tragedy of *Romeo and Juliet*'.[2] His final note on Mab leads him astray from the solid ground of moralism to a series of productive and intuitive remarks which go against the grain of humanist criticism. The logic of the afterthought, for which Mab stands as a model, colonizes the critical voice:

> The speech puts Mercutio outside the general Christian framework of the play. He is surely a pure Pagan . . . There is an angriness in him that is a link with Hamlet, Othello, Lear, Macbeth . . . Here, not in the oblivious *Liebestod* of the lovers . . . we find the true germ of Shakespeare's later development. One may suspect that Mercutio haunted this playwright, that the character and his death provided the foundation on which the later tragedies could be securely built.[3]

Just a few lines earlier, Leech refers to Mab's 'fantastic dreamworld' as making us aware of 'a *mystery* not sufficiently explicit' (my emphasis), surely a frail foundation for Shakespeare's monument to rest on. Mab sets Leech off the foundational, organicist trail. Laterality and openness have replaced closure and coherence. Mercutio – the figure, not the character – sets Leech on an oblique track across the canon. The critic's return to the concept of 'foundation' loses its credit when juxtaposed with the argument of Mercutio's *haunting* function. The logic of haunting, of boundary-crossing and lateral moves, is more germane to post-structuralism than to foundation-oriented criticism, which founders in the process.

E. Pearlman's reading of 'Shakespeare at work' in the same volume reaches the ironical conclusion that Shakespeare was at play, rather, and that 'in writing *Romeo and Juliet* he gambled again and again for extremely high stakes; his occasional losses were more than offset by great victories'[4] – yet another self-consuming exercise. 'The most wondrous of Shakespeare's additions to *Romeo and Juliet*' has in fact generated endless series of subtractions, negative critical statements as to what it is and what it does. 'Unrelated to content or plot' (120), 'retrograde to the character of its speaker' (122), the speech suffers from 'mislineation' (123) and possibly misplacement, since it 'came disorderly to the printer's hands, possibly on a sheet that was of separate origin and that was burdened with marginal insertions or pasted slips' (123). To sum up, it 'does not draw its subject matter from the play in which it is embedded, contradicts the psychological development of its speaker, is inessential to plot, barely tangential to themes and ideas, and bears the typographical signature of separate creation' (124). It invalidates, in other words, the critical notions of subject matter, character, plot, theme, idea and creation. As in Leech's commentary, the word 'mystery' is bandied about, in what seems an acknowledgement of critical helplessness: 'when Shakespeare inserted Queen Mab into Mercutio's part . . . he transformed his play from a mirror of Verona to a mirror of mystery' (124).

The last essay in the collection, Donald W. Foster's 'The Webbing of *Romeo and Juliet*', comes close to breaking new critical ground by establishing lateral links between literary text (the text as web) and computer networking (the Web).[5] It remains, however, a source study rather than a proper reading of the text, theoretically geared to a dualistic approach of the text as warp and thread, if not to a linear conception of literary influence. The 'Shaxicon Notebook' database is described as an orthogonal grid with 'more or less vertical fibers' ('those words, mannerisms, grammatical habits, that reappear throughout Shakespeare's career') and 'more or less horizontal threads' ('such stuff as one finds in a particular stage at his career') (131). The database brings to light an interesting nexus of twin texts, which according to Foster invalidate J. O. Holmer's previous findings that the Mab speech was chiefly indebted to Thomas Nashe's *Terrors of the Night* (141). Foster comes up with two other knots in the network, imported from Book I of Spenser's *Faerie Queene* and from a French primer by John Eliot (*Ortho-Epia Gallica*, 1593), where the 'grass-hopper', 'the spinner the spider's wife' whose body is 'litle bigger than a peaze' appear.[6] Foster's conclusion, however, takes on global overtones, thus missing the local and the historical: 'these few representative words and phrases from Eliot, Shakespeare and Webster[7] appear in a shared matrix of influence that extends through human time and around the globe, *a web that cannot be fully accessed*' (147, my emphasis) – yet another system failure in the source-bound, linear model. Grass-hopping, rather than world-wide-web accessing, emerges as the productive metaphor, the icon for lateral mobility and discontinuous moves. Mab navigates along non-linear, non-orthogonal paths, to be traced along cross-country migratory routes, from John Eliot and Shakespeare to Descartes via Lyotard's reading of Hamlet's 'mobled queen'.

My argument is not to demonstrate that Mab is of great relevance to the play,[8] but that it is of great relevance to textual studies in general, whether the text be literary, social or cultural. Mercutio's speech subverts the received notions of dramatic or thematic relevance, and revises linear as well as tabular modes of reading. Mab's speech provides an arachnean model, an accretive mode where non-linear concepts operate; it is spun out of a contagious 'figure' of rhetoric: paronomasia. 'Figure' must be taken in the darker sense developed by Lyotard, which relocates it in the vicinity of rhythm rather than discourse, somewhere between the signifier and the signified.[9]

A number of definitions of paronomasia to be found in two of the most famous dictionaries of rhetorical terms published in the Elizabethan period deserve closer examination. In 1577 and 1593, Henry Peacham's *Garden of Eloquence* defines paronomasia as 'a figure which *declineth* into a contrarie by a likelihood of letters, either added, changed, or taken away',[10] while George Puttenham's *Arte of English Poesie* (1589) explains that 'ye have a figure by which ye play with a couple of words or names much resembling and because the one seemes to answer th'other by manner of illusion, and doth, as it were, *nick* him'.[11] Both definitions link the figure to a form of subversion or perversion of the letter, whether one relies on Peacham's 'declension' or on Puttenham's 'nicking'. The apparently precise use of the verb 'to nick', which *OED* paraphrases as 'to tally with or suit exactly' (*OED* II 4 a), is questioned by Puttenham's adding 'as it were', as if 'nick' peddled other echoes. Puttenham's paraphrase of paronomasia as 'the Nicknamer' does not tally at all with his first use of 'nick', since the two words stem from different roots. 'Nick' carries a number of allusions to the nick or prick of time, where a 'bawdy hand' is at work, as in Mercutio's 'prick of noon' (II.iii.100.).[12] Both terms, 'decline' and 'nick', signal the deviating, devious, diabolical slant contained in the figure.

If one turns to Greek and Roman rhetoricians, the figure is not generally approved of, except by such 'early modern' writers as Lucretius, as shown by Jane McIntosh Snyder. She argues very convincingly that Aristotle 'tends to view ambiguity as a deficiency or drawback in language' and that Quintilian, (who uses the Latin term for the figure, *adnominatio*) 'disapproved of word-plays involving *amarus* and *amare* as well as *avis* and *avius* [though] these same two puns interested Vergil'.[13] Lucretius, however, made ample use of the figure, and a number of the loose etymological associations he makes anticipate, or perhaps always already reiterate, in an 'early modern' fashion, Derridean behaviours. I quote Snyder: 'Lucretius . . . was bound to look for some natural connection between the person and the *nomen* . . . In the loose association here of *Venus* with *venenum*, Lucretius hit upon the correct etymology of the name, since *venenum* (originally like the Greek *pharmakon*, in a neutral sense), *venus-tas, venus, venenor*, etc., are all from the same root.' Plautus, also, frequently associates *Venus* with *venenor*, a 'textual' or verbal form of play which turns the letter against itself, folds or invaginates the word, rewrites the text into a single-threaded, yet manyfold web. The association becomes 'looser', more lateral still, when one reads in *De rerum natura* 'Venus is used to mean *membrum virile*',[14] turning the trope into a cross-gender signifier. Other examples of

Lucretian paronomasia can be quoted, such as *fundus* (ground) against *fundere* (to pour),[15] genius/generating, close to the pun on *mater/materia/terra*. The function of such paronomastic tricks is not cosmetic but philosophical, since the permutations of the word they allow for give shape to Lucretian atomism:

> Ut potius multis communia corpora rebus
> multa putes esse, *ut verbis elementa videmus*,
> quam sine principiis ullam rem existere posse.
>
> (1.196–198)

So that rather should you think that many bodies are common to many things, just as we see many letters are common to many words, than that anything is able to exist without atoms.[16]

Such declensions of letters are a direct function of atomic swerve or clinamen. A process of word declension affects the small-scale operations of Mercutio's speech. The cases of paronomasia with which the speech opens and closes – *dream/drum, carriage/chariot* – are repeated in a number of internal declensions such as *a team/atom, courtiers/curt'sies, fingers/fees, knees/nose, tithe-pig/tickling*. Similar effects reappear in alliterative series such as *Mab/mare/maid/much/misfortune* and *blisters/because/breath*. The speech weaves in a number of *w/s* sequences, a Will Shakespeare signature tune spun into the textural fibre, to be overheard in the description of the fairy's carriage: *w*aggon-*s*pokes, *w*ings of gras-*s*hoppers, *s*mallest *s*pider *w*eb, *w*at'ry beams, *w*hip of cricket'*s* bone, her *w*aggoner a *s*mall . . . gnat.

This is where Foster's recovery of the John Eliot source can yield lateral, oblique results: the French primer is less interesting as a source than as a study in cross-linguistic reading, a visual key to foreign phonetics, an exercise in marginal gloss and quick eye motion. The facing pages of this 'double invention' force the eye into a discontinuous, grass-hopping type of reading. Marginal gloss, usually associated with biblical collation and annotation, here becomes a phonetic pursuit, geared to the operations of the ear rather than to the eye. Eliot's key to the pronunciation of French results in long lists or declensions of phonemes, vowels in the left-hand margin, consonants in the right. The text bears the mark of its author's taste for paronomasia and the pleasure of the phoneme. In his dedicatory epistle to 'the learned professors of the French', John Eliot explains, with proto-Joycean ability for word-creation, how he '*retired himself among the merrie muses*' to write: '*by the work of my pen and inke, I have dezinkhornifistibulated a fantasticall rapsody of dialogisme, to the end that I would not be found an idle drone among so many famous teachers and professors of noble languages, who are very busie dayly in devising and setting forth new bookes'*. There follows a long paronomastic series, in which an author can be seen at work, like Diogenes:

> [he] begins to belabour his roling citie, to set it going, to turn it, overturn it, spurne it, bind it, wind it, twind it, throw it, overthrow it, tumble it, rumble it, jumble it, did ring it, swing it, fling it, ding it, made it leape, skip, hip, trip, thumpe, jumpe, shake, crake, quake, washt it, swasht it, dasht it, naild it, trailt it, tipt it, tapt it, rapt it, temperd it, tamperd it, hammerd it, hoopt it, knockt it, rockt it, rubd it, tugd it, lugd it, stopt it, unstopt it, tied it fast, then losd it again, rusht it, crusht it, brusht it, pusht it, charmd it, armd it, farmd it .[17]

Like Eliot's book, where the reader is invited to use the pronunciation table as a '*Theseus* thread to guide thee out of that Labyrinth' or 'as *Mercuries* finger to direct thee in thy progresse of learning',[18] Mercutio's speech reads as a labyrinthine, paronomastic text declining the syllable 'air'. 'Thin air' reads as yet another inflection in the declensional series contained in Mab's speech, *fairy/ear/hairs*.[19] Mercutio's verse is driven with the same paronomastic energy (*wind/who/woos*) in the final, broken sonnet – two quatrains, echoed in Romeo's own final eight-lines – another version of Mercury as the wind-god.[20] Mercutio's piece addressed to Romeo declines from frozen north to dew-dropping south, to reach the homoerotic climax of the last line. The phrase 'turning *his* side to the *dew-dropping* south' (I.iv.102) repeats and declines Mab's heterosexual models into a gender-free mode. Mercutio, the utterer of verbal near-misses, cross-dresses as a near-miss.

Declension, declination or 'nicking' place Mab's fairy rhetoric in close connection with atomism. Lucretius' atoms, like Mercutio's verbal near-misses, are characterized by their minor deviations from the straight path. In *De natura rerum*, Lucretius describes his own 'teams of little Atomi' as swerving off their course. 'When the Atoms are travelling straight down through empty space by their own weight, at quite indeterminate times and places *they swerve ever so little from their course, just so much that you can call it a change of direction.*'[21] Lucretius' philosophical puns operate much like a verbal *clinamen*, based on minute differences like *paronomasia*:

> Indeed, it also makes a difference in my own verses in what order each letter is placed and with what other letter ... The difference in their positioning distinguishes the different substances. Likewise, then, with regard to things, when the assemblages of atoms and their

motion, order, position, and shapes are changed, so also the things themselves must be changed.[22]

One example of atomic-like letter change occurs in Lucretius' frequent puns on *mater* and *materies*, mother and matter. Queen Mab, a strange 'material mother',[23] and *Hamlet*'s 'mobled queen' a paronomastic body-double, equally diverge from the straight path, towards what Jean-François Lyotard has called the space of the 'figural'.

Mab and the mobled queen

As a local network of loose energies, the Queen Mab speech reads as a follow-up exercise on the play's initial question, 'can you read?' (I.ii.56). Speed rather than substance emerges from it, creating a strong sense of orality in the play's overwritten poetics. Mercutio's syncopated speech calls for a different critical beat. G. Blakemore Evans, with some critical insight, notes that Mercutio 'is wholly Shakespeare's invention – perhaps, indeed, an invention that occurred to him after he had blocked out the major lines of the play, [his] appearance in I.4. is rather sudden and one is given the impression that, along with Romeo and Benvolio, he is gate-crashing Capulet's feast'.[24] Mab, like Mercutio, is an invitation to a form of critical gate-crashing: like *Hamlet*'s 'mobled queen', as decoded by Jean-François Lyotard in the final pages of *Discours/Figure*, Queen Mab calls for philosophical reading, based on mobility. Lyotard rereads the Freudian analytic gesture as a tropism, as a case of lateral mobility:

> La question d'Hamlet . . . 'The mobled queen?' ne peut être à son tour entendue par Freud qu'en raison du caractère oscillant, *mobile* de la région où se tient la relation spectaculaire . . . Il suffira que Freud *tourne le dos* à la scène pour que l'attitude analytique s'instaure: attention flottante, mais substitution à l'œil de la seule oreille qui prépare l'entendement et le discours théorique.[25]

> Hamlet's question . . . , '*the mobled queen?*' can only be understood by Freud because of the *mobile*, labile character of the region where the spectacular relation is held . . . Freud will only have to *turn his back* to the scene for the psychoanalytic pose to begin: a floating interest, but also a substitution of the ear to the eye – an ear for 'entendement' and theoretical discourse.

Mercutio's speech, however, resists interpretation, and bars the way to the language of dreams, by becoming a waking substitute, a screen to the tale of Romeo's dream. Queen Mab's speech actually derides and deforms dreaming and the interpretation of dreams into drumming and ear-drumming. Mab's 'mobled' or muffled discourse makes it clear, to quote Deleuze and Guattari in their revision of Freud, that the unconscious operates as a crowd, a mob.[26] Both Shakespearian queens generate a language-between, an unstable lexical space, close to the portmanteau word, but yet not exactly that either, a new, infra-linguistic term that does more and less than signify, half-way between misprision and invention.

As a minor text which does not immediately cohere with the tragic discourse of the play, Mab's speech operates as what Jean-François Lyotard has termed a form-figure, which imports 'non-language within language'.[27] The space of the figural, which disturbs the logic of oppositions (a pattern that gains visibility throughout *Romeo and Juliet*'s chiasmic rhetorical effects), generates a crisis within the established critical discourse. Queen Mab's speech, as a grafted, disconnected element in the play, destabilizes patterns of oppositions through its lateral, figural, paronomastic drift. Mab can be shown to operate as a figural element, a staple ingredient in Shakespearian poetics which 'cannot be reduced to the process Jakobson designates as selection and combination' (41). Lyotard's concept of the *figure* rewrites the process of reading: what he calls *sensible reading*, based on the signifier, re-emerges as *sensory reading*, geared to the a-signifier, the infra-semantic detail, the local disturbance – to be seen at work in the use of paronomasia. Lyotard writes:

> Le mouvement par lequel le sensible se présente est toujours une gesticulation, une danse . . . Le sensible est dans un écart insuppressible avec le sensé. (41)

> (The movement by which the sensory presents itself is always a gesturing, a dance . . . The sensory insuperably deviates from sense.)

Like other figures in the Shakespearian corpus, Mab is a factor of deviation, derivation or disturbance in the play's textual procedures. The speech revises the rhetoric of chiasmic oppositions, and reactivates the play's expository puns on 'moving' and 'being moved'. Queen Mab and Hamlet's *mobled queen* both operate as puns, this time defined *against* the Saussurian grain: single-threaded, non-semiotic, paronomastic, lateral instead of literal.

To quote from Jonathan Culler's introduction to the volume *On Puns*, a pun is what makes language respond to 'the call of the phoneme, whose echoes tell of wild realms beyond the code',[28] realms close to the derivative, paronomastic landscape of Mercutio's Mab speech, itself beyond codes. The dominant code introduced in the play, based on the oxymoron, the criss-crossing of opposite pairs, is perturbed by figural elements. The time-hallowed 'figure of rhetoric' appears to give way to another, contour-less 'form-figure' such as Lyotard describes in *Discours/ Figure*. The failure of rhetorical logic is apparent in Robert Evans's attempt to isolate and classify the figures of rhetoric in *Romeo and Juliet*, and in Mercutio's speech in particular.[29] From his initial declaration that it is 'one of the most puzzling and difficult speeches to interpret', Evans moves on to the realization that 'there is *another, subtler sense* in which the entire passage is a figure of rhetoric' (84), which blatantly places classical rhetoric on shaky ground. The Mab speech limns a model of language where the oxymoronic code gives way to paronomastic forms of subversion – or Lucretian *clinamen*.

The central element of *discourse* in the speech, *dream*, is re-figured or dis-figured by a number of lateral, parasitic outgrowths and by-products, such as *drum*, which later in the play resurfaces as *dram*. Both *dream* and *drum* hark back to the Old Saxon form *drom*, mirth, noise, close to its French equivalent 'noise', trouble, which laterally ties in with the witches' trouble and toil in *Macbeth* and with Rumor in *2 Henry IV*.[30]

Mercutio's speech, like Hamlet's pun, drums another, derivative and distorted language on the eardrums of the listeners. The near-foreign tongue uttered in the process escapes what could be called the dominant code of the eye, the visual in the play – emblematized by Romeo's declaration in Juliet's garden that 'her eye discourses' (II.i.55). Mab, literally or laterally, dis-courses in different terms, in an uncouth tongue that tells of wild linguistic realms beyond the Welsh border, though nothing as stable as a Welsh origin for the word has been established by lexicographers. The Welsh word 'mab' means boy, though the first translator of the *Mabinogion* into English actually translates *mab* as 'child'.[31] Like Mercutio, the 'fairy' displays unstable gender features, taking on a 'modern' sense. She operates as a 'tympan' or eardrum, a term with which Jacques Derrida opens *Margins of Philosophy*.[32] The speech turns tragic discourse into a tympanic figure, warping *dream* into *drum* into *dram* (a 'dram of poison', V.i. 60) into *drama*, distorting signifiers into a series of lateral, mobile as well as *mobled* echoes.

Mab and the margin

Derrida's introduction to *Margins of Philosophy* resorts to a number of metaphors connecting what he calls 'the figure of the oblique' to the topography of the ear – one of Mab's and the mobled queen's main entry-ways into the *logos* of both plays. The oblique path, much like the paronomastic slant, is Derrida's topographical equivalent of deconstruction. Derrida writes:

> The membrane of the tympanum, a thin and transparent partition separating the auditory canal from the middle ear (the cavity) is stretched obliquely (*loxôs*). Obliquely from above to below, from outside to inside, and from the back to the front. There it is not perpendicular to the axis of the canal. One of the effects of this obliqueness is to increase the surface of impression and hence the capacity of vibration . . . The tympanum squints.
>
> Consequently, to luxate the philosophical ear, to set the *loxôs* in the logos to work, is to avoid frontal and symmetrical protest, opposition in all the forms of anti-, or in any case to inscribe antism and overturning, domestic denegation, in an entirely other form of ambush, of *lokhos*, of textual maneuvers.[33]

Derrida's own paronomastic word-derivation, in the one-dimensional space of the riddle that rewrites *logos* as *loxôs* and *lokhos*, parallels Mab's revision of the straight path into the swerving, deviant course of word-play. The trappings of her chariot are not very distant from Derrida's own trappings and 'traces'. Her eardrumming also leads to the ambush, or '*lokhos*', of academic and philosophical 'breaches' and 'ambuscadoes' (I.iv.84–85).

Mab, like Derrida's tympan, challenges the logic of oppositions. In the *logos* of *Romeo and Juliet*, Juliet's 'discourse of the eye' is made to squint or at least to wink. Mab's set-piece provides a side-glance at Juliet, an implicit, oblique link between her solar characteristics ('Juliet is the sun' (II.i.45)) and her *mobled*, mobile as well as muffled nature.[34] Like Gertrude, Juliet belongs with the sphere of 'mobled', mobile beings, which the Mab speech connects with the underworld of 'foul sluttish hairs' and plaited manes (I.iv.89–90). Juliet's solar name shifts throughout the play in a mobile, paronomastic fashion, from associations to *July* to *Jewel* and *Jule, Ay*, a configuration which displaces her towards another mobile character in the canon, Julius Caesar. Julius's own patronym is derived, according to Littré, from the Greek *youlos*, 'curly' – a loop-line, a loop-hole, a figure of deviance.

A migrating figure, Mab runs across the corpus in many guises and disguises. Her emergence in *Hamlet* as 'the mobled queen' reads as a paronomastic tangle. Jean-François Lyotard sees in it the key *lapsus* to the tragedy, and comments on André Gide's translation of mobled as 'encamouflée' in the following terms – 'encamouflée' being Gide's own portmanteau term:

Dans les parages de *mobled*, en associant librement, nous trouvons: *the mob*, la populace; *motley* est une *incongruous mixture* et désigne en particulier l'habit que portent les bouffons; to *wear motley*, c'est *to play the fool*. Pas beaucoup plus loin, phonétiquement, nous trouvons *mother* ... La clé de *mobled*, c'est mobilisée, la perte de l'invariance des écarts qui détermine la parenté ... une mère mobile, c'est une mère qui n'est pas à sa place, qui est là où on ne l'attend pas et pas là où l'attend, 'camouflée' parce qu'elle se dérobe et 'encanaillée', prostituée, parce qu'elle s'est donnée en violation des écarts imposés par les règles de l'échange.[35]

(Not very distant from mobled, by a process of free association, we find: the mob, the rabble; motley is an incongruous mixture and is used more specifically for the dress of the professional fool; to wear motley means to play the fool. Not much further, phonetically, one finds mother ... The key to mobled is mobilized, i.e. the loss of invariability in the degrees that determine parenthood. A mobile mother is a misplaced mother, who is found where nobody expects to see her, and not found where she is expected to be, 'camouflée' [muffled] because she keeps herself out of view [se dérobe], and 'encanaillée', a loose woman, because she has given herself in violation of the proper rules of exchange within degree of relation.)

Much like the 'motley fool', the composite, incongruous word does not speak the truth but acts it out, in the web of its lateral, semantic displacements.

As displaced and deviant as Juliet – never found where one expects her, as appears from her mother's reiterated question 'where's my daughter?' (I.iii.1) – Mab operates as a mobile element as well as as a *mob*, a collection of disconnected parts and opposite meanings floating in the same Scotch (or Welsh) broth. The scattering, disseminating energy generates Juliet's desire to atomize the body of Romeo into 'little stars' (III.ii.22). Mab's linguistic carriage, much like Lévi-Strauss's 'bricole', displaces the signifier into neighbouring paronyms, thus challenging the sense of place.[36] Mab conveys a wagonload of hybrid meanings which operate as a loose body of mobile and muffled elements. The 'good carriage' (I.iv.93) of proper social behaviour is shown to rest on the sport and disport of Mab's 'chariot' (line 78) or 'charivari', close to the spirit of carnival, though the revel occurs regardless of the tabular space of the calendar.

Juliet's name, read along such mobile, paronomastic lines, escapes its textual, logical, logos-bound affinities with the month of July and its solar imagery. The name enters a process of formal declension as 'Jule', a paronym or nickname which provides shakier lexical ground. The nurse's insistance on shaky matters in her description of Juliet's weening in Act I – ''Tis since *the earthquake* now eleven years . . . *Shake*! quoth the dove-house' – places or misplaces Juliet in close lateral connection to the character of Julius Caesar, a man of many 'seizures', whom Shakespeare chose to present as mobile, full of 'women's matters ' – *mobled* in the three senses of the word.

The names of both Juliet and Julius roam rather far from the orthogonal space of the calendar into the wilder regions of etymology. Juliet's name easily bifurcates from July to *youlos* (meaning, to quote Littré again 'curly, crisped, fleecy'), into the kinkier space of the coil, the deviation from the straight path. The same deviation is apparent in Mab's mischievous hair-curling, plaiting 'the manes of horses' and baking 'the elf-locks in foul sluttish hairs'. A sheep, in Elizabethan English, was another word for a prostitute – one straying from the right way. Juliet's secret, 'muffled' marriage places her in the mobile space of prostitution, violation and volatility, thus turning her into another *mobled*, or *Mab-led* figure in the corpus.

A number of signifiers in Mercutio's mercurial speech follow the same mobile logic. Words such as *traces, web, collars, whip* and *lash* operate both ways, as elements of discourse as well as dis/course (or figure, to borrow Lyotard's term). While 'collars' (I.iv.63) points backward, to the play's initial word-play on *collar/choler/collier/coal*, the mobile chaos out of which the text is generated, words such as 'traces' and 'lash' (lines 62, 64) shift ground. A trace is a strap, a harnessing element, but the word can tip over to its opposite meaning: trash, refuse, or riffraff – in the vicinity of an old French verb *tracier*, to hold on a leash.[37] Leash occurs in the speech in the form of 'lash' (line 64) which means a whip or constraining contraption but also its opposite, as in French 'laisser', to let go. Mab's own web is not so much made as unmade in the process, untangled and interrupted before its proper rhetorical ending – proper only if the speech is conceived of as text. As a spinning process, rather than a text, Mab's speech belongs with on-going, open-ended productions rather than closed artefacts. It reads as a curl, coiling or folding upon itself in several instances, which textual criticism identifies (rightly so, but still missing the point and the fabric) as cases of 'mislineation' or unwelcome repetitions. The outlines of Mab's progress over knees, fingers, noses and necks, delineate a fractural topography, a succession of fault lines, open throats and 'breaches'. The web breaks up before completion, to form a discourse that reads as a parody of onanist intercourse between Romeo and Mercutio.

When juxtaposed to a contemporary and thematically similar text by Michael Drayton, the mobile quality of Shakespeare's writing emerges clearly. In Drayton's poem, written in rhyming verse rather than in Shakespeare's poetic, but prose-like medium, every signifier is geared to what could be called a stable textuality:

> Her chariot of a snayles fine shell,
> Which for the colours did excell:
> The fair Queene Mab, becomming well,
> So lively was the limming:
> The seate the soft wooll of the bee;
> The cover (gallantly to see)
> The wing of a pyde butterflee
> I trowe t'was simple trimming.[38]

The slow snail has replaced the nimble gnat; the chariot is seen as a noble product of limning rather than spinning, and the resulting machine is shown equipped with 'seat' and 'cover', two elements of stability and protection. The underworld of the Mercurial fairy has metamorphosed into the world of the gallant, the excellent and the 'fair', in a judgemental, moralizing mode.

Shakespeare's 'midwife' reads, laterally, as 'mid-wife', i.e. as the woman-in-the middle rather than literally, as the assistant at childbirth. Such a *being-in-the-middle* calls for no feminist or post-feminist agenda, but for a revision of sexuality along mobile lines. Like the Mercurial god of borders – possibly Welsh borders – Mab voices her liminal status in textual as well as sexual matters, to the effect that both text and sex become misnomers for the organization of desire. As dreams drift into drums, Mab shifts into a mob of gender-free signifiers: 'Spanish blades' and 'healths five fathom deep' (I.iv.84–85) open up a mobile map of hetero- as well as homosexual desire. Rather than luxuriance and fertility, however, Mercutio's speech promotes (with the help of Romeo's 'breaking in') luxation, miscarriage, displacement.

The *mobled* fairy does not belong, however, with the Freudian *lapsus*, as Lyotard opines. Mab – and the *mobled queen* – designate the space of the *overlap* rather than the place of the lack, or of the fall. Mab's overlapping 'mad' logic is also to be found in a celebrated, contemporary text by the author of the *Discourse on Method*. The fairy and the philosopher, once reread, share the same madness in the method.

The fairy and the philosopher: madness, the *method* and manholes

Though fairy-lore is anathema to Cartesian studies, Mab's eardrumming operates in a way similar to Descartes' concept of 'entendement' (in the double sense of understanding and hearing), a word plagued with rival, lateral meanings. While 'entendre' is used by Descartes to refer to rational understanding or method, it is contaminated with tympanic effects linking the word to hearing and eardrumming – forms of madness or 'ma/b/ness'

Mab's 'team of little atomi' operate in a way quite similar to the 'airy spirits' or the 'subtle wind' Descartes refers to in many instances – a phrase he imports from Thomism and classical physiology. The philosopher is at pains to invest the phrase with a novel meaning, to sever it from its pre-modern origins. His *Treatise on Man* uses the phrase in what seems an entirely new context. Descartes' new cognitive model of 'entendement', where man is shown to operate along mechanic lines, can be shown to retain distant echoes and eardrumming effects, where what is repressed and eliminated comes back, Mab-wise, with a vengeance.[39] The following text, published in 1633 but written in 1610, treats the subject of motion in such a way as to distinguish it from premodern mutability:

> The parts of the blood which penetrate as far as the brain serve not only to nourish and sustain its substance, but also and primarily to produce in it *a certain very fine wind*, or rather a very lively and pure flame, which is called the *animal spirits* . . .
>
> Now in the same proportion as the animal spirits enter the cavities of the brain, they pass from here into the pores of its substance, and from these pores into the nerves. And depending on the varying amounts which enter (or merely tend to enter) some nerves more than others, the spirits have the power to change the shape of the muscles in which the nerves are embedded, and by this means to move all the limbs. Similarly you may have observed in the grottoes and the fountains in the royal gardens that the mere force with which the water is driven as it emerges from its source is sufficient to move various machines, and even to make them play certain instruments or utter certain words depending on the various arrangements of the pipes through which the water is conducted.[40]

Descartes' 'very fine wind' ('un certain vent très subtil'), or fire, is rewritten in the next paragraph as a liquid metaphor – a colder, clearer medium through which the philosopher describes the operations of a mechanistic body. The mobile or *mobled* element, the restless 'animal spirits' are rephrased as a pattern of disimpassioned pores and pipes, where the baroque aesthetics of 'grottoes and the fountains in the royal gardens' are relegated to a subservient, metaphorical function.

Descartes' *Treatise on Man*, however, is never far from reading as a *Treatise on Mab*. Mobility returns in the metaphorical web of the philosopher's description of motion. A number of figural elements create minor ebbing disturbances in the controlled conduits of Cartesian motion, such as Descartes' use of the word 'regard', a word which disrupts the rationality of what he calls 'entendement'. This becomes apparent in the following paragraph, where 'regard' in its technical sense is mistranslated as 'tank', instead of as *manhole*:

> Indeed, one may compare the nerves of the machines I am describing with the pipes in the works of these fountains, its muscles and tendons with the various devices and springs which serve to set them in motion, its animal spirits with the water which drives them, the heart with the source of the water, and the cavities of the brain with the storage tanks . . . External objects, which by their mere presence stimulate its sense organs and thereby cause them to move in many different ways depending on how the parts of its brain are disposed, are like visitors who enter the grottoes of these fountains and unwittingly cause the movements which take place before their eyes. For they cannot enter without stepping on certain tiles which are so arranged that if, for example, they approach a Diana who is bathing they will cause a Neptune to advance and threaten them with his trident; or if they go in another direction they will cause a sea-monster to emerge and spew water onto their faces; or other such things according to the whim of the engineers who made the fountains. And finally, when a rational soul is present in this machine it will have its principal seat in the brain, and reside there like *the fountain-keeper who must be stationed at the tanks* [manholes] to which the fountain's pipes return if he wants to produce, or prevent, or change their movements in some way.[41]

Though the baroque space of Descartes' garden seems once more rewrought into a complex network of pumps and waterpipes, with Diana symptomatically shoved out of the scene and made to hide in the bushes, a number of ob-scene, oblique, lateral elements or 'figures' perturb the philosophical 'discourse'. Descartes systematically returns or repairs to the baroque, mobile space of the garden, where the 'regard' in its technical sense of manhole is contaminated by its other, lateral, homo-phonic and theatrical equivalent – 'le regard', the gaze. There, in the space of the garden, water breaks free from its controlled, circuitous paths, to gush forth with some violence at the face of the reader or visitor. A threatening Neptune steps forth, then a spewing sea-monster, much in the way in which a number of 'floating' signifiers emerge in the philosophical discourse and threaten the safety of its lexical boundaries. Antanaclasis – *regard/gaze* and *regard/manhole*, a form of perfect paronomasia – perturbs the operations of the 'nerves of the machines'. Descartes' attempt to replace the 'regard' of individual vision or eyesight by the 'regard' of centralized supervision only partially succeeds. The fairy, airy spirit of mobility returns, with its displaced, deviant train of thought: 'manhole' redirects the reading towards the space of the Mercurial, cross-gender body, via the French homophones. Mobility re-emerges in Descartes' labile syntax, where a subject in the singular incorrectly rules a plurality of objects – a single 'fountain-keeper', who must be stationed at several 'tanks/manholes'. The return of the plural, the 'mob', perturbs the philosopher's attempt to establish the rule of the modern logos. Whatever is repressed or 'refoulé' returns in the 'press', in the twofold sense of the crowd, the mob (la foule) as well as the printed text. Mab, to return to Shakespeare, is 'the hag . . . / That *presses* them' (I.iv.92–93) in more than one way.

Notes

1 P. B. Shelley, *Poetical Works*, ed. Thomas Hutchinson (Oxford: Oxford University Press, 1990), pp. 762–835.

2 Clifford Leech, 'The Moral Tragedy of Romeo and Juliet', reprinted in Joseph A. Porter (ed.), *Critical Essays on Shakespeare's Romeo and Juliet* (New York: G. K. Hall & Co., 1997), pp. 5–22.

3 *Ibid.*, p. 21.

4 E. Pearlman, 'Shakespeare at Work: *Romeo and Juliet* ', reprinted in Porter (ed.), *Critical Essays*, pp. 107–130 (p. 127).

5 Donald W. Foster, 'The Webbing of *Romeo and Juliet*', in Porter (ed.), *Critical Essays*, pp. 131–149.

6 *Ibid.*, p. 141. See Joan Ozark Holmer, 'No "Vain fantasy": Shakespeare's Refashioning of Nashe for Dreams and Queen Mab', in Jay L. Halio (ed.), *Shakespeare's Romeo and Juliet* (Newark: University of Delaware Press, 1995), pp. 49–82. Foster refers to fol. V and V2 and L1 of 'The Parlement of Pratlers', in *Ortho-Epia Gallica* (1593). My quotations are from: John Eliot, *Ortho-Epia Gallica, Eliots Fruit For The French*, reprint (Menston: The Scholar Press Limited, 1968).

7 Foster moves on from Eliot to the propitiously named John Webster, *The Devils Law-case*, in John Webster, *The Complete Works*, ed. F. L. Lucas (New York: Gordian, 1966), vol. 2, pp. 104–106.

8 Compare Robert O. Evans, *The Osier Cage* (Lexington: University of Kentucky Press, 1966), pp. 69–86. Evans argues that the speech is replete with rhetorical figures, but the analysis seems to collapse with the statement that 'the entire speech is a rhetorical figure'. A number of intuitive remarks, however, deserve attention, including the citational title of the book, 'The osier cage', a phrase used by Friar Laurence to refer to his basket (II.ii.7) woven in a way not unlike the wickerwork of Mab's speech.

9 Jean-François Lyotard, *Discours, Figure* (Paris: Editions Klincksieck, 1971), p. 71. The translations and the emphasis are mine. A figure 'is capable of crossing the partition which severs the intelligible word from the world of the senses'.

10 Henry Peacham, *The Garden of Eloquence*, 1593, facsimile reprint with an introduction by William G. Crane (Gainesville: Scholars Facsimiles and Reprints, 1954), p. 56. My emphasis.

11 George Puttenham, *The Arte of English Poesie*, ed. Gladys D. Willcock and Alice Walker (Cambridge: Cambridge University Press, 1936), p. 202. My emphasis.

12 All quotations are from the text in *The Norton Shakespeare*, ed. Stephen Greenblatt, Walter Cohen *et al.* (London and New York: W. W. Norton and Co.), pp. 865–941.

13 Jane McIntosh Snyder, *Puns and Poetry in Lucretius' De Rerum Natura* (Amsterdam: B. R. Grüner Publishing Co., 1980), pp. 62–65.

14 *Ibid.*, p. 95.

15 *Ibid.*, p. 100.

16 *Ibid.*, p. 38.

17 'The Epistle to the French Teachers', Eliot, *Ortho-Epia Gallica*, fol. A4. The list goes on a page or so. Eliot then invites the reader to find fault with his '*pricks, nicks and tricks*' and prove them '*not worth a pin, not a point, not a pish*'. Many more examples could be quoted.

18 'Rules for French Pronunciation', *ibid.*, fol. C.

19 See Philippa Berry's study of the air/ear/heir connection in 'Hamlet's Ear', *Shakespeare Survey, 50: Shakespeare and Language*, ed. Stanley Wells (Cambridge: Cambridge University Press, 1997), pp. 57–64. See also M. D. Garnier-Giamarchi, 'Splitting Heirs: Shakespeare's Tempest and Leibnizian Folds', in C. Perault (ed.), *Shakespeare, La Tempête: Etudes critiques* (Besançon, Presses de l'Université de Franche Comté, 1994), pp. 161–168.

20 Quoted by Berry in 'Hamlet's Ear'. She bases Hamlet's relationship to air, among other elements, on examples of Renaissance iconography where Mercury is depicted as *Mercurius Ver*, which she reads, laterally, as another form of *ver* (worm) and *vers* (verse). See also the analysis of Botticelli's *Primavera*, in Charles Dempsey, *The Portrayal of Love: Botticelli's 'Primavera' and Humanist Culture at the Time of Lorenzo the Magnificent* (Princeton: Princeton University Press, 1992), p. 40.

21 Lucretius, *On the Nature of the Universe*, trans. R. E. Latham (Harmondsworth: Penguin Books, 1994), p. 44.

22 Snyder, *Puns and Poetry*, p. 45.

23 On 'materializing the word' see Margaret W. Ferguson, '*Hamlet*: Letters and Spirits', in Patricia Parker and Geoffrey Hartman (eds), *Shakespeare and the Question of Theory* (New York and London: Methuen, 1985), pp. 292–309. My reading differs slightly, the mobled queen and Mab owing less to the mat(t)erial than to the concept of mobility.

24 G. Blakemore Evans, *Romeo and Juliet* (Cambridge: Cambridge University Press, 1984), p. 21. Evans's claim that 'his set-piece on Mab' is 'a brilliant tour de force of doubtful dramatic or thematic relevance' provides no clue, however, as to where the 'tour' and the 'force' lie.

25 Lyotard, *Discours, Figure*, p. 387.

26 Gilles Deleuze and Félix Guattari, *A Thousand Plateaus*, trans. Brian Massumi, (Minneapolis: University of Minnesota Press, 1987), pp. 26–38. See especially their reading of Freud and the Wolf-Man: 'Freud tried to approach crowd phenomena from the point of view of the unconscious, but he did not see clearly, he did not see that the unconscious itself was fundamentally a crowd', p. 29. A crowd, to suit my purpose, is a mob.

27 Lyotard, *Discours Figure*, p. 51.

28 Jonathan Culler, 'The Call of the Phoneme: Introduction', in Jonathan Culler (ed.), *On Puns: The Foundation of Letters* (Ithaca: Basil Blackwell, 1988), pp. 1–16 (p. 3).

29 Evans, *The Osier Cage*, pp. 69–86.

30 See Harry Berger, 'Hydra and Rhizome', in Russ Mc Donald (ed.), *Shakespeare Reread* (Ithaca: Cornell University Press, 1994), p. 89.

31 According to Jeffrey Gantz, editor of *The Mabinogion* (Harmonsworth: Penguin Books, 1976), the word *mab* remains an obscure term. He quotes Lady Charlotte Guest, who first translated the book of tales into English in 1849 and who based her translation of the title on the idea that 'mabinogi' was a word meaning 'a story for children' and that *mabinogion* was the plural of the word, when in fact, says Gantz, the word does not exist in Welsh (p. 31). He also mentions *Mabon*, from the Celtic form Maponos, 'Great Son' (p. 17).

32 Jacques Derrida, *Margins of Philosophy*, trans. Alan Bass (Chicago: University of Chicago Press, 1982).

33 *Ibid.*, pp. xiv–xv.

34 *Mobled* may mean muffled. Mercutio when giving the Mab speech characteristically wears the mask of a beetle (I.iv.32).

35 Lyotard, *Discours Figure*, p. 386. My translation. Lyotard's use of 'se dérobe' [disrobe] to translate 'muffled' is interesting. The French verb weaves two opposed meanings: to hide oneself, and to remove a layer of clothing – the verb itself is a case of semantic mobility.

36 Lévi-Strauss's use of 'bricolage' is based on the word's association with extraneous, deviant movement: 'In its old sense, the verb *bricoler* is used for ball-games and billiards, hunting and riding, but always in order to describe an extraneous mouvement: a ball bouncing, a dog darting off, a horse swerving from the straight line to avoid an obstacle'. Claude Lévi-Strauss, *La Pensée sauvage* (Paris: Plon, 1962), p. 26, as translated in Walter Redfern, *On Puns* (Oxford: Basil Blackwell, 1984), p. 34.

37 See Ann Lecercle's reading of 'trash' and 'trace' in *The Tempest*: 'Trash dans La Tempête', in C. Perault (ed.), *Shakespeare*, La Tempête, pp. 169–184.

38 Michael Drayton, 'Nymphidia, the Court of Fayrie', in *Poems of Michael Drayton*, ed. John Buxton, 2 vols (London: Routledge and Kegan Paul, 1953), I, pp. 179–200 (lines 137–144). The date of composition, though uncertain, is probably posterior to *A Midsummer Night's Dream*.

39 See also Pierre-Alain Cahné, *Un autre Descartes: le philosophe et son langage* (Paris: 1980). Cahné shows that Descartes' writing is largely based on metaphors, and that scientific 'truth' needs to be historicized.

40 René Descartes, A *Treatise on Man*, in *The Philosophical Writings of Descartes*, trans John Cottingham *et al.*, 3 vols (Cambridge: Cambridge University Press, 1985), I, pp. 100–101. Here is the French version: 'Pour ce qui est des parties du sang qui pénètrent jusqu'au cerveau, elles n'y servent pas seulement à nourrir et entretenir sa substance, mais principalement aussi à y produire un certain vent très subtil, ou plutôt une flamme très vive et très pure, qu'on nomme les *Esprits animaux* ... Or, à mesure que ces esprits entrent ainsi dans les concavités du cerveau, ils passent de là dans les pores de sa substance, et de ces pores dans les nerfs, où selon qu'ils entrent, ou même seulement qu'ils tendent à entrer, plus ou moins dans les uns que dans les autres, ils ont la force de changer la figure des muscles en qui ces nerfs sont insérés, et par ce moyen de faire se mouvoir tous ses membres. Ainsi que vous pouvez avoir vu, dans les grottes et les fontaines qui sont aux jardins de nos rois, que la seule force dont l'eau se meut, en sortant de sa source, est suffisante pour y mouvoir diverses machines, et même pour les y faire jouer de quelques instruments, ou prononcer quelques paroles, selon la diverse disposition des tuyaux qui la conduisent.' René Descartes, *Traité de l'Homme*, in *Discours de la Méthode*, suivi d'Extraits de *La Dioptrique, des Météores, de la Vie de Descartes par Baillet, du Monde, de l'Homme, et de Lettres* (Paris: Garnier-Flammarion, 1966), pp. 242–244.

41 Descartes, *Treatise on Man*, p. 101. The original runs: 'Et véritablement l'on peut bien comparer les nerfs de la machine que je vous décris aux tuyaux des machines de ces fontaines; ses muscles et ses tendons, aux autres divers engins et ressorts qui servent à les mouvoir; ses esprits animaux à l'eau qui les remue, dont le cœur est la source, et les concavités du cerveau sont les regards ... Les objects extérieurs, qui par leur seule présence agisseent contre les organes de ses sens, ... causent eux-mêmes sans y penser les mouvements qui s'y font en leur présence: car ils n'y peuvent entrer qu'en marchant sur certains carreaux tellement disposés que, par exemple, s'ils s'approchent d'une Diane qui se baigne, ils la feront cacher dans les roseaux ... ; s'ils vont de quelque autre côté, ils en feront sortir un monstre marin qui leur vomira de l'eau contre la face ... Et enfin quand l'âme raisonnable sera en cette machine, elle y aura son siège principal dans le cerveau, et sera là comme le fontenier, qui doit être dans les regards où vont se rendre tous les tuyaux de la machine, quand il veut exciter, ou empêcher, ou changer en quelque façon leur mouvement' (Descartes, *Traité de l'Homme*, p. 244).

8

Covenant, coven, charm, *carmen*:
beyond the word–image opposition

ANN LECERCLE

The most innovative art historian in France today, Georges Didi-Huberman,[1] works on the following hypothesis:

> Beyond its recognizable history, story, *istoria*,[2] a painting knows how to be a field of possibilities [*sait être un champ de possibilités*]. What it is important to perceive here is the labyrinth into which a simple painting is capable of precipitating [*secouer*] us.[3]

This is the knowledge I wish to foreground in suggesting ways in which seeing in early modern Europe was placed under the sign of what the historian Pierre Chaunu has called the non-gesture:

> Protestant Europe posits the sacred value of the non-gesture [*non-geste*] . . .
> Hence, for the French protestant and for the puritan, the refusal of the sign of the cross, for the quaker, the refusal to salute even the King. One's hat is removed only before the Eternal. For the Anabaptists, the refusal to bear arms. Hence the gesture in the negative [*en creux*], a gestuary of the non-gesture.[4]

More particularly, in early modern England, the gesture of opening one's eyes and looking, minimal though it might seem in terms of gesture, and, beyond it, the scopic drive, Freud's *Schaulust*, are both endowed with an exceptionally high profile by the violent and renewed outbreaks of iconoclasm that lasted over a longer period in England than elsewhere on the continent.[5] Thus, of the art of the period, Ernest B. Gilman writes, in a passage that will serve as the dramatic backcloth to my argument also, before I finally come back to the drama proper of the Elizabethan theatre:

> For more than a century, from the time of the Henrician reforms of the 1530s to the Restoration in 1660, religious paintings, statues, rood

screens, and stained glass all over England fell to successive waves of iconoclastic zeal. During those same years, Protestant enemies of idolatry filled thousands of pages with arguments against the abuse of 'images' in devotion while their opponents . . . filled thousands more in reply . . .

. . . both the phenomenon of iconoclasm itself and the body of controversy it provoked are sharply etched in the literature of the period – indeed they are a crucial dilemma for the literary imagination of the sixteenth and seventeenth centuries.[6]

Gilman's formulation, it seems to me, is unnecessarily restrictive: his point holds true not only for the literature of the day but for much, if not all, representational art produced in such a context. With the revival of the biblical interdict dramatically inscribed in pride of place in their mental outlook, there ensues a heightening of acuity in the consciousness with which the gaze as gesture is both represented in artefact and experienced by audience. Interdiction not only highlights but whets the edge of desire, a desire which was a powerful spur in sending the English into the theatres wherever these were available.

In the context of the visual arts with which I am concerned here, the curtailing or cutting off of gesture adumbrated by Chaunu finds its correlate in a cutting out, a reserve, of the order of what Georges Bataille famously called *la part maudite* or 'accursed part',[7] invested by the sacred and requiring a particular strategy of the gaze, a gaze schooled in the knowledge that, in Aby Warburg's phrase, *'Der liebe Gott steckt im Detail'*: the good Lord is to be found (concealed) in the detail.[8] In the last analysis, cur-tailing and de-tailing are the two complementary faces of one logic: that of castration, foregrounded, as has been suggested, with rare drama in early modern visual culture by the spectre, or the spectacle, of iconoclasm.

In pursuing this line of investigation, it will be useful first to recall the founding scenario of the biblical – the Mosaic – *part maudite*, which ends with Moses himself in the role of 'accursed part', a turnabout which paradigmatically enshrines the logic of radical reversal attaching to such cut-off parts in Lacan's account of the fantasy. I shall then look at two late Renaissance works of art where castration is central, and in more ways than one.[9] Both works are egregious examples of the knowledge Didi-Hubermann posits in the painting: in both, the inscription of castration is present not only in the object represented but in the regarding subject, in the cognitive process suscitated by the work, one which necessitates a veritable scotomization of the image, of which Hans Holbein the Younger's famous double portrait known as *The*

Ambassadors[10] is only the most dramatic and flamboyant example. Indeed, in the case of the second work I want to look at, a distinguished piece of Elizabethan sculpture, the scotomization of the image has been taken to the extreme of misrecognition or censorship by authorized discourse of what is actually being represented. More generally, the logic these works embody throws light on the age's drama when it comes to representing the senses as processes of cognition.

Covenant and coven: the scene on Sinai and the debt

To begin at the beginning: there would seem to be two founding texts in the field of vision for Renaissance literature. One takes place in the leafy depths of the Garden of Eden under the boughs of the fateful tree, where Eve espied the apple. This is not the one pertinent to our theme here. The other, which is, takes place high on Sinai: this is the theatre where is enacted the primal scene of *not* seeing that surrounds and veritably embeds Moses' 'covenant' with his people, otherwise known as the Ten Commandments.

Those of us who are neither biblical scholars nor zealots tend to underestimate the degree to which the Ten Commandments are an isle set in a sulphurous sea of vision. The actual text of the 'covenant' is preceded by a long chapter (Deuteronomy 4) which, in contradistinction to Eve's reaction to the apple, insists on what is *not* seen:

> 11. And ye came near and stood under the mountain; and the mountain burned with fire unto the midst of heaven, with darkness, clouds and thick darkness.
>
> 12. And the Lord spake unto you out of the midst of the fire: ye heard the voice of the words, but saw no similitude; only ye heard a voice.
>
> 13. And he declared unto you his covenant, which he commanded you to perform, even ten commandments; and wrote them upon tables of stone. . . .
>
> 15. Take ye good heed unto yourselves; for ye saw no manner of similitude on the day that the Lord spake unto you in Horeb out of the midst of the fire:
>
> 16. Lest ye corrupt yourselves, and make you a graven image, the similitude of any figure, the likeness of male or female
>
> 17. The likeness of any beast that is on the earth, the likeness of any winged fowl that flieth in the air,
>
> 18. The likeness of anything that creepeth on the ground, the likeness of any fish that is in the waters beneath the earth.[11]

These injunctions are repeated with an almost numbing obsessiveness which eventually throws up the 'covenant' itself[12] in the list of the Ten Commandments.

What one tends to forget even more, however, is the revelation made by Moses half-way through the litany of Deuteronomy 4: '22. But I must die in this land, I must not go over Jordan, but ye shall go over, and possess that good land.' In other words, Moses himself, and he alone, will *not* see Israel. The act of foundation, of which he himself is the agent, comprises a debt. To come into being, empowerment requires, indeed is posited upon, disempowerment. Paradox is not only the hall-mark of tragedy, it is the birthmark of nations, at least in the Bible.

More importantly, it is the payment of this debt that prevents the covenant from crossing the knife-edge of distinction and becoming a coven, with which 'covenant' is cognate, the coven representing the reverse side of the religious coin in the mental universe of early modern Europe. What after all is a 'coven'? As the *Oxford English Dictionary* indicates, a coven is a convent of witches; it further indicates the composition as being thirteen in number, i.e. 12 + 1. It is this one that has to be lopped off. This is the symbolic debt that Moses pays to an empowerment that purports to be and presents itself as transcendental. This is what Mauss and Hubert, in their classic study of symbolic empowerment call the debt, a gift that no 'counter-gift' (*contre-don*) can reciprocate, let alone efface.[13] In other words, empowerment is predicated upon castration, which in extreme or paradigmatic cases can go as far as death.

I want now to explore how such 'cur-tailing' creeps its way into pictorial art, where, though 'cabin'd' in corners, its import is not, in Shakespeare's words, 'cribb'd' or 'confin'd' therein. Sacrality is precisely of this order, proceeding, as it does, from the act of separation, by cutting off. In this light, the corner always has something of the sanctuary.

Falcon and falchion: drapes and folds

In the collection of Renaissance works of art belonging to Count Cini (in the Palazzo Cini in Venice), one can see a late Renaissance painting by Ludovico Mazzolino[14] entitled simply *The Circumcision* (*La Circoncisione*) (reproduced here). It is, I suggest, a Renaissance allegory of the same logic of representation as that adumbrated above, but this time in the domain of vision.

The Circumcision is conceived at a point in time which, with the dissemination of printed matter, is characterized by Francis Barker as

Ludovico Mazzolino, *La Circonsione*

the 'historical transition from sight to script as the medium of political facility and encratic difficulty'; his following sentence goes veritably to the heart of the matter addressed by Mazzolino's depiction of *The Circumcision*. For Barker continues: 'that the efficient reader is also a *male castrator* no doubt recounts a corporeal history of its own'.[15] This 'corporeal history' is precisely the history that furnishes the problematic of Mazzolino's painting, which from the outset places the work under the sign of the Mosaic covenant: Moses bearing the twin tablets on Sinai is depicted in a roundel in bas-relief sculpted at the centre of the entablature above the portico before which rabbinical law is about to be enacted on the person – on the penis – of the Infant Jesus.

Mazzolino's painting is small and square in format, and classic in composition:[16] the centrepiece of the scene, the impending ritual, is to take place at the apex of a regular triangle whose base is somewhat above the lower edge of the painting; here, the innocent babe in arms about to be operated on and rightly appalled at his imminent fate, indeed bawling, is held in patriarchal arms with the instrumental blade suspended above him in the chief rabbi's hand.[17] The central characters are richly dressed, disposed on either side of the triangle which recedes into the centre of the work. Three of them, those most closely involved in the ritual, are more ostentatiously clad than the rest: each wears a magnificent badge of what appear to be large pearls, 'unions' in the parlance of the period, so that this triangle of jewelled clasps not only echoes the perspectival triangle of human figures grouped about the Infant Jesus but frames the sacred babe in the confines of the formal figure of the trinity. One member of these central triumvirate figures is the officiating rabbi, on the right of the triangle; the other two, patriarchal dignitaries of the synagogue, constitute the other side and the apex of the triangle. We notice also that the curve of the impending blade on the right is a perfect fit with the rim of the ewer on the left.

This triangle is prolonged out towards the sides by two further dignitaries. These two are armed not with the blade brandished in the background but with that other cutting edge, that other instrument of separation: the letter of the Law. That is to say, in this case, both are consulting volumes of written text with earnest scrutiny; of the dominant group, they alone are not observing the central tableau.[18] What they are occupied in observing is the Word of God.

The overall effect of both the work as object and of its internal composition is of neatness and orderliness; the internal organization is clear-cut and hieratic, immediately legible. The painting seems deliberately to eschew any attempt at originality or virtuosity. In fact, what it does do is to replicate in these unexceptionable qualities the characteristics soon to be imprinted on the infant's penis: a hopefully neat and clear-cut line which is the seal of the Law in the flesh, the emblem of integration into the social order, but first and foremost into the linguistic order canonized in the engraved tables given to Moses on the Mount enshrined in the white marble of the roundel suspended over the scene.

The structural equilibrium of Mazzolino's painting, the semantic coherence of the work and the neat symmetry of detail (e.g. the three sets of pearls underlinging the global *dispositio*), all this goes to make up, indeed it defines, what Barthes would have called the *studium*.[19] In contradistinction to the latter, piercing its overplacid, not to say complacent unity, indeed unicity,[20] is what Barthes termed the *punctum*. This is the dissymmetrical element in the ensemble, the one that upsets the balanced apple cart of symmetry and sense, so as to decentre our attention, revive a flagging or faint interest or initiate a reappraisal of what might otherwise remain bland, setting our involvement along a new tack.

Mazzolino is an artist of the Ferrara school, and his work, aesthetically, seems to bridge a north–south divide (it usually contains groups of smaller figures set against villages and houses reminiscent of contemporary northern European painting with figures on horseback wandering amidst woods and tumbling brooks with watermills). Reindert Falkenberg[21] has interpreted such 'inserts' in terms of what he calls *Simultanbilder* (simultaneous images) or *Erziehungsbilder* (instructive images). For Falkenberg the technique required to interpret these works is based on the principle that 'the inconspicuous is the key to the full understanding of the work'.[22] Barthes's concept is a resurrection, unspoken if not perhaps unwitting, of this principle.

In Mazzolino's *Circumcision*, as far removed from the centre of the scene as is spatially possible, in the front right-hand corner, there is a detail portrayed with the naturalism of a Douanier Rousseau, very different from the relative blandness and unremarkability elsewhere in the painting. The object depicted is a pair of spectacles, executed with preternatural precision of line, perched on the nose of the temple elder down on the extreme right, who is reading, or rather scrutinizing, the tomes of rabbinic dispensation. It is the only such detail in the work, which elsewhere confines itself to a harmonious grouping of conventional visages and vestments. Initially Mazzolino's spectacles conform to the same logic as Barthes's *punctum*: in both cases a partial object or body part is isolated and highlighted. It is true of course that one may need glasses to read; it is equally true that spectacles were of recent invention and the object of interest, even wonder. However, the bespectacled character is a vignette unto himself, the only foregrounded character in something approaching a realistic style, which goes along with wholly *un*adorned vestments. And what strikes me is that this plainness of apparel permits the highlighting of a detail which is an essential part of the meaning of the whole. This detail is the half-circle of white drapes around the fleshy neck and bowed head, buried, bespectacled, in the Book. These drapes are precisely complemented by what is presumably a white swaddling cloth at the centre of the painting. This swirl of white cloth, under the baby's bottom and up his groin, is to be read, I suggest, as a displaced continuation of the bespectacled reader's neckcloth. This second central swirl of white cloth circumscribes the 'anatomy theatre', so to speak, where the circumcision is about to be performed.

The circle thus constituted by these two complementary semicircles brings together two representations rarely juxtaposed: to the inscription on the penis of the law of the Fathers, Mazzolino adds a supplement that addresses the eye. To the orthodoxy of the law concerning both generation (the incest taboo separating generations) and gender (the male alone is concerned by circumcision) is added the orthopaedia of vision, confining it to the straight and narrow path which is here represented in its paradigmatic form: the Book, the written text of the Law, the assimilation and respect of which the naturalistic spectacles are here designed to accommodate. The spectacles poised on the elder's nose emblematically inscribe vision with the Law, just as, in the *studium*, the blade poised over the babe's penis inscribes sexuality with the Law. Since it is in the nature of things that babes in arms do not wear spectacles, the latter have been attributed to the uncannily well-named 'elder' who represents a later stage of the babe's development and is nearer to us who behold him – nearer both in age and pictorial space. For the bespectacled character is noticeably younger than the imposingly bearded triumvirate officiating at the centre of the canvas.

This is not all. For the swaddling cloth of the Infant Jesus and the neckcloth of Bespectacled Man are the only two parts of the canvas addressed so far where we see a uniquely and conspicuously folded surface, a *plissé*, both of them white. In fact, however, there is a third region of white *plissé* directly opposite Bespectacled Man. Together with the neckcloth and swaddling cloth, this third region of white *plissé* inscribes a new triangle, slightly below and parallel to the main triangle of bald heads and jewelled clasps that constitutes the principal *ligne de force* of the composition. The *plissé* this time is not the softly curving swathe of folds previously encountered. Above all, the representation in question gives the strange impression of being enigmatically related, even unattached, to the torsos of any of the darkly clad figures of whom it might appear to constitute a plausible appendage. The effect is weird, and it is highlighted by the purest white of the entire canvas, from which this *plissé* emerges, tighter and straighter than elsewhere. I suggest here that we first remember the recommendation of Alberti, that the place of the sacred, the place of a *jouissance* forbidden to Man be depicted in visual art by the colour white – which was also, in Protestant lands, the white of whitewash – and not, as hitherto, by the application of gold leaf.

I suggest moreover that we turn for a moment to one of the most famous, not to say notorious, examples of such a form in Renaissance art, which is also white. I am thinking of the only subject which Titian painted no fewer than three times, and a favourite amongst sexually titillating *epyllia* of the period: *Tarquin and Lucrece*. One of Titian's versions belonged to Arundel, the great seventeenth-century art collector, and then passed into the collection of Charles I,[23] now to be seen in the Musée des Beaux-Arts at Bordeaux (and in desperate need of a clean), the second, its sumptuous colours in a better state of repair, hangs in the Fitzwilliam Museum in Cambridge, while the third is in the Akademie der Bildenden Künste in Vienna.[24] The moment Titian, like Mazzolino, chooses to depict is that evoked by Shakespeare in lines 505–511 of *The Rape of Lucrece*, when the blade is poised above the horrified victim whose genital integrity is at stake:

> This said, he shakes aloft his Roman blade,
> Which like a falcon tow'ring in the skies,
> Coucheth the fowl below with his wings'shade,
> Whose crooked beak threats, if he mount he dies:[25]
> So under his insulting falchion lies
> Harmless Lucretia, marking what he tells
> With trembling fear, as fowl hear falcon's bells.[26]

(Notice how the word 'falchion' is framed by the double occurrence, before and after, of 'falcon'.)

Titian's treatment of this moment contains something absent from the Viennese study.[27] In the bottom left-hand foreground in both Mazzolino and Titian we remark the same type of representation. In Titian it appears as a white drape that falls from the bed in preternatural fashion between the naked legs of the lady and the knickerbockered legs of the lord. This is a classic pun, a witty visualization of the invisible phallus – of the erect 'i' that appears in the middle of Shakespeare's 'fal-con': fall-con (cunt). It never does to underestimate the materiality and plasticity capable of investing the minutest part of the picture in such cases.[28]

This is where the parallel between Titian and Mazzolino becomes instructive. For in *The Circumcision*, which is a celebration not of law-less lust but of the Law itself, the tip of this fantomatic form seems to have been lopped off, leaving at the top a neat concave rim. This effect is underlined by two arms that bar the *plissé*: the lower arm points to Bespectacled Man opposite, indeed to the spectacles themselves, while the upper arm contains another book, this time closed, but whose corner points upwards to the frieze in bas-relief, also in white, showing the ghostly Moses brandishing the Tables of the Law. This 'phallic phantom', to borrow a phrase from Lacan,[29] is, I suggest, the Symbolic Phallus, the correlate and creation of circumcision.

I will conclude with a hypothesis which I take from Deleuze's essay on the baroque and Leibniz, called *Le Pli*. My hypothesis concerns the *plissé* in *The Circumcision* which from this point of view anticipates later developments. The trait of the baroque, says Deleuze, is the fold (*le pli*). He then proceeds by distinguishing two orders of fold, and two orders of infinity, 'as if infinity were composed of two storeys [*comme si l'infini avait deux étages*]: the folds of matter, and the folds of/in the soul [*les replis de la matière, et les replis dans l'âme*]'[30]. In *The Circumcision*, the folds of matter are the folds of flesh which embody the corporeal site of *jouissance*; these the temple elder is precisely in the act of exploring so as to wield the knife. This is the first stage/storey and occupies the strategic centre of the composition. The second series, the transcendent folding, is, I suggest, represented by the threefold *plissé* of Albertian, meta-physical white.

But, one may object, the High Renaissance art of Italy is one thing, English, Elizabethan, art quite another, even though, via the influence of France, notably from Francis I onwards, it was not without a certain impact on cultivated English tastes. It is to meet such an objection that I propose now to turn to indigenous artistic creation, and, the better to address the point, to an artist that was, more typically of England, a craftsman rather than an artist in the sense defined by those whose names are immortalized in the annals of the history of European 'high art'. Here too, I believe, we can detect an analogous logic of representation at work.

Charm and *carmen*: the Knole Mermaid frieze

In his youth, the Father of English tragedy, Thomas Sackville (1536–1608), had composed a verse drama in which each section had been conceived with appropriate accompanying music. This was *The Tragedie of Gorboduc* (1565), which paved the way for Shakespeare's compositions in the same genre. But Thomas Sackville turned his back on poetry, preferring a life of politics and rising in rank to end up as Queen Elizabeth's Lord Treasurer. In the process of this upward mobility he came into possession of the noble palace of Knole in Kent,[31] and added to his name the titles of Baron Buckhurst and First Earl of Dorset. The Lord Treasurer was passionately interested in music and filled Knole with its strains, employing his own consort of viol players and lutenists, and his own singers, not only in the chapel and the minstrel's gallery but in the main living hall, now called the Ballroom, where the frieze I want to look at is to be seen. When he died, Sackville made special mention of his musicians for the contentment and solace they afforded him when, weary of work and the world, he would return to Knole and to the healing harmony they dispensed; he also remembered them in the beautifully carved musical instruments that decorate the chimney piece in the same room.[32] Both the frieze (see detail reproduced here) and the

Detail of the frieze from the Ballroom at Knole

musical instruments are the work of the most eminent woodcarver money at the time could buy, the royal Master Carpenter, William Portington, who long served not only Elizabeth but also James. (Under the latter monarch he was responsible notably for realizing the complex stage sets for the court masques.) The official description of the frieze, which we owe to the pen of Oliver Garnett of the National Trust, which now owns Knole, evokes 'this strange world of mermaids and make-believe ... and squatting figures like Sumo wrestlers'.[33] A propos of 'strangeness' what strikes me is that the undoubtedly well-informed author of these lines has eyes but seemingly no sight, let alone vision in the nobler sense of the word.

The frieze, as I said, is complementary to a group of exquisitely carved musical instruments such as one might have expected to find in, or at least on the wall of, any self-respecting Renaissance *studiolo*. But neither is the frieze with the mermaids 'make-believe' nor is the figure on the right any fat and flabby Sumo wrestler. The frieze may be a complement, it may even be an 'elaborate thank you' to Elizabeth – hence the Tudor rose – but it is more, and other, than this. In fact, I would see it as a variant, a lay variant in the domain of hearing, of what Mazzolino's little picture portrays in terms of sight. Above all, perhaps, it is a feminine realization of the same underlying logic of representation.

The disposition is very close to that of *The Circumcision* except that, nature being what it is, here the cornerstone of the Symbolic, the Tudor rose, grows up from the lower edge of the ensemble, where God's original deputy on earth, Moses, surveys the scene from above. Both moreover duly occupy the centre of an overwhelming symmetry (the mermaids), with a leftover, or supplement, depending on which way you look at it, namely the odd male figure – here shown on the right, like Bespectacled Man.

The mermaids hold not their traditional mirrors but a garland, and this above the Tudor rose. Now the garland is not only the conventional emblem of pre-eminence: it is here, I suggest, a composite representation, of the organ of aural fascination, the mouth, whence issues the charming voice and its *carmina*, but at the same time of their sexual charms, for in sixteenth to seventeenth-century slang a 'mermaid', as Garnett rightly points out, signified a lady of charms which were for sale – and not of the musical kind (which was why brothels often advertized themselves using this emblem). If, according to Todorov's principle, the fantastic realizes the literal in the figurative, then this frieze is, amongst other things, a witty *concetto* on the representation of the charm-*carmen*. But it is also much more than that.

The polysemic 'O' so familiar to Elizabethan audiences explains why the little Tudor rose pops so perkily up from the ground, because this way it can thrust its head and slender neck through the 'ring' expectantly awaiting it (note how its leaves point downwards so as to facilitate the passage). To put it bluntly, the complementarity phallicizes the rose, but it does so in the symbolic, and thus, in so doing, castrates the male figure on the right, which embodies, and as it were channels off, the potentially demonic in the charm, for the point is that the 'Sumo wrestler' has cloven hoofs. This is why the flower is discreetly, delicately phallicized – and of course the Queen as we know was not only Virgo but equally, and increasingly, Virago, 'the wonderful old Virago' as A. L. Rowse called her. Thus, in veritable visual counterpoint, the penis is portrayed clamped into a male chastity belt and battened down, for it points vertically downwards to a space between the cloven hoofs. At the same time, this figure sports two round breasts. This is not simply a reworking of Ulysses attached to the ship's mast. Portington was the foremost woodcarver in the land, and his talent went primarily into masque sets themselves orchestrated in terms of counterpoint and symbol.[34]

The ring and the chastity belt are the correlates to the round spectacles and the rabbi's knife in *The Circumcision*. In either case there is, as it were, a hard and a soft version of the same representation. In either case too, there is a discreet undercurrent of the comic. But this is no mere conceit. The thin line of the Knole frieze operates, like the rabbi's knife, along the cutting edge between *carmen* and charm: another name for which is castration.

In the last analysis, what these two images oppose are two types of imprint in the domain of the senses – the imprint inscribed by passion, and that inscribed by castration. The first takes us back to Aristotle, who conceives the mechanism of vision, for instance, rather differently from those who explain it as an emission from eye to object and back. For Aristotle vision is a *zoographema*, an imprint marked as on a receptive, 'passive' wax-block:

> Passion produced by a sensation in the soul and in the part of the body which possesses the sensation is something like a drawing . . . The movement which is produced marks as it were an imprint of the thing perceived, as happens when one apposes a seal with thanks to a seal-ring.[35]

This is the same metaphor used by Freud of the *Bahnungen*, the traces of a lack at the root of 'passion'. What these two images superimpose is in either case the inscription, circumscription, circumcision that is the *other* imprint, that of the Law.

In my introduction I started out from what Pierre Chaunu calls a gestuary of the non-gesture, a curtailing or cutting off of gesture that finds its correlate in a certain reserve, which, in the last analysis, is not unrelated, in the visual arts, to what a French philosopher of language, Jean-Jacques Lecercle, has baptized the remainder (*'le reste)'*.[36] In other words, what I am suggesting is the pertinence of a supplement to the classic model of cognition which is that of analogy, of the system of harmony and proportion of the human body conceived as microcosm, of 'Vitruvian man', perfectly inscribed from his centrepoint in the circle and the square, the image which, in the phrase of Rudolf Wittkower, 'haunted the imagination' of the Renaissance.[37] As Daniel Arasse, the author of the above quotation, points out in the essay it is excerpted from, and as Georges Didi-Huberman develops in his work on the detail, the image has a deviously perverse tendency not to stay put but, far from reflecting any divine dispensation, ultimately to upset the apple cart. Small – the 'micro-' in 'microcosm' – is not only beautiful, as a popular adage would have it, it is also eminently unstable, not to say subversive. One can suggest here two potent early modern instances of this proposition. The first is the definition of a figure that much preoccupied the Renaissance, Antichrist, as the fourth beast of the apocalypse, as the prince 'remarkably small amongst all'.[38] The second is the dramatic instantiation of curtailing that is suspended over Shakespeare's first English tragedy, *Richard III*, who is *'part maudite'* made man, and, for the Elizabethan audience, Antichrist to boot:

> I that am rudely stamp'd and want love's majesty
> To strut before a wanton ambling nymph:
> I, that am curtail'd of this fair proportion,
> Cheated of feature by dissembling Nature,
> Deform'd, unfinish'd, sent before my time
> Into this breathing world scarce half made up –
> And that so lamely and unfashionable
> That dogs bark at me . . . therefore . . .
> I am determined to prove a villain[39]

What is important as an account of early modern knowledge is the ongoing tension between the analogical model and the supplement thus defined.

Notes

1 The originality of his research as art historian is reflected in an evolution which, by French standards, is eminently atypical. Trained as a philosopher and at present a

lecturer at the Ecole des Hautes Etudes en Sciences Sociales in Paris, Georges Didi-Huberman started out by working on the Holy Shroud of Turin, then moved on to the photographic archives of the Mental Hospital at the Salpétrière in Paris on the eve of the historic moment of transition from psychiatry to psychoanalysis, from Charcot to Freud. This produced a book-length study entitled *L'Invention de l'Hystérie: Charcot et l'Iconographie photographique de la Salpétrière* (Paris: Editions Macula, 1982), closely followed by an edition and presentation of Charcot's and Richer's *Les Démoniaques dans l'art* (Paris: Editions Macula, 1984). Between these two volumes, still in the field of such medical *mirabilia* and their representation in visual (and textual) documents, he wrote *Mémorandum de la peste: le fléau d'imaginer* (Paris: Christian Bourgois, 1983). This trilogy evinces a solid grasp and above all a sensitive use of psychoanalytic concepts in the field of iconography. From this he moved on to a ground-breaking study, *La Peinture incarnée* (Paris: Editions de Minuit, 1985), which bridged the gap between psychiatric imagery and pictorial art: inspired by Honoré de Balzac's short story *Le Chef d'oeuvre inconnu*, the theme was the representation of human flesh in painting, and more particularly of what in art goes by the name of 'flesh tints'. Then came a fascinating essay on Fra Angelico (*Fra Angelico: dissemblance et figuration* (Paris: Flammarion, 1990)), and a reappraisal of art history as (scientific?) field of investigation (*Devant l'image: question posée aux fins d'une histoire de l'art* (Paris: Editions de Minuit, 1990)). Most notable amongst his later productions is *Ce que nous voyons, ce qui nous regarde* (Paris: Editions de Minuit, 1992), which explores the implications of the 'inevitable scission of seeing'.

2   The French term *histoire* in this context contains all three notions. For a thorough-going investigation of the whole concept of '*istoria*' and its place in the study of Renaissance art see Alain Laframboise, *Istoria et théorie de l'art: Italie, XVe et XVIe siècles* (Montreal: Presses de l'Université de Montréal, 1989).

3   Didi-Huberman, *Fra Angelico*, p. 253.

4   Pierre Chaunu, *Eglise, culture et société: essais sur Réforme et Contre-Réforme (1517– 1620)* (Paris: Société d'Editions de l'Enseignement Superieur, 1981), p. 276. Translation mine.

5   See, notably, Ernest B. Gilman, *Iconoclasm and Poetry in the English Reformation: Down Went Dagon* (Chicago: Chicago University Press, 1986).

6   *Ibid.*, p. 1.

7   The long essay (prefaced by William Blake's maxim that exuberance is beauty), published under the title *La Part maudite* (Paris: Editions de Minuit, 1967) is a reflection that matured during the 1930s notably under the influence of Marcel Mauss's seminal study of the gift which Claude Lévi-Strauss dates from the first years of the twentieth century. Claude Lévi-Strauss, in Marcel Mauss, *Sociologie et anthropologie* (Paris: Presses Universitaires de France, 1968), p. xxxii. In its turn, Bataille's concept of the 'accursed part' is a probable influence on the notion of the 'objet petit a', object and cause of desire, in the work of Jacques Lacan, Bataille's friend in the Surrealist group in Paris (the two even exchanged an 'object of desire' in the form of Sylvia Bataille who left the philosopher to become Sylvia Lacan).

8   Quoted by Daniel Arasse at the beginning of the introduction to his monumental study of the detail in the visual arts, *Le Détail; Pour une histoire rapprochée de la peinture* (Paris: Flammarion, 1992), p. 10.

9   In Lacanian terms this programme corresponds to looking at the *Urtext* with its institution of the Symbolic – of the Law, and of (a given) culture with its various discriminations and dispensations – before turning the prism more towards the Imaginary – notably the treasury of fetishizable members – in the pictorial representation of the human body.

10   This hangs in the National Gallery in London, where it has recently undergone a highly controversial cleaning that would seem to have affected certain crucial details such as the line of the anamorphic jawbone of the death's head, the detail that imprints the law of castration on the two resplendent French noblemen dispatched by François I to the court of Henry VIII, arrayed in all their pomp and circumstance and in the glory of the Renaissance *savoirs* displayed emblematically around them.

11   Cited from the Authorized King James's Version of the Bible (London & New York: Collins, n.d.).

12   To be precise, the same injunctions are restated from verse 22 onwards, and also at the beginning of chapter 5, the chapter which finally discloses the precise contents of the inscribed 'tables' (of course, they figure high on the list of priorities addressed by the Ten Commandments themselves).

13   See Mauss, *Sociologie et anthropologie*, p. 200.

14   Ludovico Mazzolino lived c. 1480–1528(?) His earliest surviving work is the triptych of 1509, now in Berlin.

15   Francis Barker, *The Tremulous Private Body* (London and New York: Methuen, 1984), p. 20 (emphasis mine).

16   With the notable exception of the large canvases that date from his last year of activity, the opus of this artist largely consists of small pictures adapted to small family chambers, such as chapels or bedrooms, or the *studioli* of private *palazzi*.

17   'Despite the atmosphere of activity however, everyone and everything in these episodes seems fixed in an attitude of immobile expectation': such is the characteristic of all the artist's work, as pointed out here by the catalogue of the exhibition entitled *From Borso to Cesare d'Este: The School of Ferrara 1450–1628* (London: Matthiesen Fine Arts Publications, n.d.), p. 81.

18   If one excepts the gaze of the face turned to the Virgin, watching from behind, who thus serves as relay.

19   I am thinking here, of course, of Roland Barthes's seminal essay on photography *La Chambre claire: note sur la photographie* (Paris: Seuil/Cahiers du Cinéma, 1980). In a nutshell, the *studium* is the repository of culturally conditioned frames, forms and features, while, as it were rebelling against and subverting this disposition, the *punctum* is the detail that refuses to remain, or has never been inscribed, within what classic aesthetic exegesis in France calls *les grandes lignes*, the *studium*, of a work.

20   This unicity is no other than the formal celebration of the One defined by the ethologist Pierre Clastres in the following passage: 'coextensive with the entire history of western civilisation concerning what human society is and what it should be, [we find] the certainty expressed from the Greek dawn of . . . political thought, of the *polis*, in the fragments of Heraclitus. Namely that the representation of society as such should be embodied in the figure of the One external to society, in a hierarchical disposition of political space, in the function of the commander, the king or the despot.' Pierre Clastres, *Archéologie de la violence* (Paris: Aube, 1997), p. 7 (translation mine).

21 Curator of the Mauritshuis in The Hague, in a lecture delivered in the Series 'De la Puissance de l'Image' in the Auditorium of the Louvre, 27 March 1997. There has been considerable work published in France on this subject in recent years: apart from Daniel Arasse's monumental volume already cited, see Georges Didi-Huberman 'L'art de ne pas décrire: une aporie du détail chez Vermeer', *La Part de l'Oeil*, 2 (1986) pp. 103ff. On the detail more generally, notably in the literary text, see the interesting collection of essays edited by Liliane Louvel, *Le Détail* (Poitiers: Publications de la Licorne, 1998).

22 My personal notes taken at the lecture mentioned in note 21.

23 Rarely can a painting have had a more distinguished series of owners: Titian's version of the Rape of Lucrece was sought by the foremost collectors of the day: from the royal collection of Charles I, where it was seen by Ridolfi in 1648, it crossed the Channel after that sovereign's demise, entering the collection of Cardinal Mazarin in 1649; the latter finally offered it as a gift to the 'Sun King' in 1661 before it disappeared, to be unearthed in the Bordeaux region in 1927. Of the trio of versions, the Bordeaux version is deemed to be the original. See Corrado Cagli and Francesco Valcanover, *Tiziano: l'opera completa* (Milan: Rizzoli, 1969, 1978), p. 498.

24 In the Vienna version, unlike the other two, the lady is minimally clad in more or less diaphanous drapes. Moreover the lower third of the other two versions has been suppressed, nothing lower than the thighs of the two figures being visible. For good measure too, the eyes and attitude of the lady are less expressive of terror, this version being more decorous all round.

25 One cannot but help remark how the predatory, not to say ravening, aspect of Eros, only thinly masked by the constraints of courtly decorum and rhetorical diction, is foregrounded with urgent immediacy in Shakespeare's early poetic opus, where the bird of prey swoops on its mesmerized victim long before this passage from *The Rape of Lucrece*: already in *Venus and Adonis*, the spectacle of rabid dismemberment urged by the pangs of erotic passion is expressed with an almost identical image:

> Even as an empty eagle, sharp by fast,
> Tires with her beak on feathers, flesh and bone,
> Shaking her wings, devouring all in haste,
> Till either gorge be stuff'd or prey be gone:
> Even so she kiss'd his brow, his cheek, his chin,
> And where she ends she doth anew begin.
> (stanza 10, lines 55–60)

Venus and Adonis, in William Shakespeare, *The Poems*, ed. F. T. Prince (New York: Routledge, 1960), p. 6.

26 Shakespeare, *The Poems*, ed. Prince, p. 91.

27 This suggests that it might have been a preparatory version.

28 Just how far this can hold true was evidenced by the papers read by members of a panel organized on this very theme by Philippa Berry with Patricia Parker and myself at the recent annual conference of the Shakespeare Association of America under the title 'The Materiality of the Shakespearean Text' (3 April 1999 at San Francisco).

29 See the section on the gaze ('Du regard comme "objet petit a"'), in *Le Séminaire, Livre XI: les quatre concepts fondamentaux de la pyschanalyse*, edited by Jacques-Alain

Miller (Paris: Le Seuil, 1973), p. 82 (the seminar in question is the publication of Lacan's teaching of the year 1963).

30 G. Deleuze, *Le Pli* (Paris: Editions de Minuit, 1988), p. 5 (translation mine).

31 Knole is the largest private house in the country. The earliest part can be traced back to 1456, but in 1603 it was significantly augmented and enhanced by Thomas Sackville, to whom it had been given in gift by Queen Elizabeth for services rendered.

32 The room in question is at present known as the Ballroom, and is elaborately decorated in the early seventeenth-century style of wood panelling, ornate plasterwork alternating squares and circles, or rectangles and ovals, on ceilings and walls (adding stuccowork arabesquerie to the latter). The magnificent chimneypiece and overmantel are in marble and alabaster.

33 *National Trust Magazine*, 80 (Spring 1997), p. 72.

34 There is also a secondary contrapuntal effect between the floral ring and the firm metal yoke which constitutes the upper section of the penile clamp.

35 Quoted in G. Agamben, *Stanze* (Paris: Rivages, 1994), p. 126.

36 Jean-Jacques Lecercle, *The Violence of Language* (London & New York: Routledge, 1990).

37 Daniel Arasse, 'Le Corps fictif de Sébastien et le coup d'oeil d'Antonello', in I. Almeida, D. Arasse C. Bérard, P. Fédida and C. Hart-Nibbrig (eds), *Le Corps et ses fictions* (Paris: Editions de Minuit, 1983), p. 56.

38 See my 'Corps, regard, parole', in D. Goy-Blanquet and R. Marienstras (eds), *Le Tyran: Shakespeare contre Richard III* (Amiens: Presses de l'Université de Picardie. n.d.), p. 40.

39 William Shakespeare, *King Richard III*, ed. Antony Hammond (London: Methuen, 1981), I.i.16–30.

— part four —

Locating self-knowledge

9

'I do not know my selfe': the topography and politics of self-knowledge in Ben Jonson's *Bartholomew Fair*

MARGARET TUDEAU-CLAYTON

As *Bartholomew Fair*, the play by Ben Jonson performed at the Hope public theatre on 31 October 1614, moves towards the puppet-play which constitutes its climax, the following pre-performance exchange takes place between Lanterne (alias Leatherhead), the producer-cum-stage-manager, with a streetwise eye firmly on audience ratings, and Bartholomew Cokes, his principal customer-spectator, whose name signals a privileged, indeed almost eponymous, relation to the play or fair within which the puppet-play is staged.

> *Cok.* But doe you play it according to the printed booke? I have read that.
> *Lan.* By no meanes, Sir.
> *Cok.* No? How then?
> *Lan.* A better way, Sir, that is too learned, and poeticall for our audience; what doe they know what *Hellespont* is? Guilty of true loves blood? or what *Abidos* is? or the other *Sestos* hight?
> *Cok.* Th' art in the right, I do not know my selfe.
> *Lan.* No, I have entreated Master *Littlewit*, to take a little paines to reduce it to a more familiar straine for our people.
> (V.iii.106–117)[1]

In performance a particularly able actor might just capture the grammatical and semantic ambiguity of 'I do not know my selfe' ('my selfe' may be taken as object of the verb as well as in apposition to 'I'). But it is an ambiguity above all for *readers* to recognize and relish, especially those readers who inhabit the universe of 'learned, and poeticall' discourse which the cited placenames evoke by synecdoche and to which Cokes – literate but without the necessary symbolic capital – has no effective access. The ironic ramifications of the ambiguity for these readers include recognition that Cokes's incapacity to understand learned and poetical discourse and his lack of self-knowledge constitute one and the same condition. It is, moreover, a condition they are invited to recognize not only as that of the type of spectator for whom Leatherhead caters but also as that of his 'Play-fellowes in wit' ('The Induction', line 57) – the public theatre spectators of *Bartholomew Fair*. For 'according to the printed booke' of the play (printed 1631, published in the 1640 Folio), according, more precisely, to the figures and places – the topoi – of learned and poetical discourse it mobilizes, *Bartholomew Fair* is encoded for learned readers as an allegory of its own conditions as performance in the public theatre. These are troped specifically as the conditions of an 'underworld', a universe of lack or negation 'below' inhabited by such as Bartholomew Cokes, who are without understanding and, especially, without the privileged form of knowledge – self-knowledge – acquired by means of an education in learned and poetical discourse.[2]

I do not want, however, simply to offer another interpretation of this particular play-text, or to contest the prevailing narrative of Jonson's authorial development which it has been used to underwrite, although what follows will do both these things.[3] I want rather to examine *Bartholomew Fair* for its illustration of more general questions: first, the 'ends' of a bourgeois humanist education, specifically, the exclusions, repressions or negations called for by its model of self-knowledge, and, second, the intertextual and ideological relations between what Jonson calls 'learned and poeticall' discourse and other universes of discourse or knowledge, here the popular culture of the fair and the public theatre. Indeed, the play explicitly dramatizes the humanist's traditional, and arguably ongoing, 'project' (a key word) as 'overseer' (another key word): to provide moral and spiritual education, and to judge and master through judgement. This dramatization is effected primarily through the figure of Cokes's kinsman, Justice Overdo, who is precisely a would-be humanist overseer, quoting from Virgil, Cicero and Horace, amongst other humanist (re)sources, in his aspirations to educate, judge and so master the world of the fair, and through whom Jonson, more specifically, engages critically with Shakespeare's figure of the learned (over)seer, Prospero. Overdo, of course, turns out to be a fool, or, in the terms of the play, an 'ass'. Seen where he would see, judged where he would judge, he is 'a kinne to the *Cokeses*' (II.vi.19), not only literally but also, for readers, figuratively, inasmuch as he belongs, with Cokes, in the class of those identified by the printed book as spectator-asses without understanding and without self-knowledge.

Overdo's failure to gain any degree of control over the world of the fair, together with his subsequent humiliation, would seem to call for recognition that learned and poetical discourse can have no moral or epistemological purchase on such places, and for the consequent renunciation of the humanist's project as overseer. This view is endorsed by the general amnesty of the close, which replaces judgement with feasting, and which critics have tended to take as symptomatic of a more benevolent older Jonson's renunciation of the implied or explicit moral 'high ground' of earlier plays.[4] However, if this 'high ground' is renounced in performance, it is recuperated for learned and poetical discourse, and, for learned readers and author, in the 'printed booke of the play'. For this invites recognition that the performed renunciation of the humanist project is to be taken ironically as a function of the conditions of production in the public theatre, a place which is mirrored by the world of the fair, and identified, like and with it, as an 'underworld'.[5]

To aspire to the humanist project in the 'underworld' of such places is shown, finally, to be out of place, a breach of decorum. More specifically, like the 'o'erdoing' of nature by Hamlet's bad actors, who fail to 'Suit the action to the word, the word to the action', it is to fail to suit the word and action to the place of production, and: 'anything so *overdone* is from the purpose of playing, whose end, . . . was and is to hold, as 'twere, the mirror up to nature: . . . Now, this *overdone* . . . though it makes the unskilful laugh, cannot but make the judicious grieve.'[6] If, as my italics are intended to suggest, the name of Overdo glances at the recurring (overdone?) term of Hamlet's discourse on playing, the allusion serves to underscore how this figure functions in the play's encoding of its own conditions of production as performance, and, specifically, its argument that to aspire to oversee the underworld of the fair or public theatre, as Overdo does, is to 'overdo' the humanist project.[7] It is precisely for its 'overdoing' of this 'project' that, I shall suggest, *The Tempest* is criticized. For Shakespeare's most recent production is criticized not simply for its unrealistic mode but more specifically for its failure to 'speake to the capacity of . . . hearers'[8] such as Cokes, who are shown to be, like Hamlet's 'groundlings' 'for the most part, . . . capable of nothing but inexplicable dumb shows and noise' (*Hamlet* III.2.10–11), and incapable of education into the redeeming grace of self-knowledge. This is 'shown', on the one hand, by the framing of Cokes as spectacle in relation to the shows of the fair, especially the puppet-play, with which *The Tempest* is explicitly linked in 'The Induction' (lines 127–134), and, on the other, by an explicit allegorization of Cokes's loss of his betrothed Grace, which ironically evokes the final awakening to self-knowledge of Shakespeare's figure of unredeemed nature, Caliban, and his aspiration to be 'wise hereafter, / And seek for grace'.[9]

'Bartholmew, and Bartholmew Fayre' (I.v.66–67)

It is the Horatian epigraph on the title page of *Bartholomew Fair* that announces to educated readers that spectators in the public theatre (and hence the conditions of its own production as performance) are the objects of this 'printed booke'.

> *Si foret in terris, rideret* Democritus: *nam*
> *Spectaret populum ludis attentius ipsis,*
> *Ut sibi praebentem, mimo spectacula plura.*
> *Scriptores autem narrare putaret assello*
> *Fabellam surdo.*   Hor.lib.2.Epist.I.

> If Democritus were on the earth today he would laugh! For he would look more attentively at the crowd than the plays themselves, as providing him with more shows than the stage. As for the authors – he would think they were telling their tale to a deaf ass.[10]

Usually, although not always, a term of abuse, 'ass' is used at least thirteen times in *Bartholomew Fair*, and of no character as frequently as of Cokes, whose identification with the Horatian deaf ass of a spectator is, in addition, encoded in his name – 'cokes' being 'as the learned term, an ass'.[11] Although all those who gaze at, or participate in, the fair's shows may be viewed by the reader from the place of the epigraph as 'spectacula', it is Cokes who is singled out as the embodiment of the Horatian deaf ass of a spectator-spectacle and so as the mirror image of public theatre spectators at the Hope. This relation is signalled just prior to the performance of the puppet-play in a description of Cokes which echoes a description of the Hope spectators in 'The Induction'. A figure called 'Booke-holder', taking over from another called 'Stage-keeper', derisively dismisses the latter's claim to 'judgement' only to qualify this dismissal by conceding that 'hee may' pretend to judgement 'i'the most o'this matter', 'For the *Author* hath writ it just to his *Meridian*, and the *Scale* of the grounded Judgements here, his Play-fellowes in wit' ('The Induction', lines 54, 55–57). To Michael Bristol's suggestion that the expulsion of the stage-keeper 'objectifies the displacement of a popular, improvisatory and extra-official participatory tradition',[12] we might add that this tradition is glanced at in the phrase 'Play-fellowes', which is here used to class spectators and stage-keeper together – as childlike, participatory spectators – as it will later be used to class Cokes with them.[13]

The family likeness is underscored by the first evocation of the Horatian figure of the deaf ass. Addressing the Hope audience as

'*Gentlemen*' (line 1), with a deference like that shown by Leatherhead towards Cokes in the pre-performance exchange quoted above, the Stage-keeper caustically criticizes the '*Play*' that is about to begin, derisively quoting the response of 'the *Poet*' (lines 7–8) to his ideas: 'I am an Asse! I!' (line 36). From the place of the Horatian epigraph the Stage-keeper's irony is framed and undercut by a second level of ironic commentary which makes him an ass indeed, the object of a derisive, intellectual, non-participatory gaze – the gaze, we might say, of Democritus – shared by the implied community of learned humanist author and readers.

It is by one of the group of characters (Quarlous, Win-Wife and Grace) through whom the ironic non-participatory gaze of Democriticus is articulated within the play that the phrase 'play-fellowes' is used of Cokes: '*Win-W.* Looke yonder's your *Cokes* gotten in among his play-fellowes; I thought we could not misse him, at such a Spectacle' (V.iv.1–3). Deictically framing Cokes as a spectacle-within-the spectacle (within-the-spectacle), this identifies him more particularly as a child-like participatory spectator – a mirror image of 'his play-fellowes', the public theatre spectators. In his relation to the puppet-play he is actually described as a child – 'Hee is a Child i'faith' (V.iv.227–228) – a description which is confirmed by his own language and behaviour as well as by other characters' comments. To be childlike is not of course a privileged condition of being and knowing (as for the Romantics), but, on the contrary, a condition of deficiency or lack, like the condition of animals.[14] The representation of Cokes as a child thus simply serves to confirm his association with the Horatian deaf ass of a spectator-spectacle.

This association is prominently advertised in another comment by Win-Wife at the outset of the play proper of *Bartholomew Fair*.

> *Win-W.* Did you ever see a fellowes face more accuse him for an Asse?
> *Quar.* Accuse him? it confesses him one without accusing. What pitty
>   'tis yonder wench should marry such a *Cokes*?
>
>   (I.v.49–53)

Again framing Cokes as spectacle, this comment turns his face as visual sign into the object of a derisive and judgemental gaze ('accuse' and 'confesses' evoke the courtroom). This 'makes an ass' of him, as the subtext of 'such a Cokes' – such an ass – confirms for readers (see above, p. 180). This objectifying of Cokes as spectacle continues after he has entered the fair, most patently in a comment by Quarlous: 'Wee had wonderfull ill lucke, to misse this prologue o'the purse, but the best is, we shall have five *Acts* of him ere night: hee'le be spectacle enough! I'le answer for't' (III.ii.1–3). It is, of course, not only readers who are invited by this comment to regard Cokes as a spectacle, co-extensive with the day at the fair (and with the rest of the play of *Bartholomew Fair*). But it is only readers reading from the place of the epigraph who will recognize in this 'spectacle' the Horatian 'spectacula' of deaf asses of spectators and consequently the mirror image it provides of public theatre spectators, the play-fellows of Bartholomew Cokes. The spectators are thus taken in (both included and duped) by the derisive gaze of learned readers for whom spectators are part of the 'spectacle' – deaf asses who do not realize that in laughing at Bartholomew Cokes they are laughing at themselves.

That the play holds up a mirror to such asses is unwittingly pointed up by Cokes himself: 'I call't my *Fayre*, because of *Bartholmew*: you know my name is *Bartholmew*, and *Bartholmew Fayre*' (I.v.65–67). The grammatical lapse here confirms the condition of Cokes as a child without the capacity properly to separate and structure which grammar both furnishes and figures. His incapacity to separate is illustrated too by his appropriation of the fair – an appropriation which suggests, as the puppet-play will demonstrate, that if *Bartholomew Fair* had not been 'writ . . . just to his Meridian, and the Scale of . . . his Play-fellowes in wit' ('The Induction', lines 56–57), the deaf ass of a spectator would have reduced it to this scale – remaking it in the image of his own mind. This is indeed the thrust of the following comment by Cokes's guardian Waspe, a would-be overseer,[15] who observes and frames his charge:

> he that had the meanes to travell your head, now, should meet finer sights then any are i'the *Fayre*; and make a finer voyage on't; to see it all hung with cockleshels, pebbles, fine wheat-strawes, and here and there a chicken's feather, and a cob-web. (I.v.93–97)

Although Waspe himself is overseen and framed, made an object of derision (an 'ass') by Quarlous and Win-Wife, this has a pertinence, like other comments he makes, which he does not fully grasp.[16] For the voyage through the fair is here represented as a voyage through the empty fullness of the mind of a spectator immersed in the immediate, heterogeneous, trivial and ephemeral material objects of his desires, which constitute the universe of what 'hee knowes' (The Induction', line 115), constitute indeed his 'self'.

For learned readers this voyage is encoded as a modern descent into Hades by the commentary of Quarlous and Win-Wife on their arrival at the fair (II.v). For they draw comparisons, at once comic and serious, between the figures of Smithfield and figures from learned and poetical narratives of the underworld. First, on seeing (and hearing) Leatherhead, Quarlous exclaims: 'S'lid! heere's *Orpheus* among the beasts, with his Fiddle, and all!' (II.v.8–9). The comparison serves both to identify Leatherhead as an author figure and to point up the ironic distance between the corrupt contemporary figure who produces 'wares' with an eye on commercial profit, and the ideal classical model, Orpheus, described in Horace's *Ars poetica* as 'priest, and speaker for the Gods', whose art exerted such powerful moral and civilizing effects that he 'Was Tigers, said, and Lyons fierce to tame'.[17] This power 'to tame' is illustrated by the descent of Orpheus into Hades in pursuit of his lost wife Eurydice when he held 'the very halls of Hell . . . spell-bound, and inmost Tartarus, and the Furies'[18] and when he moved even Proserpina, the queen of the underworld.[19] It is to Proserpina that Quarlous alludes in his next comparison, likening Joanne Trash, the gingerbread woman, to '*Ceres* selling her daughters picture in Ginger-worke!' (lines 11–12). Immediately ironic in the difference between the two universes, these evocations are ironic at another level for the learned reader, who recognizes that the universe of the fair may indeed be viewed as an 'underworld', inasmuch as it a place of contingent and ephemeral matter without ideal or spiritual essence, the body without soul, a place or condition of lack to which Leatherhead's vendor's cry – 'What doe you lacke?' (II.v.4) – echoing like a refrain throughout the scenes at the fair (II.ii.29–30; II.iv.3; III.ii.34 etc.) – may be taken to allude ironically. For according to the dominant (neo-Platonic) exegetical tradition, the underworlds of learned and poetical discourse, especially the Virgilian underworld of *Aeneid* 6, were understood to figure the 'sublunary or terrestrial world' (*OED*), as this, one of the first meanings of the word 'underworld', indicates.[20] A place at once below and without, this underworld of material and temporal confinement was a place, specifically, without the single, indivisible and essential condition of the soul, 'forgotten' in the descent into the division, and unstable plurality of matter. To recover knowledge of this condition was to recover the self-knowledge called for by the ancient oracular imperative 'know thyself', and such self-knowledge was the purpose of an education in the arts – of reading 'learned and poetical' discourse – for 'what the Latins call reading the Greeks call recovered knowledge'.[21] The comparisons made by Quarlous, especially his identification of the occupants of Smithfield with beasts, indicate for readers that this is a place of those who remain uneducated by learned and poetical discourse (the voice of Orpheus) into recovered (self-)knowledge. They remain, that is, like and with their 'true customer' (II.v.18–19) Cokes, confined within the terms (language and limits) of the body, without the recovered knowledge of an original, essential and spiritual self, a knowledge which distinguishes the human from the animal, and the child.

That the terms of this place are those of the body is announced at the close by Quarlous. Reminding Overdo of his first name Adam, Quarlous makes of the shared condition of 'flesh and blood' (V.vi.97) a reason for Overdo to renounce his project as overseer. It is, however, in the language used of, and by, a woman who likens herself to the wife of Adam that the significance of the fair as body is most explicitly signalled. A massive, sweating pig-woman, the figure of Ursula consti- tutes, with her oven – to which 'Hell' is a 'a kind of cold cellar' (II.ii.44) – the figurative and visual focus of the fair.[22] On observing her Quarlous exclaims, 'Body o'the *Fayre*! what's this? mother o'the Bawds?' (II.v.73– 74), to which Win-Wife adds, 'Mother o'the *Furies*, I thinke, by her firebrand' (line 77). Translating 'matri Eumenidem' (*Aeneid* 6, line 250), this evokes the moment just prior to Aeneas's descent, when he makes sacrifices, to Proserpine as well as to the mother of the furies (lines 250– 252). Similarly at the outset of their voyage through the fair, Win-Wife consciously draws a parallel with the descent of Aeneas. More import- antly, his exchange with Quarlous economically weaves a constellation of terms around Ursula linking them with each other as well as with her: the body, the fair and a mother from hell/Hades. Such associations are underscored by her own description of herself as 'all fire, and fat' (II.ii.50) liable 'to melt away to the first woman' (lines 50–51), the first mother, Eve. Ursula is subsequently described by Overdo as 'the very *wombe*, . . . of enormitie' (II.ii.106) and by Busy as 'the fleshly woman . . . the Flesh' (III.vi.33, 36–37). At one level comic, these descriptions carry a metaphysical level of significance, which fuses biblical and philo- sophical traditions, especially the putative etymological connection made by neo-Platonists between *mater* and *materia*. Ursula is thus identified as an emblem of the 'body of the fair' – the 'underworld' of *mater– materia*, the 'womb' engendering both physical and moral corruption. Through her name this significance is, moreover, extended to the place which the fair mirrors. For her name alludes to the bear-baiting practised at the Hope theatre,[23] as her colleague Knockem points up in a jocular address which includes the title of the play: 'What! my little leane *Ursla*! my shee-Beare! art thou alive yet? with thy litter of pigges, to grunt out another *Bartholmew Fayre*?' (II.iii.1–3). That these two places share the characteristic properties of the underworld of *mater–materia* is also foregrounded in 'The Induction' by the scrivener's ironic comment that 'the place' of the Hope theatre is 'as durty as *Smithfield*, and as stinking every whit' (lines 159–160).

Smithfield is indeed dominated by the body and its functions, especially the female body, and its overflowings of matter: in urinating (a woman's need to urinate twice furnishes crucial plot motivation), in breeding (a pregnant woman's 'longings' are made a pretext for going to the fair) and in vomiting. This last is particularly significant for it is Adam Overdo's literal wife, under the influence, we might say, of his figurative wife Ursula–Eve, who vomits, and the overflowing of matter from her mouth is what finally silences her husband's flow of words and his project to oversee and judge the fair. This assimilation of what comes out of women's mouths with the flux of matter is anticipated by Win-Wife, who earlier comments that Ursula's language 'grows greasier then her Pigs' (II.v.133–134). As Patricia Parker suggests, Ursula's language, in its tendency to spread or dilate, epitomizes 'the multiplication of vernaculars or mother tongues'[24] in a play which the scrivener describes as 'full' of 'noise' ('The Induction', line 82) – another indication that the play and fair are places of heterogeneous plurality, the underworld of *mater–materia*.

Whether or not we wish to accept, as Parker also suggests, that 'grease' 'punningly echoes grace' (*ibid.*), the figure of Ursula clearly stands in an oppositional relation to the figure of Grace WellBorn in the play's system of representation, and its encoding of the conditions of production as performance. For Grace is joined to Bartholomew Cokes in a bond that may be taken as the figurative correlate to the bond of Adam Overdo to Ursula–Eve. This is signalled by an explicit allegorization of Cokes's loss of Grace, which takes place during his voyage through the fair. A 'process of being plucked and picked clean',[25] this voyage ironically echoes learned and poetical narratives of Hades as a site of loss – Orpheus loses Eurydice, Ceres, Proserpine – and the neo-Platonic troping of it as a site of the loss, or forgetting of the (self-)knowledge which it is grace to recover. This is pointed up in an exchange between Win-Wife and Grace at the end of the scene during which Cokes loses her.

> *Win-W.* You see what care they have on you, to leave you thus.
> *Gra.* Faith, the same they have of themselves, Sir.
>
> (III.v.288–290)

Towards the close of his voyage when he has sustained the final loss – of his sword, cloak and hat – Cokes seems momentarily to awaken into understanding that he has 'lost' his 'self' (as well as Grace) when, addressing the madman Trouble-all, he laments:

Friend, doe you know who I am? or where I lye? I doe not my selfe, I'll be sworne ... I ha'lost my selfe, and my cloake and my hat; and my fine sword, and my sister, and *Numps*, and Mistris *Grace*, (a Gentlewoman that I should ha' marryed) and a cut-worke handkercher, shee ga' mee, and two purses to day. And my bargaine o'Hobby-horses and Ginger-bread, which grieves me worst of all. (IV.ii.78–86)

Initial pathos here evaporates as the lament for the loss of identity merges with an indiscriminate list of losses in which people are jumbled with things, and the only distinction made is to the loss of the bargain of hobby horses and gingerbread, which is prioritized as 'the worst of all'. This priority, together with the failure to discriminate a self from material ephemeral objects of desire and the loosely co-ordinated syntax – 'and ... and ... and ... and ...' – identify Cokes again as a child (an identification that just been underscored by Edgworth as he watches Cokes scramble for pears like a schoolboy (IV.ii.38–40)). As such he lacks a stable transcendent self to 'know' as Edgworth remarks in a comment immediately before the speech quoted above, which serves to frame it. 'Talke of him to have a soule?' heart, if hee have any more than a thing given him in stead of salt, onely to keepe him from stinking, I'le be hanged afore my time, presently: where should it be trow?' (IV.ii.54–57)

That this condition of Cokes mirrors that of the typical public theatre spectator is signalled not only by the exchange with Leatherhead which I quoted at the outset but also by the staging of the loss of Grace, which takes place while Cokes is absorbed as spectator in the perform-ance of the sonsgter Nightingale. During this performance he sustains another, more overt material loss – of a purse – to which the explicit allegorization of the loss of Grace is linked. This material loss itself repeats a loss – the 'prologue o' the purse' (III.ii.1) as Quarlous calls it – which takes place as soon as Cokes arrives at the fair (II.vi), when he is stopped in his tracks by the spectacle of his disguised brother-in-law Adam Overdo (whom he does not recognize), denonouncing the evils of drink and tobacco in his attempt to exercise moral control over the fair. In this exquisitely comic scene, it is not only the deaf ass of a spectator Cokes who fails both to recognize Overdo and to realize when his purse is cut by Edgworth, but Cokes's would-be overseer, Waspe (nicknamed 'Numps'), who neither recognizes Overdo nor sees when Edgworth cuts Cokes's purse. Their shared condition of blindness – the not-seeing of Hades[26] – is pointed up by the negations in the exchange made as Edgworth cuts the purse.

Cok. Who would ha' mist this, Sister?
Over. Not any body, but *Numps.*
Cok. He do's not understand.
Edg. Nor you feele.   *Hee*
                              picketh
                              his purse.

(II.vi.55–58, SD)

Thanks to Edgworth's comment here, spectators off-stage do not share in the blindness, but are granted the twofold pleasure of perceiving what is going on and the superiority of their own perceptions over those of characters watching on-stage – the pleasure, in short, of the overseer. For the reader, however, the spectators' pleasure and power are undercut by recognition that what is being staged mirrors a regular 'drama' of the public theatre, which was frequented by cutpurses.[27] As Bristol points out, the actor Will Kemp recounts how cutpurses were regularly pilloried on the stage 'for all people to wonder at, when at a play they are taken pilfering', an improvised transformation of 'unplanned social drama' into performance[28] which this scene seems to will to produce. At any rate its business – the sheer number of characters and actions on stage – requires just such concentration on the part of the theatre spectator as encourages the cutpurse to do his job.

Attention is drawn to the fact that purses are regularly cut '*At Playes*' (III.v.120) in the ballad sung by Nightingale in the second scene, which not only repeats the first – Edgworth cuts a second purse from Cokes – but reflects ironically on the implied authorial complicity with cutpurses. For the songster Nightingale is precisely an accomplice to the cutpurse, who slips the purse to him once he has cut it, as Win-Wife remarks to Quarlous (lines 163–164) in a commentary which again ensures that spectators off-stage will not fail to see what is going on as the characters watching on-stage fail. Nightingale's corrupt practices – treating his songs both as objects of material exchange and as a cover for theft – are in ironic contradiction both with his name – the nightingale is a traditional figure of the ideal poet – and with the advertisement of his song as 'a gentle admonition . . . to the purse-cutter, and the purse-bearer' (lines 65–66), as, that is, a song with the traditional humanist purpose of moral (as distinct from commercial) profit.[29] However, the most spectacular (!) irony is that this song holds up an accurate mirror to its principal listener, who fails to understand its relevance to himself. Identified again as a child – Nightingale's ballads remind him of his nursery (lines 49–51), a place he appears never to have left – and then again as an ass – Cokes derisively quotes Waspe's characterization of him, 'I am an Asse, I cannot keepe my purse' (line 144), just before his purse is cut – Cokes is entirely taken in by the spectacle, that is, included and duped, indeed duped because included. In his abandonment to the pleasure of such participation Cokes pursues his own loss, as Waspe anticipates – 'Why so! hee's flowne to another lime-bush, there he will flutter as long more; till hee ha ne'er a feather left' (lines 17–19) – although the would-be overseer Waspe also fails to see the loss of the purse which bears out his prediction.

More importantly, Waspe fails to see the loss of Grace, which takes place at the same time as the song and the purse-cutting. He consequently fails to understand the allegorical level of significance to his own derisive reply to Cokes's comment 'is there any harme i'this?' (line 109): 'To tell you true, 'tis too good for you, 'lesse you had grace to follow it' (lines 110–111). For readers (who 'follow'), the loss of Grace is here allegorized to represent the incapacity of the deaf ass of a spectator to understand what he sees in relation to himself and to act accordingly, in short, to reap moral profit (rather than material loss) from the spectacle. Were Cokes to 'follow' he would begin to be educated, led out of the underworld he inhabits, into the 'upper air' which is the grace of recovered (self-)knowledge.[30] That he is incapable of such education, incapable of grace, is precisely the ironic thrust of his loss of Grace here.

At the outset of the play, the engagement of Cokes to Grace is advertised (I.i.3–7) with a glance perhaps at the final words of Caliban, to suggest that grace has not only been sought but found. Yet the subsequent loss of Grace indicates that such contemporary, local instances of brutish unredeemed nature as Cokes (and the public theatre spectators he represents) are incapable of being awakened into self-knowledge. For they are destined to remain childlike asses transfixed by 'trash' (*The Tempest* IV.i.224), participating in spectacles to their own loss, ripped off by such as Leatherhead, *Trash* and Nightingale, who produce 'wares' with an eye not on moral profit for their spectator-customers but on commercial profit for themselves.

This commercial motive is pointed up in a self-congratulatory speech by Leatherhead, in an exchange with two door-keepers, pointedly named Sharkwell and Filcher, which is structurally parallel to 'The Induction' to *Bartholomew Fair* (V.i.1–19). Leatherhead's declared purpose – to 'please the people' (line 6) – is motivated precisely by economic criteria, the audience being judged as 'an eighteene or twenty pence audience' (line 13) and the plays according to their 'get-penny' (line 12) earning power. The 'best' productions, he argues, are 'home-borne projects' which are 'easie and familiar', 'they put too much learning i'their things now o'dayes' (lines 14–16). Though at one level as obviously ironic for the learned reader as Leatherhead's dismissal of the 'printed booke' of *Hero and Leander* in the exchange with Cokes two scenes later, the point, at a second level, is that Leatherhead is right: to make money he must please such as Cokes and to please such as Cokes learned and poetical discourse must be 'reduced' to the scale of his (little) wit, as Little-Wit has reduced the printed book of *Hero and Leander*, which has been '*Metamorphos'd*' (V.iii.127) into the terms of the underworld of Smithfield – and the Hope public theatre.

Surrounded by children on his arrival at the puppet-play (V.iii.14–15) and associated by Win-Wife with 'his play-fellowes' (V.iv.1–2) the actors – here mere inanimate matter (puppets) – the child-ass of a spectator Cokes then makes a spectacle and ass of himself by participating, as before, through a running commentary. A little uncomfortable at first on account of (very unsophisticated) word-play, which he does not follow, Cokes relaxes on hearing the word 'Pandar' – 'He sayes he is no *Pandar*. 'Tis a fine language; I understand it, now' (lines 163–164). Unlike the learned and poetical language of the printed book, this is a language he understands. But he takes the process of metamorphosis one step further by representing the characters of the narrative 'as' the objects he has purchased in the fair.[31] '*Hero* shall be my fayring: But, which of my fayrings? (Le'me see) i'faith, my *fiddle!* and *Leander* my *fiddle-sticke*: Then *Damon*, my *drum*; and *Pythias*, my *Pipe*, and the ghost of *Dionysius*, my *hobby-horse*. All fitted' (V.iii.133–137). His commentary is then made in terms of these character-objects: 'But my Fiddle-sticke do's fiddle in and out too much' (V.iv.192–193); 'where is the friendship, all this while, betweene my Drum, *Damon*; and my pipe, *Pythias?*' (lines 219–220); 'You think my Hobby-horse is forgotten, too; no,' (line 222). Though absurd, this dramatizes how the deaf ass of a spectator appropriates and transforms what he sees into the material, heterogeneous objects of what 'he knowes' ('The Induction', line 115), the objects which fill his mind and which are confused with his 'self'.

Given such conditions of production there can be no place for learned and poetical discourse, which will fall on deaf ears, like the words of Grace: 'What a Rogue in apprehension is this! to understand her language no better' (I.v.136–137). This comment by Quarlous anticipates the loss of Grace to himself and Win-Wife – the group through whom the ironic non-participatory gaze of Democriticus is articulated within the play for learned readers. Indeed, the 'restrain'd scorne' (I.v.57–58) observed by Win-Wife in Grace's relation to Cokes might well be applied to the relation which learned readers are invited to assume towards the fair and the public theatre. It is, finally, either thus, in restrained scorn, or in silence, that Grace relates both to Cokes and more generally to 'his' fair. For those who inhabit the universe of learned and poetical discourse – the place of the recovered self-knowledge of Grace – silence or controlled, detached irony are the only modes of relation that may be had with the 'underworld' of the fair/public theatre.[32]

'an Asse, and ... kinne to the *Cokeses*' (II.vi.19): Adam Overdo

Since there is no place for learned and poetical discourse, any attempt to use it to engage with such places will be out of place, absurd. This is dramatized through the figure of Adam Overdo, who may recall earlier Jonsonian authority figures as well as the literary type of the disguised duke, as others have suggested, but who also, more specifically, recalls Shakespeare's figure of the learned (over)seer, Prospero.[33] This is done, first, through Overdo's repeated use of 'project', a word not often used in the Shakespearian corpus, except in *The Tempest*, where it is used, first, by Ariel and Prospero of Prospero's political and moral purpose within the play (II.i.294 and V.i.1); second, by Ariel of the counter-plot of Caliban and company (IV.i.175); and, finally, by Prospero, as actor as well as *dramatis persona*, of the purpose of the play, which, he says, invoking one half of the Horatian formula, 'was to please' ('Epilogue', line 13). While this is the declared purpose (with commercial profit the underlying motive) of Leatherhead's 'home-borne projects', as we have just seen, Overdo's projects are rather aimed at the other half of the Horatian formula: moral profit. In this they are like Prospero's 'project' within the play, a project which he achieves in part thanks to the learned and poetical Virgilian spectacle of the harpy, which has a '*grace* ... devouring' (*The Tempest*, III.iii.84, italics added) in bringing about the moral awakening of Alonso.

Overdo begins one of his monologues: 'I cannot beget a *Project*, with all my politicall braine, yet; my *Project* is how to fetch off this proper young man from his debaucht company' (III.v.1–3). The clumsy repetition draws attention not only to the overdoing of the word but also to the posturing in such a self-conscious assumption of the role of learned humanist as moral overseer.[34] Overdo's specific project is of course patently absurd to spectators and readers alike, who have seen that 'the proper young man' he refers to – Edgworth – is just as 'debaucht' as his 'company', and, specifically, that he has used Overdo's earlier performance as a cover for the cutting of Cokes's purse. Overdo's blindness both at the level of perception and at the level of moral judgement is typical: intent on his project as would-be overseer, inhabiting a universe of learned and poetical discourse which gives him no purchase on the universe of the fair, he is blind to what goes on and fails to exercise the control to which he aspires. He is indeed judged and punished where he would judge and punish, turned, finally, into another spectacle and humiliated, both verbally – through the derisive framing comments of Grace, Win-Wife and Quarlous (II.v.27–30 and II.v.265–270) – and physically: he is beaten up and put in the stocks.

The significance of the failure of Overdo's project in relation to the projects of Prospero (and of *The Tempest*) is pointed up by contrasts furnished within the play by Leatherhead and Quarlous. For immediately after Overdo has used 'project' (as a verb), Leatherhead uses it (as a noun) in the phrase 'home-borne projects', which draws attention to the contrast in their strategies. Leatherhead succeeds where Overdo fails because he adapts his 'projects' to those he addresses, speaking to their 'capacity', which he understands and so manages to penetrate and control, making the commercial profit he wants. In these self-interested managerial skills he is like Quarlous, who, as Haynes comments, 'plunges into' the fair, managing 'to manipulate the symbol system' and so 'to master its noise and confusion', while Win-Wife and Grace rather 'stay aloof'.[35] Though participation of a kind, this is not collective 'festive' participation, but entrepreneurial, self-interested participation. Still more importantly, while Leatherhead simply dismisses learned and poetical discourse as irrelevant to the fair, Quarlous uses it, not, like Overdo, to attempt to engage with this universe, but, on the contrary, to *disengage* from it. When, having employed the cutpurse Edgworth, he finds he is being offered a share in his prostitute, Quarlous repulses him with 'Keepe it for your companions in beastlinesse, I am none of 'hem, Sir' (IV.vi.22–23), adding, once Edgworth has left, 'I am sorry I employ'd this fellow; for he thinks me such: *Facinus quos inquinat, aequat.*' (lines 28–30). Denying, even as it announces, the levelling effect of such participation in the fair as Quarlous has engaged in, the quotation works, specifically, to distance Quarlous 'as' learned humanist both from Edgworth (and the universe of the fair) and from Edgworth's 'companions in beastliness', or play-fellows, which include those in the public theatre audience without the capacity to understand the quotation.[36]

These contrasts within the play point up the futility of the humanist project to engage with, and to seek to educate the world of the fair and the theatre through learned and poetical discourse, which, as the puppet-play dramatizes, will be appropriated and transformed into the material terms of these underworlds. This is underscored at the close when Overdo finally steps forward, Prospero-like, to reveal himself and make his discoveries. For, having interrupted the puppet-play, which he brings to an end through a gesture of would-be authority like the gestures which close earlier Jonsonian comedies,[37] and having begun his 'project' of moral exposure and judgement, he is himself interrupted by a cry from his intoxicated wife whom he has failed to notice amongst the spectators at the puppet-play. The stage directions – '*Mistresse* Overdo *is sicke: and her husband is silenc'd*' (V.vi.68 SD) – concisely articulate the reversal staged by this interruption: the flow of words from a male would-be moral overseer through which he would master and close the universe of the fair and the play – the universe of *mater–materia* – is interrupted and closed by a flow precisely of matter from the woman to whom he is bound by wedlock as he is bound in the play's system of representations to the woman who has made her drunk – Ursula–Eve – a bond which I have suggested is the figurative correlate of the bond with Grace lost by Cokes. This is pointed up by Quarlous's reminder to Overdo that he is 'but *Adam*, Flesh, and blood! you have your frailty' (V.vi.96–97). On account of this common frailty Quarlous proposes, as a more appropriate project than that of moral overseer, a general amnesty and an invitation to supper (line 98). His project is, moreover, endorsed by an implied authorial renunciation of control. For the last lines are given not to Overdo, nor even to Quarlous, but to Bartholomew Cokes, who, to Overdo's 'lead on' (a phrase with which an earlier play might have closed) adds: 'Yes, and bring the *Actors* along, wee'll ha' the rest o'the *Play* at home' (line 114–115) An indefatigable, participatory spectator to the end (and beyond), Cokes projects an indefinite deferral of closure of (the) play in a universe which includes the public theatre spectators of *Bartholomew Fair* (note the referential ambiguity of 'the *Play*'). It is an open form of closure which is in absolute contrast to the close of earlier plays, such as *Poetaster*. For if Virgil in *Poetaster* is silenced, like Overdo, by interruption from a figure associated with the body and its 'underworld' humours, this figure is quickly brought under control, his mouth literally stopped, and Virgil restored as overseer to make the final judgement and (with Augustus) to close (the) play.[38]

This contrast would seem to indicate authorial recognition of the futility of the attempt to contain the universe of *mater–materia*, and, specifically, of the project of learned and poetical discourse to oversee and contain through judgement the universe of the fair or public theatre.

But this recognition is, in turn, cancelled in the places of production outside the place of the public theatre: the printed book for learned readers, as we have seen, and the court. For the frames which are provided in both places precisely circumscribe – contain and close – the universe of the fair and the public theatre, and restore the position of overseer which 'the author' and Overdo renounce within it.

The frame for the performance at court is provided by an added prologue and epilogue which are addressed to 'the King' (H&S, vol. 6, pp. 11, 141). While the prologue emphasizes the specificity of the place of the play and fair, and its language – 'a Fayre / Such place, such men such language and such ware' (line 2) – implying the difference, and distance, of the place of the court and its language, the epilogue places 'the King', as he is placed in the masques, as the place from which the play is to be properly seen and judged. This cancels the 'agreement' of 'the author' in 'The Induction' – and its implied authorial endorsement of the criteria of such as Leatherhead – to allow a hierarchy of judgement according to the price of the spectator's place ('The Induction', lines 85–91). For the only judgement that counts here is that of 'the King' (line 12), who is, and has the last word.

More importantly still, the position of the overseer is restored in the frame provided by the Horatian epigraph for learned readers.[39] As we have seen, this key or master text invites the reader to assume the position of overseer and to read the play as an allegory of the conditions of its production in the public theatre, conditions constituted by spectators such as Cokes, childlike deaf asses incapable of understanding learned and poetical discourse as they are incapable of the redeeming grace of self-knowledge it bestows. That Cokes should 'close' the performed public theatre play, and so ambiguously, is thus, for such readers, simply, if ironically, appropriate – a decorous confirmation that this is indeed 'his' play. Such recognitions of irony serve to confirm the learned reader's position as overseer. This position is in turn underwritten by the playtext's topography of learned and poetical discourse, which maps this universe as an 'underworld' – a place 'below' of negation or lack, especially of self-knowledge. Cokes and the public theatre spectators he represents are thus included as objects of knowledge for learned readers, but excluded as subjects of (self-)knowledge, and consequently as properly human, by a discourse which confirms its own – and its users' – normative, and superior value by locating those without this discourse, together with their participatory culture, in/as a place 'below' of negation. They are thus excluded from the community of human equals to whom, as Charles Taylor puts it, respect is due by virtue of inclusion.[40] Herein then lies the politics of the printed book's topography of self-knowledge. Mapped over and across the traditional hierarchy according to birth (and by birth Cokes belongs to the elite if to its lower orders), Jonson's bourgeois alternative defines 'high' and 'low' according to what is acquired by means of a humanist education – the symbolic capital of learned and poetical discourse and the self-knowledge which the reading of such discourse bestows. This mode of self-knowledge is defined in and by separation from the multiple differences of embodied existence as well as from participatory, historically embedded, forms of culture, including theatrical performance. To a self thus defined, participation in the multiple differences of embodied experience threatens to 'trouble all' (the name of the figure of the madman to whom Cokes's lament of self-loss is addressed): to unsettle, that is, the sense of a bounded, unified and transcendent self and reduce it to the childlike 'confusion' illustrated by Cokes. Although from such 'confusion' – such undoing of the integrity of the self – may emerge new forms of self-knowledge, as in Shakespeare's tragedies, especially *King Lear*, and although participatory forms of culture including theatrical performance may offer alternative forms of knowledge, as Shakespeare's plays imply they do, Jonson's playtext defines such confusion as the ignorance or blindness of Hades. Its topography of self-knowledge thus furnishes, finally, a topography of the psychic repression as well as the political exclusion constitutive of the transcendent, unifed and stable bourgeois subject.

Notes

1 Throughout I refer to the text given in *Ben Jonson*, ed. C. H. Herford, Evelyn and Percy Simpson, 11 vols (Oxford: Clarendon Press, 1925–1952), vol. 6, pp. 1–141, modernizing the names and the *i/j*, *u/v* spelling forms. (Further references to this edition will be given in the abbreviated form *H&S*, followed by the volume number.)

2 For a different discussion of the supplementary material given in the printed text, which, however, does not mention the Horatian epigraph on the title page, which I take to be the most significant, see Leah S. Marcus, 'Of Mire and Authorship', in David L. Smith, Richard Strier and David Bevington (eds), *The Theatrical City: Culture, Theatre and Politics in London, 1576–1649* (Cambridge: Cambridge University Press, 1995), pp. 170–181.

3 To read texts as allegories of lives seems to me fraught with problems, but it is worth noting that, where this play is concerned, two different approaches end up by saying much the same, namely, that the play is symptomatic either of Jonson's conscious tolerance of, or his unconscious identification with, the squalid, immoral and licentious universe of the fair, which he officially condemns. For representative examples see Thomas Cartelli, 'Bartholomew Fair as Urban Arcadia: Jonson Responds to

Shakespeare', *Renaissance Drama* 14 (1983), 151–172; Marcus, 'Of Mire and Authorship', and Peter Stallybrass and Allon White, *The Politics and Poetics of Transgression* (Ithaca: Cornell University Press, 1986), pp. 27–79. Without contesting the interest of these approaches, I want to focus rather on the printed text's system of representation, or ideology, to show, specifically, how it underwrites not only the authority and pre- rogatives of the king (as Marcus argues in an earlier reading) but also, and more importantly, the authority and prerogatives of a community of learned humanist readers and authors and the learned and poetical discourse they share. See Leah S. Marcus, *The Politics of Mirth: Jonson, Herrick, Milton, Marvell and the Defense of Old Holiday Pastimes* (Chicago: University of Chicago Press, 1986), pp. 38–63.

4 For a summary of this critical opinion see Cartelli, 'Bartholomew Fair as Urban Arcadia', pp. 154–155, especially note 11.

5 Jonson's association of the world of theatrical spectacle with the Virgilian underworld and the ideological implications of his elaboration of this association in the direction of the modern senses of the word *underworld* are explored further in Margaret Tudeau-Clayton, '"Underwor(l)ds", l'ancien et le nouveau: de Virgile à Ben Jonson', in François Laroque and Franck Lessay (eds), *Esthétiques de la nouveauté à la Renais- sance* (Paris: Presses de la Sorbonne Nouvelle, 2001), pp. 59–76.

6 William Shakespeare, *Hamlet*, ed. G. R. Hibbard (Oxford and New York: Oxford University Press, reprint, 1994), III.2.12–13, 18–21, 23–25 (italics added).

7 The word 'overdo' is explicitly linked to a would-be author's excessive intellectual aspirations in a mocking comment by Quarlous on the 'ambitious wit' of Little-Wit (author of the puppet-play): 'You grow so insolent with it, and overdoing, John' (I.v.71, 74–75).

8 From a passage in *Timber* (*H&S*, vol. 8, p. 587), which, as others have noted, echoes not only the criticism of *The Tempest* in *Bartholomew Fair* but also a related passage in the preface to the 1612 quarto of *The Alchemist*.

9 William Shakespeare, *The Tempest*, ed. Frank Kermode (London and New York: Routledge, reprint, 1994), V.i.294–295. References throughout will be to this edition.

10 *H&S*, vol. 6, p. 9 (my translation). The epigraph is a modification of a passage from the first of Horace's second book of epistles. See *Horace, Satires, Epistles and Ars Poetica*, trans. H. R. Fairclough (Cambridge, Mass.: Harvard University Press; London: William Heinmannn, rev. edn. 1978), pp. 396–419 (lines 194–200). Jonson has omitted two lines from the middle of the passage (lines 195–196) and has replaced 'seu' with 'nam'. In the Loeb edition 'nimio' is given for 'mimo' (line 198); the epigraph's 'assello' is a misprint for 'asello'. The epigraph has not received much attention from critics, although Richard Dutton takes it as 'a riposte' to popular theatre audiences and argues that there is a 'duality' of perspective throughout. Richard Dutton, *Ben Jonson: To the First Folio* (Cambridge: Cambridge University Press, 1983), p. 174. He does not discuss the specific dualities produced by reading from the place of the epigraph.

11 John Ford, *The Lover's Melancholy*, IV.ii.179–180, in John Ford, *'Tis Pity She's a Whore and Other Plays*, ed. Marion Lomax (Oxford: Clarendon Press, 1995) (cf. *H&S*, vol. 10, p. 171). Despite the hints in his name, Cokes has not received more than cursory attention from critics who tend, moreover, to consider him no more

than 'a blessed naïf and a booby squire'. See Francis Teague, *The Curious History of Bartholomew Fair* (London and Toronto: Associated University Presses, 1985), p. 15.

12 Michael D. Bristol, *Carnival and Theater: Plebeian Culture and the Structure of Authority in Renaissance England* (New York and London: Routledge, 1985), p. 119.

13 The *OED* glosses 'playfellow': 'A companion in play or amusement: usually said of children or young people'. Quoting relevant passages from *Timber*, Barish argues that playgoing is generally treated by Jonson 'as a symbol of childishness'. Jonas Barish, 'Jonson, and the Loathed Stage', in W. Blissett, Julian Patrick and R. W. Van Fossen (eds), *A Celebration of Ben Jonson* (Toronto: University of Toronto Press, 1973), p. 40.

14 See, for example, Elisabeth Badinter, *L'amour en plus: histoire de l'amour maternel* (Paris: Flammarion, 1980), chapter 2.

15 The word 'Overseer' is actually used, mockingly, of Waspe (by Edgworth) at IV.ii.61.

16 Quarlous describes Waspe as a 'serious Asse' (III.v.265) before instigating the plot that will make him one. The likeness to Overdo is advertised by Grace: 'Justice Overdo . . . is answerable to that description, in every haire of him' (lines 269–270).

17 Jonson's translation of 'sacer, interpresque Deorum / . . . / Dictus lenire tigres, rapidosque leones' (*H&S*, vol. 8, pp. 326–327). Less than a hundred lines later a corrupt poet who pays for approval of his work is likened to 'a Crier / That to the sale of Wares calls every Buyer' (*ibid.*, pp. 332–333). These lines may bear on Jonson's central figure of literary productions as 'wares' especially since, according to Drummond's *Conversations*, he included, in a preface to his translation of the *Ars*, 'ane apologie of a Play of his St Bartholomees faire' (*H&S*, vol. 1, p. 134). Unfortunately lost in the fire of 1623 (*H&S*, vol. 11, p. 110), this 'apologie' perhaps made explicit the play's treatment of its own conditions of production, specifically the departure from classical and Renaissance humanist ideals occasioned by the treatment of literary products as objects of economic exchange (wares), a corruption illustrated by Leatherhead, whose criterion of judgement is commercial profit (see below, pp. 188–189). In this perspective the representation of the play as itself a 'ware' ('The Induction', line 161) is particularly ironic.

18 *Georgics* 4, lines 481–483, in *Virgil, trans.* H. R. Fairclough, 2 vols (Cambridge, Mass.: Harvard University Press; London: William Heinemann, reprint, 1974).

19 *Metamorphoses* 10, lines 45–47 in *Publius Ovidius Naso, Metamorphoses*, trans. Frank Justus Miller (Cambridge, Mass.: Harvard University Press; London: William Heinemann, 3rd edn, 1977), vol. 2.

20 See Tudeau-Clayton, '"Underwor(l)ds"', especially pp. 63–64.

21 See Ambrosius Theodosius Macrobius, *Commentarii in somnium scipionis*, ed. J. Willis (Leipzig: Teubner, 1970), pp. 40–60 (quotation from p. 49; my translation).

22 R. B. Parker suggests that Ursula's booth would have been placed stage-left in the place of the traditional entry to hell in 'The Themes and Staging of *Bartholomew Fair*', *University of Toronto Quarterly* 39:4 (1970), 294. On the association of Ursula with the body see, for example, Jonathan Haynes, 'Festivity and the Dramatic Economy of Bartholomew Fair', in Harold Bloom (ed.), *Ben Jonson* (New York, New Haven and Philadelphia: Chelsea House Publishers, 1987), pp. 141–162 (p. 143), and Teague, *The Curious History*, pp. 14–15.

23 Andrew Gurr, *The Shakespearean Stage 1574–1642* (Cambridge: Cambridge University Press, 3rd edn, 1992), p. 154.

24 Patricia Parker, *Literary Fat Ladies: Rhetoric, Gender, Property* (London and New York: Methuen, 1987), pp. 24–25.

25 Ben Jonson, *Bartholomew Fair*, ed. G. R. Hibbard (London: A. & C. Black; New York: W. W. Norton, reprint, 1991), p. xxiv.

26 To 'not see' is the putative etymological origin of the Greek for Hades.

27 Gurr, *The Shakespearean Stage*, pp. 223–225.

28 Bristol, *Carnival and Theater*, p. 143.

29 In Virgil's narrative of the loss of Eurydice in *Georgics* 4 an extended simile compares the grieving Orpheus – the ideal figure of the moral, civilizing poet to whom Leatherhead is ironically compared, as we saw earlier – to a nightingale mourning her young (*Georgics* 4, lines 511–515).

30 I allude here to the lines of the Sibyl to Aeneas which describe those few permitted by Jove to escape from Hades into the upper air (*Aeneid* 6, 129–131) and which Jonson quotes elsewhere, in association with the word 'grace'. John Dryden use the word 'Grace' in his translation of the lines. See Tudeau-Clayton, "'Underwor(l)ds"'. pp. 65–68.

31 Pressure from the allegory appears to have led Jonson into an (unusual) inconsistency at the level of plot: Cokes has by this time lost all his purchases and no recuperation of them has been staged.

32 Compare Haynes on the group formed by Win-Wife, Quarlous and Grace, separate and aloof from the community of the fair, 'their own little society' 'based on the . . . values of self-possession and the manners that reflect a gentlemanly bearing' (Haynes, 'Festivity', p. 149).

33 In their efforts to 'discover' who lies behind Overdo, critics have almost outdone Overdo. For the parodic version of earlier Jonsonian authority figures see Jonas Barish, *Ben Jonson and the Language of Prose* Comedy (Cambridge, Mass.: Harvard University Press, 1960), pp. 212–213, Douglas Duncan, *Ben Jonson and the Lucianic Tradition* (Cambridge: Cambridge University Press, 1979), p. 206. For the parodic imitation of the type of disguised duke and allusions to specific historical characters see D. McPherson, 'The Origins of Overdo: A Study in Jonsonian Invention', *Modern Language Quarterly* 37 (1976), 229–233, and for parodic allusions to James see Dutton, *Ben Jonson: To the First Folio*, p. 173.

34 The historically specific semantics of the word 'project' are relevant here. Lorna Hutson has shown how it was 'practically synonymous' with 'plat/plot', arguing that skill in discerning and making plots or projects was a function of humanist reading (and writing) strategies, in short, of an education in learned and poetical discourse. Lorna Hutson, 'Fortunate Travelers: Reading for the Plot in Sixteenth Century England', *Representations* 41 (Winter 1993), especially pp. 86–87.

35 Haynes, 'Festivity', pp. 657, 655.

36 The quotation, from Lucan's *Pharsalia*, is rendered 'Crime puts those it corrupts on the same footing' in Ben Jonson, *Bartholomew Fair*, ed. Hibbard, p. 136.

37 See Peter Womack, *Ben Jonson* (Oxford: Basil Blackwell, 1986), p. 156.

38 See Margaret Tudeau-Clayton, *Jonson, Shakespeare and Early Modern Virgil* (Cambridge: Cambridge University Press, 1998), pp. 160–161, 174–175.

39 Typically, Jonson thus works in the interest at once of a bourgeois ideology and the political structure of an absolute monarchy. See further Tudeau-Clayton, *Jonson, Shakespeare and Early Modern Virgil*, pp. 11–12, p. 118.

40 Charles Taylor, *Sources of the Self: The Making of the Modern Identity* (Cambridge, Mass.: Harvard University Press, 1989), p. 5. Jonson's exclusionary humanism belongs to a tradition outlined by Robert Kaster: 'the oldest article of faith in the literary culture, extending back to Isocrates, repeated through the Renaissance and beyond' is that 'the eloquent man' (i.e. the man educated in learned and peotical discourse) is 'nothing less than a distinct . . . species'. Robert A. Kaster, *Guardians of Language: The Grammarian and Society in Late Antiquity* (Berkeley: University of California Press, 1988), p. 17.

10

Knowing her place: Anne Clifford and the politics of retreat

SUSAN WISEMAN

Property, lineage, politics

IF, IN THEORY, the absence of women was part of what guaranteed the sanctity of the political sphere in Renaissance or early modern England, how can we conceptualize the relationship of women to that sphere? What follows argues that an examination of the discourses of law, place and lineage makes a response to this question possible. Although the places of land and lineage in political cultures are understood as highly politicized, texts by women on such topics are more often than other texts interpreted as 'private' instead of part of social and political culture. Yet some such texts were understood by their writers and readers as participating in debates with political dimensions and implications. As the case of Anne Clifford clearly shows, such writings and texts were not always part of networks in which political commentary was naturalised (or socialised) as gossip. Anne Clifford (1590–1676), as the daughter of the Earl and Countess of Cumberland, was a seventeenth-century heiress of very high social standing. When she was disinherited, then, we can see in her response a politics of place and family which repays study.

The texts that Clifford produced are marked by a self-consciousness of family and place which is oriented not only towards family, but also – in monuments and buildings as well as in paintings – towards what must, at times, be understood as a much wider range of interpreters. Thus, using Clifford's various texts, this essay argues that textualizations of property, land, and images need to be seen as participating in politicized understandings of lineage, place and estate – and hence in political discourses. Clifford's textual production (from the fragmentary diaries of the 1610s and 1620s to the highly systematic narratives, building and images of her later years) repeatedly asserts her legal status as heir, and therefore as full legal and propertied subject. It also, therefore, offers an opportunity to explore the way in which aristocratic claims to land and family were understood as both inherently political and as politicized by their specific circumstances.

Although Clifford does offer, as Alice Friedman aptly puts it, a 'subject through which to examine the representation of the self', this self is enunciated in a context where family and politics are overlapping categories.[1] Clifford's texts offer a substantial case against understanding texts articulating feminine subjectivity as either private or guilelessly self-revelatory. The assumption that the personal and private are dominant in Clifford's texts, an assumption held by a recent editor, anachronistically binds a varied body of texts to a modern conception of private life.[2] Moreover, the early diary, on which such a picture of Clifford substantially rests, cannot be productively assessed in complete isolation from other things Clifford commissioned, built and signed – texts and artefacts which consistently invite us to question the separation of private and public that concentration on the personal implies. Indeed, the strategies these texts use to interweave familial happenings and politics suggest that they address a readership which is imagined with increasing fullness and precision through Clifford's writing life. Clifford's very neglect of some public events, particularly pronounced towards the end of her life, suggests not that she had no views of government or wider world but that we should look elsewhere for the interpretative narratives she used.[3]

As I have suggested, concentration on Clifford's diary of her early years, where Anne features as a subject fissured by mutability and loss, has produced some critical assessments of Clifford's writing as 'essentially . . . very personal'. However, as Katherine Acheson indicates, Clifford produced several types of 'autobiographical discourse' (diary, chronicles and 'annual summaries', and the 'Life of Me'), each highly systematic in their return to her status as heir.[4] As many writers on Clifford recognize, such texts manifest 'sustained public opposition to . . . property settlements'.[5] When we recall, as Margaret Ezell and Helen Wilcox both remind us, that early modern diaries cannot be understood as private in a modern sense, then it becomes more obviously possible not to treat diaries and buildings as equivalently 'public' but to trace some of the connections between the two.[6]

Clifford's texts produced between 1605 and her death in 1676 begin with a response to her father's will and her very public deprivation of her legal rights. Grounded in the twin experiences of entitlement and deprivation, they announce legal claims which can be understood in part in political terms. As Acheson's invaluable research suggests, Clifford's case was based on the 'interpretation of laws and practices regarding the inheritability of baronies by female issue'.[7] Specifically, Clifford's case rested on the status of an entail of lands on heirs male or female (the case brought by Clifford's mother in 1606) and on tenure (the 'physical possession of estates') which was heard in the Court of Wards in April 1608.[8] Further suits were heard in the Court of Common Pleas (1615), before the Council of the North (1616) and James I gave judgement in favour of the Earl of Cumberland's designated heir, his brother Francis Clifford in 1617. When Francis died in 1628 Clifford renewed her suits.[9] The law case itself was far from private and involved the interests of powerful families around the King.

In this case it is precisely Clifford's status as an unusual, elite woman which illuminates so vividly the politicized implications of diaries, images, monuments. As an heiress and landholder in a prominent family (sole child and heir of George, Third Earl of Cumberland) Clifford occupied, potentially, a position usually reserved for the masculine elite. As Samuel Daniel's poem to her stresses, she was one that 'such a faire advantage have / Both by your birth and happy pow'rs'.[10] Clifford's elite status and later wealth, the very circumstances that enabled her to produce her texts, make her far from representative but the discourses she used – legal, familial, lineal – extended throughout Stuart and Civil War society, tying feminine identity to the political sphere.[11] Clifford's focus on property acts to illuminate conceptions of self as tied to a network including the local and the national. In a situation where property is bound to ties of land and genealogy as well as capital, it illuminates wider cultural networks. Thus, Clifford's exceptional status, wealth and creativity were brought to the fore by her lawsuit, and in turn bring into view the operations of discourses and self-understandings usually seen only intermittently, in the courtroom. Her elite cultural production, emphasizing the place of honour and family (things bound to other discourses such as loyalty and duty), also enunciates political identity.[12]

1616: Montaigne and monuments

On 9 November 1616 Clifford was having Montaigne read to her: 'I sat at my Work & heard Rivers and Marsh read Montaigne's *Essays*.'[13] Florio's translation had included a commendatory poem by her tutor, Samuel Daniel, punning on 'estate' by characterizing Montaigne (a 'Prince') as one who 'Hath more adventur'd of his own estate' than any before.[14] Was Clifford, in meditating on her own 'estate', influenced by Montaigne's project or methods?

The evidence suggests that even in the apparently fragmentary diary of 1616 we find Clifford shaping the material which she was to use to assert and later to celebrate her legal status retrospectively. Indeed, it is hard to imagine that, given her pride in her father's achievements – she had his voyages copied out at Christmas 1618 – Clifford did not read 'Of the Cannibals', with its final rhetorical address to the reader: 'All that is not very ill; but what of that? They wear no kinde of breeches nor hosen.'[15] This essay's ironic questioning of self and other, as Michel de Certeau notes, foregrounds the twin problems of presence and of reading – the reader whose missing presence authorizes textual production. As he puts it, 'writing arises from the separation that makes this presence the inaccessible other of the text'.[16] The question of the possible reader and either adversarial or benign interpreter is a figure consistently imagined in the labyrinthine and spatialized plotting of Clifford's 1616 diary.

Unlike Montaigne's retirement, Clifford's sequestration in 1616 was largely enforced. Isolated at Knole, her husband's house in Kent, sometimes in London, Clifford was embattled, already, in the legal case that came to be the reference point of all her writing. While the connections the reader finds in Montaigne's texts open outwards to many, overlayered, ways of thinking about presence and absence, reading and writing, Clifford's chains of association are secured by reference to her law case and drawn back to twin themes of lineage and place.

Like Montaigne's essays, though, Clifford's Stuart diary does seem to imagine a reader, as is suggested by the juxtaposition of narrative and annotations. This is January 1616:

> Upon New Year's Day (7) I kept to my chamber all day, my Lady Rich and my Sister Sackville supping with me, but my Lord and all the Company at Dorset House went to see the Mask at Court. Upon the 6th, being the Twelfth day, I supped with my Lady of Arundel & sat with her in the Ladyship's Box to see the Mask which was the second time it was presented before the King and Queen.[17]

Although the existing texts are later copies, it is still clear that spatial and comparative principles are at work. Apparently trivial, 'personal' and quotidian details are imbued with significance. Characteristically, what seems to be a casual detail in the narrative turns out to be a motif of the diary. The note – 'Jan. 1616. the 1st day Sir Geo. Villiers was made Master of the Horse & My Lord Worcester Privy Seal' – refers to the rising star of James I's new favourite, linking the rise of Villiers (who replaced Sir Robert Carr, Duke of Somerset) with that of her own husband. Clifford herself, meanwhile, is caught between the King and her husband, with whom negotiation over her land in Westmorland caused endless disputation and punishment as Clifford insists on her legal position.

The reader, even if that reader was perhaps initially imagined only as Clifford herself, is invited to decode Clifford's relationship to court politics through textual juxtapositions. Clifford's mood was determined not by life around her but 'as I had news from London' about the case: and the tension between local life, the lawsuit, and events in the wider world are articulated in her use of marginal notes.[18] Her stubbornness produced a situation where, after an interview with the Sackville relatives and the Archbishop of Canterbury, when 'Much persuasion was used by him and all the company, sometimes terrifying and sometimes flattering me', she was permitted to consult her mother.[19] She sees her mother in March 1616: 'Upon the 22nd, my Lady & I went in a Coach to Whingfield and rode about the park and saw all the woods.' As she was visiting her mother, happenings in court and in London (the wider world, but also a corollary for Clifford's own experiences) were recorded, her editor tells us, in marginal notes: 'Upon the 24th my Lady Somerset was sent by water from Blackfriars as Prisoner to the Tower.'[20] Francis Howard, Countess of Somerset, the wife of the king's favourite Robert Carr, was soon to be infamous as the poisoner of Sir Thomas Overbury. Here, however, she provides an analogue for Clifford's own ill-treatment by James. In May Clifford takes up the story, recording that 'my Lady Somerset arraigned and condemned at Westminster hall where she confessed her fault and asked the King's Mercy, & was much pitied by all beholders'. Like Howard, Clifford suffers public opprobrium and is to be pitied. Once again there is a marginal note:

> Upon the 24th, being Friday, between the hours of 6 and 9 at night died my dear Mother at Brougham, in the same Chamber where my father was born, 13 years and 2 months after the death of Queen Elizabeth and ten years and 7 months after the death of my father. I being 26 years and five months, and the Child 2 years wanting a month.[21]

How is such a juxtaposition to be interpreted? The death of Clifford's mother left her vulnerable; her mother had orchestrated the campaign for the lands and had been Clifford's mainstay. The text uses coincidence or repetition to lend depth and significance to the past. Yet it occurs in a note, forcing the reader to move between national and familial narratives. This note is not inviting the reader to 'read the text twice: once by continuing straight through the sentence, the second time via the detour of the note', as in Michel Butor's analysis of the relationship between text and marginal notes.[22] Rather, a more complex and less clearly hierarchized relationship is suggested whereby the information of Clifford's mother's death, of central importance to Clifford's legal struggle resonated with other indications of the quality of James's court, as opposed to that of Elizabeth. Diary and note, James and Elizabeth, Francis Howard and Clifford are all in relations of comparison. The reader is invited to make appropriate connections.

Who the reader would be for this autobiographical text remains enigmatic. Where Clifford's less fragmentary texts clearly were intended for circulation, this might have acted as a prompt to memory. Thus, she would fit in news of her mother's death, heard later, at the appropriate point. Whether or not this was the pattern of the diary, with circumstances textually producing her mother's death as marginal, the recorded events in turn imply that there is significance in the worldly timing and the page's positioning of what happened. Moreover, the repeated return to significant events and places play an even larger part in Clifford's later less fragmentary texts, including her narratives and the *Great Picture*.

In this diary juxtaposition is used to invite the imagined reader's sympathy by putting the affecting aspects of political events in a comparative relationship to Clifford's own situation. The reader is not addressed directly, as is Montaigne's reader, but is implied as a textually imagined and responding presence. The juxtapositions exist, then, to generate, a reader's interpretation (and this is true even if the initially imagined reader *was* Clifford alone). The addressee is invited to make the links which Clifford's intermittent physical sequestration in the country tended to obscure – between her husband's ill-treatment of her, James's endorsement of that, and what Clifford regards as the palpable injustices of Stuart rule. The elaborate pattern of connection works to vindicate Clifford and produce her as an object of sympathy and regard. Thus, the note for the day after the death of her mother, the 25th, concerns masculine behaviour: 'Upon the 25th my Lord Somerset was arraigned & condemned in the same place & stood much upon his innocency.'[23] Somerset's protestation is clearly contrasted with Frances Howard's plea for mercy.

The diary also textualizes spatial struggle in the household and elsewhere. What has been characterized as 'the cleft stick between the

minimum of social rights they [women] can obtain . . . and the psychological or physical price they have to pay'[24] seems, in Clifford's case, to
have involved domestic space. The great tracts of land were fought for
in battles over personal movement and space focusing on Clifford's
chamber, to which she was often confined, or self-confined. Her husband
was 'much abroad' while 'I stayed in the Countrey'.[25] She sulks in her
chamber. Her husband, wanting to discuss 'the business' must come
there. When she returns from the north, bad relations with her husband
may be signalled by separate chambers.[26]

Even this early diary – the text which is the linchpin of critical
accounts of Clifford as a private writer isolated from the wider world –
offers strong evidence that Clifford sees herself, and invites her reader
to see her, in the highly politicized contexts of the law, the contrast
between the Elizabethan and Jacobean courts, and by using historical
analogy. In this period Clifford was attempting to influence that wider
public, even political, world. In 1620, just after the first diary breaks off,
she set up a monument to Edmund Spenser in Westminster Abbey.[27]
Chamber and monument seem to be linked by at least one diarized
detail; on 28 January she records, 'Rivers used to read to me in
Montaigne's *Plays* and Moll Neville in *The Fairy Queene*'.[28] Spenser
had dedicated *The Fairie Queene* to Clifford's father and the *Four Hymns*
to her mother. As Richard Helgerson notes, the Spenserian poets
and the chorographers were, by the 1610s, at least potentially 'politically
dangerous'.[29] And as Michelle O'Callaghan observes, William Browne's
Britannia's Pastorals uses the failure to build Spenser's monument to
discuss an exilic poetic voice.[30] The monument's memorialization of
the Elizabethan past might be interpreted as a criticism of James.[31]
Certainly, it is a politicized statement about the Elizabethan poet. The
monument, asserting a political through an aesthetic stance, announced
Spenser's greatness, that of his deceased patron, and that of the patron's
daughter – Clifford.

Although apparently at polar extremes of 'private' versus 'public'
statements, diary and monument both assert familial and political
demands. In their implicitly pejorative contrast of good Elizabethan
past with Jacobean present, both, in different modes, articulate a 'desiring narrative', the 'direction and force' of which is 'always a future-past,
a deferment of experience in the direction of origin and . . . the point
where narrative begins/ends'.[32] And in each case the desiring narrative
blends familial and politicized issues. The apparently open fragments of
the 1616 diary thus draw the reader into a world which is one in which
apparently private events reverberate in relation to the lawsuit, the court,

aristocratic virtue and status. And the Spenser monument announced Clifford's aesthetic, but also lineal, claims to the world.

1643, 1649: loss and reparation

Twenty-three years after the Spenser monument was set up, Clifford, because of a sequence of deaths, did inherit her lands. The end of the war (at Charles I's execution) is marked by her escape from her 'place of refuge', the London house of her second husband, the boorish Earl of Pembroke. Here she describes her return to her estates:

> The 3d of June in 1649 I took my last leave of my 2d husband, the Earl of Pembroke in his lodging in the Cockpitt near Whitehall which was the last time that he & I ever saw one another, it being then Sunday, and that same day I went from thence to my Daughter Northamptons house at Islington, which was the first time I was ever in any of her Lords houses, nor have I been in any of them since. And methinkes ye destinie, yt she should be settled at Islington so near Clerkenwell, where my mother & I lived long in my childhood, & yt her Lords chief house of Ashby, should be so near Lillford in Northampton-shire, where both my Mor. and my self in our younger yeers had our breeding, as also yt my younger daughter of Thanett should be settled at Hothfield in Kent, not far from Sutton, where my blessed Mor. & I lived together a good while . . . And the 11th day of July 1649 having a little afore in the Barnards Castle, taken my leave of my 2 daughters & their Lords & my grandchildren, did I go out of London onwards on my journey towards Skipton . . . I came to Skipton the 18th day of yt. Month into my Castle there, it being ye. first time of my coming into it, after ye pulling down of most of ye. old Castle which was done some 6 months before, by order of Parliament, because it had been a garrison in ye late Civil War, & I was never till now in any part of yt Castle since I was 9 or 10 weeks old.[33]

Such narratives, produced after her lands were restored, present a refining and consolidation of the complex stories of the early diaries. Clifford here repositions moments and incidents to make a single story of the triumph of law and lineage.

Land, buildings and writing all come to signify her redeemed estate as she re-encodes the past.[34] In reasserting the issue of tenure so import-ant in her law case, Clifford's insistence on her re-entry into her Skipton castle as life-defining event makes a point about lineage, and the fruits of time. Forty-four years since her disinheritance by her father (despite the protection of an entail), six years since she inherited (spent in

London because of the civil wars), and six months after Charles I's execution, Skipton castle, her birthplace, is returned to Clifford. Skipton, like her other lands, had passed from her uncle Francis to his son Henry.[35] This passage recording Clifford's entry into her Westmorland lands in July 1649 might, on first reading, seem to record solely personal triumph. Certainly, it celebrates the continuity of her line and the connections between past and present in terms of her youth – as the heir of her family – and the parallels between that and her daughters' fortunes. However, the narrative emphasis on the significance of places, connections of past and present are the organizing principles of a narrative that blends legal, national, familial and monarchical significance. The movement towards the climactic moment at which she inherits her lands dominates the writing of the 1650s.[36] Clifford's frequent repetition of this narrative, the way she weaves together places, events and genealogy, convey to the reader that providence has restored her to her right.

Even as Clifford used the moment of inheritance to reshape disparate events into a narrative with places imbued with present and past significance all pointing towards the happy ending of her restoration to baronial power, she also used it to rework her relationship to space by marking various objects. Thus, the overlayering of place, person and incident with significance that is found in the early diary is here reshaped as the narrative of her loss, triumph and return with fixed moments of significance and transformation. There is much evidence that when she returned to her lands, as well as building and labelling her lands and houses, Clifford revisited the artefacts and texts of her past and had them rearticulated to proclaim her restoration.[37]

The locations to which she returned were also textualized to proclaim her renewed familial position and paradoxical autonomy as female heir and widow. The law, used against her, she now used to evict tenants whose leases did not accord with her view.[38] A further tension between quasi-'feudal' modes and languages and an 'improving' or modernizing tendency is suggested in the textualization of buildings organized to enunciate her genealogical greatness, clearly evidenced in the almshouse which she had built at Appleby, virtually within sight of her castle.[39] While the interior gave the inmates small chambers, dependency, safety, the exterior records Clifford's own change of fortune from supplicant and litigant to benefactor. The almshouse her mother had built at Beameley, restored by Clifford, was also textualized as 'more perfectly finished by her only child, the Lady Anne Clifford, now Countess Dowager of Pembroke, Dorsett, and Montgomery'. The Appleby building bears the legend of her patronage and lineage on its stonework and provides evidence of her newly powerful situation, as well as of her 'familial' relationship to her tenants. She notes the building's completion:

> And in the beginning of this year was my Almshouse here at Appleby quite finished, which had been almost 2 yeers a building, so as I now put into it 12 poor women, 11 of them being widdows, & the 12th a maimed maid.[40]

The text records the building, which itself, in its rules and inscriptions, publicizes Clifford's local, familial and implicitly national position.

The Books of Record written up in these years further elaborate Clifford's relationship to the place, using documents as well as narrative to assert legal and national claims. The women in the almshouses – so lacking in control over their lives that we know them only in Clifford's records – are uncannily reminiscent of Clifford's earlier life at Knole.[41] The women, in their need, underwrite Clifford's longed-for and now achieved autonomy in terms which suggest the importance of feudal, local connection. To house them in her narrativized building, to include them as part of the story of what she has done, is to build her story.

Clifford's philanthropy narrativizes space, time and the identity of others under the sign of her inheritance and importance. The inscriptions on her land rework the emphasis on fullness of presence and description found in chorography. Although she was apparently no bookworm, it does seem likely that Clifford, as the pupil of Daniel, memorializer of Spenser and reader of Camden's *Britannia*, was aware of the ability of chorography to assert a politics of retreat. Camden's *Britannia* mobilizes many different discourses and forms of representation to produce as full an image, narrative and understanding of the place as possible.[42] Whilst in chorographic texts the land is rearticulated through representation, Clifford's land *itself* tells the story of her ownership and significance. Chorographers made public and circulated the specifics and power relations of place, but anyone passing through the actual landscape of Clifford's domain would find her story inscribed upon it. As Richard Helgerson has suggested of chorography, these inscribed buildings expressed local claims with wider political implications.[43]

Thus it seems that, on her return to Westmorland, Clifford used the textualization of land and genealogy to assert a politics of localism and princely retreat. Clifford's retrospective narratives shift decisively towards an assertion of her landed status. The retreat from the metropolitan centre, followed by a building programme textualized to insist upon location and family, emphasizes the importance of these structures *against* the world she has left. The resumption of ownership of land is accompanied by an assertion of quasi-Elizabethan ideologies of place – location as bound to status. The memorializing of 'place' was continued in Clifford's most significant monuments, that for her mother and the *Great Picture*.

Reading the *Great Picture*

Clifford's loss and its reparation are both vividly inscribed on the landscape by Clifford's monument to her mother. In 1616, after the visit to her lands recorded in the Knole diary, Anne and her mother parted, her mother 'bringing me a quarter of a mile upon the way'. Though neither suspected it at the time, this was to be their last meeting, for Margaret Clifford, Anne's staunch ally in the lawsuits, was to die before they could meet again. Many years later, when she returned to her lands, Anne caused the meeting to be commemorated in a genealogical monument, on the very spot of the encounter – where it remains.

While many of Clifford's post-1649 texts, including her mother's tomb with its amazingly elaborate genealogy, seek to elide the misery of loss in an obsessive narrative of triumph, this monument speaks of loss and compensation. A *merkmal*, it ambiguously marks the place where loss took place, but also commemorates Anne's power to take control of that loss and, as far as possible, to compensate through memorialization. The monument is, in Susan Stewart's sense, 'a structure of desire' which describes the full relationship between mother and daughter and its loss.[44] As such it articulates the dynamics of Clifford's cultural production, with its characteristic recursive movement by which past and present, loss and reparation are both made present to the viewer or reader who is, in turn, imagined as informed, even won over, by the narrative of the past.

The tension between loss and compensation, erased from the obsessive narratives of Clifford's triumph discussed in the last section, appears also in the *Great Picture* (reproduced here) painted in London probably in the 1640s soon after her inheritance was confirmed. The politics of Clifford's retreat is illuminated by the totemic placing of relatives, and, in two panels, of books. The chorographic and chronicle impulses attempt to repair an imagined rupture of appropriate relations between self and land, present and past, and at the same time aim to transcend that problem by asserting the full presence of the present subject in relation to land and chronicle. This painting is of a mixed mode,

above and facing] Jan Van Belcamp (?), *Great Picture*. Centre panel

partly portraiture, partly genealogical, partly biographical, commemorative and memorial. In its status as narrative of Clifford's life and genealogical proof of her entitlement the painting, as Richard Wendorf suggests, calls attention to the 'fundamental relation ... between portraiture and documentation'.[45] It also serves as a reminder of what Clifford may have learnt from her contact with the Arundels and from the paintings at Wilton.

The painting itself may have been done by Jan Van Belcamp, a copyist who had been keeper of Charles I's pictures since 1640.[46] The *Great Picture* is the enigmatic product of Clifford's restoration and retreat.

Left-hand panel   Right-hand panel

It speaks of her social and physical location in visual language that asserts her national importance but also requires complex reading processes. The image unites the genealogical and spatial, even chorographic, desire to make the land speak of her ownership and place, demanding distinct and overlayered modes of interpretation all of which serve to situate Clifford at the heart of land (Westmorland), family (heir) and, therefore, as political agent – sheriff. As a triptych the image combines the narrative and spatial strategies of Clifford's textualization of her world after she succeeded to her inheritance. It represents the times of loss and restoration as chambers furnished with items of significance including portraits, books, animals, armour, and inscriptions. The viewer is required to combine spatial and temporal interpretation, and to move between a representational image and narrative, captioning and genealogy. The triptych's interpretative focus is on the period of Clifford's family, her intellectual and political formation, and the present. The Elizabethan moment of the central image provides a moment of political and familial stability which exists both to be disrupted (in the reign of James) and to be fulfilled (in Clifford herself and her relation to her genealogy).

Thus, the image is both complex and simple; it repeats the pattern of Clifford's written and built texts in using the moment of her inheritance as the point of closure. The histories that permit that end to be constituted are at least double. Two starting places are proposed – the opening of Clifford's life as suggested by the central panel copied from images made a month after her conception and the moment, memorialized in the first panel, at which she was deprived of her right (although, of course, the compositional present provides another starting place). Each starting place is out of sequence and separate, yet they make no sense except in relation to each other, undoing and complimenting each other in Clifford's progress towards her final plenitude.

Each chamber represents a significant moment in Clifford's life, yet the painting cannot be precisely read from left to right. The central panel presents in a chamber the earliest events in the image – before Anne's birth. It contains eight differently sized portraits, including Anne's brothers Sir Robert Clifford and Francis Lord Clifford (who died in 1589 and 1591 respectively), next to them her mother (central to this panel and therefore to the whole composition), and next to her Clifford's father, the will-maker. We are told these were copied from images painted in June 1589 when Lady Cumberland and her sons were staying in 'Channell Row', just after Anne was conceived.[47] The point of the panel, clearly, is that Anne is expected.

The four other portraits in the panel indicate Clifford's chosen connections. These are images of Clifford's aunts: Anne, Countess of Warwick, and Elizabeth, Countess of Bath, were maternal aunts, from the side of the family not usually strongest in the making of political alliances. Here Clifford (as in her early narrative of Elizabeth I's funeral) keeps the viewer and reader's attention on maternal networks of kinship connected to the Elizabethan court.[48] Even as Clifford claims the discourse of lineage to support her case first for legal redress and later to endorse the fullness of her enfranchisement, it is inflected by her situation. Thus the central panel foregrounds masculine power, lineage and control. Yet, apparently mere background, the images of the aunts and the inscriptions foregrounding female agency, longevity and courtly virtue set up a dynamic, dependent on the viewer's knowledge of the fates of Anne's brothers and subsequent events, whereby feminine inheritance challenges and outlasts masculine, as is suggested by the gestures both parents are making towards the two male heirs.

Clifford's very survival enabled her to select and shape the narrative. The left-hand panel shows Clifford at fifteen, at the moment of her father's death. Anxieties and deprivations are present in the picture, but, as in the later writing, here figured as overcome with full inheritance – as the relationship between this image and that of the older Clifford makes clear. The presence of Anne on the left of the image signals the start of a second story, not the one of her lineage and inheritance but of the loss and recovery of her lands. The inscriptions tell us: 'When shee was 15 yeares and 8 months old, her father died in Savoy Hous, London, the 30 of Oct: 1605: And presently after hir Moother comensed great suits in Law for hir sayd onely daughters right to the Baro: of Clifford.' The inscription goes on to chart the death of Margaret Russell, Clifford's widowhood and her remarriage.[49] The inscription of the final panel takes up the narrative of her life after the death of the Duke of Dorset, detailing her marriage to Pembroke. It closes with the death of Henry Clifford, Francis Clifford's son, the fact that even though he died in 1643 the 'Civill warrs kept her from having profits of those lands for a good while after'.[50]

Evidently the triptych requires us to hold word and image in a dynamic relation while making absolutely explicit that the point of the narrative is that the final panel is reached – in which, after the expectation in the central panel and the deprivation implicit in the left-hand panel, Clifford is a full and completed subject. Once again the text invites the reader to tease out the relationship between the details given. The titles and placing of the books enable the reader – as with the Knole diary – to weave Clifford's claims into a commentary on public and political issues. What emerges is an articulate politics of retreat and endurance, mediated by an emphasis on place, entitlement and family. The books in Clifford's images suggest that her estate in Westmorland was its own polity, a princedom set up within, and in response to, first republican and then restored Stuart politics.

The books, as much as the genealogies, assert Clifford's ambitions, making the link between virtue and stoic self-discipline and the claims to an architecturally and chrographically articulated claim to a kind of princehood.[51] History, chorography and the imagining of the self are represented by the poetical and historical writings of her tutor, Samuel Daniel, William Camden's *Britannia*, the *Manuell* of Epictetus, Boethius's *Consolations of Philosophy* and Montaigne's *Essays*, which we found her reading at Knole in 1616, in exile and disinheritance. The books suggest, perhaps, sources of literary sustenance during the years that she fought for her inheritance but more significant is the way, both open and shut, their choice and organization also indicate a dynamic between the formation and discipline of the self and the shaping of the world. Thus, poetry of her tutor, Daniel, including his poem on the civil wars of York and Lancaster clearly addresses the shaping of the ruler and the self and, depending on the edition Clifford is using, included a poem to the young Clifford, predicting, 'Such are your holy bounds, who must convay / (If God so please) the honourable bloud / Of *Clifford*, and of *Russell*'.[52] Loys le Roy's *Of the Interchangable Course, or Variety of Things in the Whole World* (1594), alluding to mutability and transformation, seems to suggest the change in Clifford's fortunes in her middle years.

The right-hand panel, showing Clifford at the moment of composition, is turned towards the image of her younger self, adressed across the image of the Cumberland family. Of central importance to both these figures is William Camden's *Britannia*, which Clifford's tutor might have read to her. If we open Camden, we find how *Britannia* describes the locations of Clifford's power, lost and regained. The early editions contain maps, including one of Westmorland, with Latin etymologies and discourses on precisely the places of Clifford's inheritance – Skipton, Appleby, Brougham all of which turn out to have significant British or Roman pasts. Noting Clifford's acquisition of this 'very proper and a strong Castle', Camden likens Skipton: 'in the middest' of 'craggy stones, hanging rocks, and rugged waies' to '*Latium* in Italie'.[53] Of Appleby he contrastingly comments, 'were it not that by reason of antiquity it had deserved to be counted the chiefe towene of the shire', it would be 'little better than a village'.[54] Finally, Brougham is significant for 'huge stones in forme of Pyramides . . . which may seeme to have beene pitched and erected for to continue the memoriall of some act there atchieved'.[55] Thus *Britannia* illuminates Clifford's pedigree, gives a desirable historical narrative to her lands, and situates those lands in relation to the whole of the nation. The stoic self-discipline of the books in the first image has been transformed into a tripartite claim to possession and virtue grounded in lineage, place and nation.

The final image of Clifford implies her highly public, landholder's virtues. The books in the third panel – tumbled on the shelf above and behind Anne – are evidently her present resources. These books suggest the overlayering of 'public' and 'private', personal and political, in their combination of, for example, George Strode's *The Anatomie of Mortality* and Henry Wotton's *Elements of Architecture*. The selection of Wotton's text, integrating the classical and homely, suggests the assertive localism implicit in the politics of Clifford's retreat. The second part of Wotton's book begins:

> Every Mans proper *Mansion* House and *Home*, being the *Theater* of his *Hospitality*, the *Seate* of *Selfe-fruition*, the *Comfortablest* part of his owne *Life*, the *Noblest* of his Sonnes *Inheritance*, a kinde of private *Princedome*; Nay, to the *Possessors* thereof, an *Epitomie* of the whole World . . .[56]

Clifford's building programme, like her repeated self-representation, was at the heart of her northern creation of a princedom.[57] Wotton's architecture made available European configurations of social space and, displayed here, suggests that Clifford's project was conceived in terms of the building of a principality. These choices demonstrate her insistence on family, lineage and place as implying a conception of political and national status. They underpin an assertion of retreat with an implicit evaluation of renewed Stuart rule.

The books in the *Great Picture* show us the materials which Clifford used to build a dual subjecthood: an inner life ordered around her fortuitously restored status as 'heir' and an external life of a northern Renaissance prince. They indicate her resources in structuring a recapitulation of the story of deprivation and inheritance as a textual and spatial narrative of power restored. That she selected Wotton on architecture, Montaigne on the self, Daniel on poetry and history and Camden's chorography to stand for her concerns indicates her sense of the wider implications of her localist interventions linking land to the nation. To write a 'memoriall' of 'mee', to repair a castle, build, sign and organize an almshouse, regulate one's lands and assert control of ones tenantry is, as the presence of these books demonstrate, to be sharply aware of contemporary discourses of antiquarianism as they impinge on understandings of law (in terms of precedent), place and nation.[58]

The books in the *Great Picture* make biographical claims for Clifford as they situate her and the things and writings she has produced in relation to space, time and status. In her discussion of Clifford's use of history Mihoko Suzuki sees her as sceptical of 'male-centred historiography' and in the *Great Picture* she gets to reshape history and space around her, turning the meaning of historical events towards her own life.[59] Yet – perhaps because of its very impulse to include all connections and meanings – the image is a more open text than any other that Clifford produced, for all that this image appears to be a final and definitive statement. The books act as markers of knowledge and status but also indicate the web of discourses that organized the late Stuart perceptions of the estate and countryside. Drawing as they do on Italian models hybridized with more English understandings of the pastoral virtues associated with the House, the discourses permeated Clifford's thinking on her place in the estates of Westmorland. It would be simultaneously inadequate and excessive to say that she conceived of Westmorland on the model of the Palladian estate or that she understood herself as recreating Renaissance Italy amongst the lakes and moors. As Vita Sackville-West notes, she did spend years, 'lording it over the north' governing 'from the midst of a little court of her own'.[60] She did, it seems, see her land as a kind of princedom built from the resources of a library, memory, buildings and genealogy. But she also needed to have those claims recognized and that may be why the story or stories imaged in the *Great Picture* are oriented both towards an inward audience of family (who need to know and accept Clifford's narrative) and towards the outer world – at least to those who came into her castle.

'She buildeth her House'

It is now possible to say a little more about the two central issues I have been pursuing; the relationship between the private and the political in Clifford's texts and the nature of the politics I have found there. As the *Great Picture* and the early diaries make equally clear, private and public, joined by the law case which is the (visually) unrepresented core of the *Great Picture*, are linked throughout Clifford's textual production. The individual subject of the diaries is, through both family and circumstances, politicized. Clifford's assertion of her status as subject, constituted by discourses of law, property and lineage, can be more certainly traced than an affective interiority split off from such discourses. These very discourses of law, land, lineage, enunciated throughout her textual production, themselves tie her texts to a particular politics. Clifford clearly had a low opinion of the male Stuarts, especially James I and Charles II (as monarchs Elizabeth I, Anne of Denmark, Henrietta Maria found greater favour). This is not, of course, to say that she favoured the republic or Protectorate against whose agents she fought unremittingly. Rather, we can find in her texts a politics of retreat. In such a context, the writing of history and memoir were – as her reading and

annotation of Anthony Weldon's history of the court of James I shows
– politicized activities. Beside an unflattering description Clifford wrote
'a right desciption of King James'.[61] Her continued interest, in later life,
in the writings of William Camden, is equally significant.[62] For those
writing about land, as for Clifford, the relationship between state and
estate was no idle pun; to claim land was to claim a political place. Seen
in this context, her sponsorship of the monument to Spenser in 1620
looks like a cultural intervention with strong political implications about
remembering the claims of locality, lineage and place.

In part a paradoxically modernising assertion of a Tudor view of
the aristocracy as governors in private princedoms, Clifford's politics of
retreat was far from 'private' in its insistence on textuality. As Juliet
Fleming notes, even Clifford's most apparently 'domestic' textualization
– that of the interior space of the household, by marking of 'her Wals,
her Beds, her Hangings' with significant sayings and her 'causing her
servants to write them in papers' – demonstrates didactic purpose.[63]
Moreover, from a critical point of view, her writings and building are
resistant to naturalization as parochial aristocratic women's networking,
for each text, each building, seeks to mark permanently an assertion of
a highly particular family politics against opponents now disappeared
but to her all too vivid.

Clifford's retreat to her estates and textualisation of land, buildings
and life can be set alongside the claims of other texts of the 1640s and
1650s. There is an analogy in the complex assertion of county primacy
found in the building works of the Duke of Newcastle. The two
Nottinghamshire structures, Welbeck and Bolsover, continued to play a
huge part in William Cavendish's psychic and, importantly, political life
when he retired abroad after defeat at Marston Moor. On his flight
abroad he wrote of his 'Divorce' from Welbeck in terms which explicitly
join personal, and political, and later his brother compounded for
Bolsover at the astronomical cost of £5,000.[64] Clifford's texts need to
be seen in terms of retirement as an assertion of the politics of law and
lineage expressed in cultural terms; her case makes clear that throughout the mid seventeenth century there were, beside the official political
sphere, though by no means remote from it, highly politicized vocabu-
laries of place, estate and location. And as the interwoven relationships
of familial and political issues in diaries, buildings and land make clear,
where the law of inheritance intersected with aristocratic privilege, a
politics of things and places was an assumed knowledge which, when
traced, reveals not a 'personal' life but a highly politicized, and worldly,
enunciation of retreat.

Notes

For comments and discussion I am grateful to Dr Philippa Berry, Dr Margaret Tudeau and to Dr Erica Fudge, Dr Hilary Hinds, Dr Michelle O'Callaghan, Ms Sarah McKenzie, Dr Paul Salzman, Professor Peter Widdowson.

1   Alice T. Friedman 'Constructing an Identity in Prose, Plaster and Paint: Lady Anne Clifford as Writer and Patron of the Arts', in Lucy Gent (ed.), *Albion's Classicism: The Visual Arts in Britain, 1550–1660* (New Haven and London: Yale University Press, 1995), pp. 359–376; especially pp. 359, 361.

2   *The Diaries of Lady Anne Clifford*, ed. D. J. H. Clifford (Stroud: Alan Sutton, 1992), p. xii.

3   See e.g. *The Diary of Lady Anne Clifford*, ed. V. Sackville-West (London: Heinneman, 1923), p. xliv; discussed in Paul Salzman, 'Revenants: Vita Sackville-West's Evocation of Anne Clifford and Aphra Behn', forthcoming.

4   *The Diary of Lady Anne Clifford 1616–1619*, ed. Katherine O. Acheson (New York: Garland, 1995), p. 14.

5   *The Diaries*, ed. Clifford, p. xii. For further discussion of this see Barbara K. Lewalski, *Writing Women in Jacobean England* (Cambridge, Mass.: Harvard University Press, 1993), pp. 125–153; p. 125; *Her Own Life*, ed. Elspeth Graham *et al.* (London: Routledge, 1992).

6   Margaret J. M. Ezell, *Writing Women's Literary History* (Baltimore and London Johns Hopkins University Press, 1993), pp. 34–35, 41.

7   *The Diary*, ed. Acheson, p. 3.

8   *Ibid.*, pp. 3–5.

9   *Ibid.*, pp. 2–3.

10 'To the Ladie Anne Clifford', in Samuel Daniel, *The Whole Workes of Samuel Daniel Esquire in Poetrie* (London: 1623), pp. 71–73.

11 Amy Louise Erickson, *Women and Property in Early Modern England* (London and New York: Routledge, 1993), p. 4. Erickson notes that the concentration on the elite transfer of property is problematic in generalizing with regard to family relations.

12 Erickson, *Women and Property*, pp. 3–21.

13 *The Dairies*, ed. Clifford, p. 41.

14 Samuel Daniel, '*To my deare brother and friend* M. John Florio, *one of the Gentlemen of hir Maiesties most* Royall Privie Chamber', in Michel de Montaigne, *Essayes Written in French*, trans. John Florio (London: 1603), fols A3r–A4r, A3v.

15 'A Brief Relation of the several Voyages undertaken and performed by George Earl of Cumberland, against the King of Spain's fleets etc., 1586–1598', written out for Lady Anne Clifford at Christmas 1618; WD/Hoth 7, Kendal Record Office. Florio, 'Of the Canniballes', in *Essayes*, I, p. 107.

16 Michel de Certeau, 'Montaigne's "Of Cannibals"', in *Heterologies: Discourse on the Other*, trans Brian Massumi (Manchester: Manchester University Press, 1986), pp. 67–79 (p. 79).

17 *The Diaries*, ed. Clifford, p. 28.

18 *Ibid.*, p. 28.

19 *Ibid.*, p. 29.

20 *Ibid.*, p. 30.

21 *Ibid.*, p. 35.

22 Michel Butor, 'The Book as Object', in Richard Howard (ed.), *Inventory* (London: Jonathan Cape, 1970), pp. 39–56 (p. 50).

23 *The Diaries*, ed. Clifford, p. 36.

24 Luce Irigaray, 'Sexuate Rights', quoted in Drucilla Cornell, 'Gender, Sex, and Equivalent Rights', in Judith Butler and Joan W. Scott (eds), *Feminists Theorise the Political* (London: Routledge, 1992), p. 291.

25 *The Diaries*, ed. Clifford, p. 33.

26 *Ibid.*, p. 35.

27 George C. Williamson, *Lady Anne Clifford* (Kendal: Titus Wilson and Son, 1922), p. 63. Williamson quotes the notebook of Nicholas Stone from *Walpole Society Proceedings*, vol. VII (n.d.), p. 54. The statue was restored in marble in 1778.

28 *The Diaries*, ed. Clifford, pp. 48–49. I am assuming that the plays are the essays.

29 See George C. Williamson, *George, Third Earl of Cumberland* (Cambridge: Cambridge University Press, 1920), fol. a4r; Richard Helgerson, *Forms of Nationhood* (Chicago: University of Chicago Press, 1992), p. 131.

30 Michelle O'Callaghan, *The 'Shepheards Nation': Jacobean Spenserians and Early Stuart Political Culture, 1612–1625* (Oxford: Oxford University Press, 2000), pp. 112–113; see also pp. 1–3, 10–11.

31 Helgerson's argument that during Clifford's lifetime chorographies came to set out the pedigrees and manors of local gentry and nobility is supported by Clifford's use of Daniel and her possession of Camden's *Britannia*. Helgerson, *Forms of Nationhood*, p. 133; Williamson thinks that the edition shown in the *Great Picture* is 1578, 1600 or 1607 (Williamson, *George, Third Earl of Cumberland*, p. 341).

32 Susan Stewart, *On Longing* (Durham and London: Duke University Press, 1993), p. x.

33 BL Harleian Ms 6177, fols 67r–v. This is a transcription of an earlier manuscript. See also *The Diaries*, ed. Clifford, p. 100.

34 She described her husband's house in Clerkenwell as 'a house full of riches', where she remained 'in my owne Chamber without removing, 6 years & 9 months'. The house was 'a place of refuge for me to hide my selfe in' from 1643.

35 Harl. Ms 6177, fol. 67v.

36 This shape is to an extent obscured by D. J. H. Clifford's narrativisation of her life. The diaries seem to have been written up retrospectively – from notes – and though it is possible to weld them into a 'life' this involves ignoring, for example, the presence of part of the actual 'memoriall' in the third Book of Record begun in 1649, in which the memorial of 'my owne life' (fol. 226) follows two and a half substantial volumes on lineage, including copies of documents, coloured pedigrees etc.

37 It may have been at this point that her portrait at thirty is inscribed: 'Lady Anne Clifford, only Daughter and Heir to George Earl of Cumberland'. See also Richard T. Spence, *Lady Anne Clifford* (Stroud: Sutton Publishing, 1997), pp. 261–262.

38 She struggled with Robert Atkinson, the Protectorate governor of Appleby Castle (later hanged for his part in the Kaber Rigg rebellion) and wrangled with tenants. See Alan Marshall, *Intelligence and Espionage in the Reign of Charles II* (Cambridge: Cambridge University Press, 1993), p. 110.

39 Williamson, *Lady Anne* Clifford, pp. 310–311.

40 Harl Ms 6177, fols 70r. See Williamson, *Lady Anne Clifford*, p. 372.

41 The invisibility of these women, existing in the anonymity of tenant–lord relations, is vividly illustrated by one of the warrants of admission; 1 March 1726 when Mary Mopson is to be admitted because 'Her son served me as footman and Butler faithfully for at least seven years' – signed Thanet. WD/Hoth EC2, Warrants of Admission, Westmorland Record Office.

42 Melanie Hansen, 'Identity and Ownership: Narratives of Land in the English Renaissance', in William Zunder and Suzanne Trill (eds), *Writing and the English Renaissance* (London and New York: Longman, 1996), pp. 87–105, p. 88.

43 Helgerson, *Forms of Nationhood*, pp. 128–136.

44 Stewart, *On Longing*, p. ix.

45 Richard Wendorf, *The Elements of Life* (Oxford: Clarendon Press, 1990), p. 9.

46 Francis Haskell, 'Charles I's Collection of Pictures', in Arthur MacGregor (ed.), *The Late King's Goods* (London and Oxford: Alistair McAlpine in association with Oxford University Press, 1989), p. 226.

47 Williamson, *Lady Anne Clifford*, p. 335. One brother, we read, died while her mother was pregnant with Anne, the other was 'a child endowed with many perfections'. *Ibid.*, p. 493.

48 Christine Kalpische-Zuber, *Women, Family and Ritual in Renaissance Italy*, trans. Lydia Cochrane (Chicago and London: University of Chicago Press, 1985), pp. 75–85; *The Diaries*, ed. Clifford, pp. 21–27. Connections to Clifford are emphasized, and some, like an aunt's marriage to Lord Wotton, are picked up in the books represented. Lady Ann Russell, Countess of Warwick, her maternal aunt, is described as having (like Anne and her mother) 'Founded an Almehouse' and 'she served Q.Eliz. most part of her life, . . . an Excellent Courtier'. Further, she and her sisters Margaret Russell (Anne's mother) and Elizabeth, Countess of Bath, are described as 'the 3 sisters of the greatest for honor, and goodness, of any 3 sisters that lived in theire tyme in this kingdome' (Williamson, *Lady Anne Clifford*, p. 492). The final image is of Lady Elizabeth Russell, who 'lived . . . a country life'. Lady Margaret Clifford, Countess of Darby, was 'eldest child to Henry Clifford, 2 Earle of Cumberland' and she was 'a deere lover of hir brother by the halfe-blood' of George, Earle of Cumberland – Clifford's father. This aunt was, like Anne, an eldest child and daughter, she, like Anne, was a potential heir (Williamson, *Lady Anne Clifford*, p. 491). Lady Frances Clifford was the Second Earl of Cumberland's child, the first child by his second wife. Her female child, 'hir eldest and deerest childe, Margaret Wharton, borne in Skipton castle, is now widdow to the Lo. Wotton, a woeman of great goodnes and worth' (Williamson, *Lady Anne Clifford*, p. 492).

49 Williamson, *Lady Anne Clifford*, pp. 494, 495.

50 *Ibid.*, p. 507.

51 The image's central panel contains four books: the Bible, Thomas Lodge's translation of Seneca, a manuscript book 'of Alkumiste Exstractions of Distillations and excellent medicines' which might have been assembled by her mother, and *The Psalmes of David* in the countess's left hand (Williamson, *Lady Anne Clifford*, pp. 498–499).

52 Daniel, *Workes*, p. 73.

53 William Camden, *Britain, or A Chorographical description of . . . England, Scotland, and Ireland . . .* (London: 1637), p. 694.

54 *Ibid.*, p. 761.

55 *Ibid.*, p. 762.

56 Henry Wotton, *The Elements of Architecture* (London: 1624), p. 82.

57 See also Katharine Hodgkin, 'The Diary of Lady Anne Clifford: A Study of Class and Gender in the Seventeenth Century', *History Workshop* 19 (Spring 1985), 148–161, especially p. 155.

58 What is missing is legal books, though, of course the great Books of Record are full of legal precedent and proof.

59 Mihoko Suzuki, 'Anne Clifford and the Gendering of History', *Clio* 30:2 (2001), 195–229 (p. 211).

60 *The Diary*, ed. Sackville-West, pp. xxxviii, xxxiv, xlv.

61 Anthony Weldon, *The Court and Character of King James* (London: 1650/1), p. 165; see p. 79 for positive comment on Somerset. Kendal Record Office.

62 See Melanie Hansen, 'Identiy and Ownership', p. 70; on law see Helgerson, *Forms of Nationhood*, pp. 63–104.

63 Juliet Fleming, *Graffiti and the Writing Arts of Early Modern England* (London: Reaktion, 2001), p. 48. Edward Rainbow, *A Sermon Preached at the Funeral of the Right Honourable Countess of Pembroke* (London: 1677), pp. 39–40. The sermon significantly takes as its theme the doubly intended '*She buildeth her House*', *Ibid.*, p. 15.

64 'The Divorce', Portland Collection, University of Nottingham, 'Poems & Plays Ms Duke of Newcastle', PwV26, fol. 131. A. S. Turberville, *A History of Welbeck Abbey and Its Owners* (London: Faber and Faber, 1938), vol. 1, 133–134; See also Mark Girouard, *Robert Smythson & the Elizabethan Country House* (New Haven and London: Yale University Press, 1983), p. 183.

—index—